P9-CRN-863

#69832-1

AFTER WORDS:

SUICIDE AND AUTHORSHIP IN TWENTIETH-CENTURY ITALY

ELIZABETH LEAKE

After Words

Suicide and Authorship in Twentieth-Century Italy

UNIVERSITY OF TORONTO PRESS
Toronto Buffalo London

© University of Toronto Press Incorporated 2011
Toronto Buffalo London
www.utppublishing.com
Printed in Canada

ISBN 978-0-8020-9279-3

∞

Printed on acid-free, 100% post-consumer recycled paper
with vegetable-based inks.

Library and Archives Canada Cataloguing in Publication

Leake, Elizabeth
After words : suicide and authorship in twentieth-century Italy /
Elizabeth Leake.

(Toronto Italian studies series)
Includes bibliographical references and index.
ISBN 978-0-8020-9279-3

1. Suicide and literature – Italy – History – 20th century. 2. Suicide
victims' writings, Italian – History and criticism. 3. Italian literature –
20th century – History and criticism. 4. Authors, Italian – 20th
century – Suicidal behavior. 5. Authors and readers – Italy – History –
20th century. I. Title. II. Series: Toronto Italian studies

PQ4088.L42 2010   850.9'3561   C2010-906443-7

This book has been published with the help of a grant from Columbia
University.

University of Toronto Press acknowledges the financial assistance to its
publishing program of the Canada Council for the Arts and the Ontario
Arts Council.

 Canada Council   Conseil des Arts   ONTARIO ARTS COUNCIL
for the Arts   du Canada   CONSEIL DES ARTS DE L'ONTARIO

University of Toronto Press acknowledges the financial support for its
publishing activities of the Government of Canada through the Canada
Book Fund.

Contents

Acknowledgments   vii

Introduction: The Death of the Author   3

1 The Posthumous Author: Guido Morselli, Giuseppe Rensi, Jacques Monod   20

2 The Corpus and the Corpse: Amelia Rosselli, Jacques Derrida, Sylvia Plath, Sarah Kofman   65

3 The Post-Biological Author: Cesare Pavese, Gianni Vattimo, Emanuele Severino   104

4 Commemoration and Erasure: Primo Levi, Giorgio Agamben, Avishai Margalit   138

Postscript: Learning from the Dead   165

Notes   173

Works Consulted   227

Index   245

Acknowledgments

This book benefited hugely from exceptional colleagues at extraordinary institutions. The Italian Department at Rutgers University granted me a timely sabbatical leave, without which this project would have languished. A Rutgers University Humanities Research Council Grant provided very useful material support. I am also very grateful to the Department of Italian and the Faculty of Arts and Sciences at Columbia University for their generous support of the publication of this book. At University of Toronto Press, editors Ron Schoeffel and Anne Laughlin were praiseworthy in the highest, as was copyeditor Judith Williams.

Conversations with Amy Boylan, Allison Cooper, Piero Garofalo, Brian Hupp, Catherine Leake, and Heather Webb helped me clarify my ideas. Cristian Muscelli brought me to Severino and Borgna; Giovanni Falaschi shared a veritable treasure trove of Levi materials; and Lucia Re's gift of her and Paul Vangelisti's splendid translation of *War Variations* was tremendously valuable to me. Sandy Waters and Maria Kager were exceptionally able research assistants. Henriette Skovhøj Pedersen, Lotte Simonsen, and Gaiva Velzyte provided writing time, and even more crucial, peace of mind.

Portions of the project were read and commented on by Mary Bly, David Brewer, Cynthia Eller, Amy Shire, Peter Sidi, Arlene Stein, Lisa Trusiani, and Laura Wittman. These early incarnations of the book benefited in countless ways from their engagement with it. Once the manuscript was complete, Paola Gambarota, Daragh O'Connell, Ruth Glynn, Dana Renga, and Alessandro Vettori made this a far better book than it would otherwise have been. I am particularly grateful to Dana Renga and to Allison Cooper, for the brilliance of their minds but also for the joys of their friendship.

Finally, there aren't enough superlatives for Søren Germer, for giving so selflessly of his intelligence, his kindness, and his humour. Without him, this book – and everything else – would be greatly diminished. And since in some ways, this book about suicide is also very much about life, I dedicate this book to those who have so greatly enriched mine: Frederik, Alexandra, and Søren.

The thirty-line extract ('Dying / ... Do not think I underestimate your great concern') from 'Lady Lazarus' from *Ariel* by Sylvia Plath, copyright © 1963 by Ted Hughes, is reprinted by permission of HarperCollins Publishers.

Extracts from Amelia Rosselli, *Sleep: poesie in inglese* / 1992, Garzanti, © Garzanti Editore s.p.a., 1992, and from Primo Levi, *Ad ora incerta* / 1984, Garzanti, © Garzanti Editore s.p.a., 1984, 1990, 1998; © 2004, Garzanti Libri s.p.a., Milano, are reprinted by permission of Garazanti Libri.

AFTER WORDS:
SUICIDE AND AUTHORSHIP IN TWENTIETH-CENTURY ITALY

Introduction: The Death of the Author

This study begins with a gunshot wound, an overdose of sleeping pills, and two falls from great heights: these methods hastened the deaths of four of Italy's greatest twentieth-century authors. Although all but one of the authors described above enjoyed some degree of international fame when they died, it was these authors' suicides, and not their literature, that captivated both the scholarly community and the general public.[1] The suicide of any public figure instigates public debate. But why do we care particularly when it is an author who dies by his or her own hand? How does that care manifest itself when we read their works? What kinds of expectations do we as readers have about authors' lives, and about our access to them via their writings? To take a familiar example, it is easy to imagine knowing that Ernest Hemingway killed himself (and perhaps even that his granddaughter did as well) without having read his work: it is the kind of fact that circulates outside literary circles. The inverse, however, is not necessarily true. I have read a good deal of Graham Greene, but do not happen to know how he died; it is not familiarity with the author or his works that determines that knowledge. When an author commits suicide, in other words, she or he makes news.

This study investigates the interrelations between suicide and reading: both how the suicide of an author informs critical and popular interpretations of his or her writings, and how, after suicide, an author's life becomes a text to be read.[2] I will argue that suicide functions as a hermeneutical tool with which readers, critics, publicists, and the author him- or herself reconstruct the author's life. The utmost example of the 'intrinsically posthumous character of the literary voice,'[3] the authoring of one's own death emends the critical reception of a work, readers' received knowledge about the work, indeed the work itself. I focus specifically on four Italian writers who rank among the most important voices in twentieth-century Italian literature. The most familiar to North American readers are Primo Levi, best known for writings that deal with his experience as a Holocaust survivor, and Cesare Pavese, a novelist whose works frequently address the role of the intellectual during Fascism. The other two figures are much less familiar to non-Italian readers, though within the Italian context their deaths became front-page news. Guido Morselli was a prolific novelist who was published only after his suicide, analogous perhaps to the American novelist John Kennedy Toole, whose book *A Confederacy of Dunces* was awarded a posthumous Pulitzer Prize. Amelia Rosselli is known for her innovative poetry, but perhaps even more for her suicide, which was enacted on the anniversary of Sylvia Plath's suicide.

My selection of these authors was governed by aesthetic considerations but also by their relations to history (or counter-history, in Morselli's case): the inevitable initial premise of canonical readings of each of these authors is that their private lives were overwhelmed by the immediate historical context in which they were embedded. They are also representative of a variety of structural positions occupied by suicide within their lives and works. One woman and three men, young, old, and middle-aged, they offer case studies of different categories of suicide when it is considered within the arc of writerly production and reception: before the successful publication of any fiction (Morselli); in full professional bloom (Pavese); in a dialogue with another famous suicide (Rosselli); and at the end of a highly celebrated career (Levi). The questions that inform my research, writ large, have to do with what authorial suicide can teach us about authorship, about reading, and about suicide more generally. Suicide is not the only connection; the linkages between these authors and their texts are various and deep enough to make for a productive avenue of research. They speak to and about each other at the level of both production and reception, as historical figures in and beyond the Italian cultural landscape, and as subjects of psychoanalysis, for example. This study engages each of them at the points at which they impact what we as readers bring to, and confront in, the texts.

The genesis of this project can be traced to my interest in the impact of watershed events on the interrelations between the life of the author and his or her critical and popular reception. In this sense, it is an extension of my previous research on Ignazio Silone,[4] a figure whose self-reconstruction as a former Communist militant turned novelist had far-reaching ramifications for his readership, both before and after his double life as a Fascist informer was revealed. Silone's case is a dramatic one, both because of the ideological nature of his writings and because of the fact that his life and those of his fictional protagonists were identical in the public eye. In the end, the force of readerly interventions into the creation of Silone's authorial persona was so incontrovertible that I could argue that not only did the man create the books; so did the books create the man. Silone is an extreme example of the always complex relationship between an author's published works and his private history; but even less contradictory figures provide us with the raw materials with which to create a hypothesis about the centrality of the reader to the writing of a text. This in itself is not a new idea; in the world of literary theory one of the most influential assertions of the last forty years has revolved around Barthes's so-called 'death of the author,' by which is meant the detachment of texts from the subject who created them, a result of the recognition of the lack of any ultimate existential truth whose authority anchors a text's meaning in the identity of its author.[5] The ramifications are as far-reaching for writing (Copernican, Pirandello might say, insofar as they displace the writer from the centre of his or her text) as they are for our own identities as readers, since according to this logic we become the producers of meaning. But if we agree that as good postmodernists and post-historicists, we cannot seek the explanation of a work wholly in its producer, we are nonetheless confronted with the *facts* of him or her, if only because (as Alfred Hitchcock has so vividly shown) there is nothing so difficult to get rid of as a body! Indeed, if the identity of the writing body is lost in writing, what happens to that body? We are left, then, in a bind. For a Barthes who reads against the dubious tradition of interpreting authorial intentions (here I use his name as shorthand for a poststructuralist, anti-humanist re-dimensioning of the role of the author), an author's suicide becomes another of the many signs that endows a text with meaning. For the popular, that is, non-scholarly reader, however, knowledge about the author (whose dimensions are demarcated in time and space and, frequently, to some extent, recast in the image of the reader) marks him or her very precisely as the guarantor of meaning, no more and no less.[6] If we understand authorial suicide to represent the definitive rewriting of the author's opus, then suicide offers a clear vantage point from which to study the moorings that bind us to the person of the author, however loose they may be.

This book's point of departure is the observation that when we think of certain authors, we cannot help thinking of their suicides, with significant consequences for our reading: indeed, we might say that we have *never* read these authors, that is, read them free of or untainted by our knowledge of their ends. The trauma of suicide (it is inevitably a trauma, in both the Freudian sense involving latency and repression, and in Caruth's sense meaning belated, ineluctable, and subject to repetition)[7] changes our reading, because we cannot help but renegotiate 'the relationship between the book and the body, the corpus and the corpse.'[8]

It is common for responses to an author's suicide to involve one of two extremes: either expurgating suicide from the record, making no mention of it whatsoever; or removing the author's opus from the context in which his or her works have conventionally been considered, and reclassifying them, to be mentioned henceforth in the company of authors of disparate provenance with little else in common but their purposeful deaths. A third impulse is to return to the author's works in order to ferret out any possible mention of suicide, death, hardship, or depression, so that reading becomes a game whose aim is to enumerate the maximum number of non-life-affirming moments possible. To my mind, these responses to authorial suicide are untenable; we cannot pretend we do not know that they killed themselves, we ought not to strip them of their literary kinships in order to privilege membership in some tragic fraternity, nor can we claim, after the fact, that an author's suicidal tendencies leap from every page.[9] Such gestures are reductive, since we must also consider that people have lives outside of their writing, and at best these gestures function as indices of our own anxieties about the unholy trinity of life, death, and writing. If we have read an author before his suicide, for example, we may revise our understanding of that text in light of the author's death. Similarly, we may bring our knowledge of an author's suicide to a first reading: his or her death, known only retrospectively, becomes *prospective* – it changes our awareness of certain aspects of the text, causing us to privilege themes or events in the writings that might otherwise go unnoticed. Instead, I prefer the image of *looming*: authorial suicide looms both in the sense of 'hovers,' perhaps ghostlike (an idea to which I will return presently), and in the sense of 'weaves,' actively shaping our understanding of a text, giving it colour and texture. Suicide, then, is both a form of authorship and a form of revision, both on the part of the author, who has written the final scene, as it were, and revised the 'natural' course of his or her life, as well as on the part of the reader, who consequently revises that author's works in an effort to make sense of the final act of writing. It is by way of this doubly inflected looming that we may determine suicide's legitimate place (neither over-determined nor deliberately ignored) as a hermeneutical tool.

Often the first response by friends and family members after a suicide is a study of the victim's writings (not just suicide notes but also letters, journals, marginalia in books, and so on); it is part of the process of mourning.[10] By looking to their words for a response to the many questions suicides pose (*why* chief among them), survivors seek to close the book on that death. We imbue these textual remains with an almost supernatural authority, as we might a voice from beyond the grave. My first premise, therefore, stems from the circularity of these practices of mutual illumination – we look to the texts to understand the deaths, and we look to the deaths to understand the texts.[11] Moreover, these practices are not unique to nonprofessional readers, but are also implemented by scholars (such as Barthes, Foucault, Derrida) whose critical stances otherwise resist such contaminations. In fact, the trauma of suicide fundamentally alters the interpretive practices of those readers whose intellectual identities hinge on distinguishing the corpus of writing from the corpse. Where once the aesthetics of the text reigned supreme, after a suicide it is the text's mimetic quotient that seems to matter most. Similarly, my second premise holds that suicide creates strange bedfellows – that is, when it is an author who commits suicide, conventional scholarly determinations about his or her literary relations are discarded and a new, posthumous identity emerges. Taken together, the stakes of these premises are high. They turn suicide into critical kryptonite; the act threatens to reverse some of the fundamental tenets of poststructuralist theory and post-Barthes reading practices, ultimately betraying some of those practices' most dearly held precepts in favour of a popular-culture romanticizing of the individual subject visible, say, in a newspaper obituary.[12]

Suicide under Scrutiny

The way popular and scholarly discourses are deployed depends to some degree on which of the many definitions of suicide is in use. For the purposes of this study, suicide will mean voluntary death.[13] It is not my intention here to take a stance in the millennial debates about definitions of suicide, nor do I wish to belittle the importance of definitions for healthcare providers, legal specialists, or the families and friends of suicides or potential suicides. For these and for all people, definitions matter greatly: hence the frequency with which suicide is contested.[14] The contestation is, moreover, a juridical question as much as it is one of posthumous reputation. In Great Britain, for example, rulings of suicide are rare in the absence of proof (such as a note stating intent).[15] The motive that subtends the practical questions of such a ruling gives voice to our reluctance to accept suicide. Indeed, suicides have been debated since Socrates drank his cup of hemlock. Merely to have intimated suicidal thoughts is difficult for some to countenance, particularly when it is a public figure whose death is under scrutiny, especially if she or he is one of those few with whom we associate virtue or courage.[16] Thus any definition, juridical or otherwise, must tangle with the issue of the subject him- or herself – with what we, as readers, believe about his or her character and circumstances.[17] The notion of altruistic self-sacrifice as suicide's virtuous twin, too, would seem to be contestable and contingent upon the cultural and historical context of its enactment, creating slippery distinctions between what philosopher Robert Martin calls 'impermissible' and 'permissible' suicides.[18] In other words, even the most casual conversation about suicide is already vexed, in some ways, by a deep-seated reluctance (at least in Western culture) to accept the term. But for my purposes it is more important that there be a general consensus among scholars, readers, family members, and the press that a suicide has taken place – in fact, it is the consensus that matters most, since I am interested in what the general assumption of an author's suicide does to that author's readership.

I am certainly not the first to note the general discomfort with which the subject of suicide is broached or ignored. Nor is it surprising that the cultural and historical vicissitudes of suicide are functions of their time and place. For scholars, the indeterminacy of suicide, and of death in general, is what makes it endlessly fascinating. Both cause and result of this fascination, suicide figures or is figured simultaneously within many disparate scholarly discourses: those of literature and/or writing more broadly conceived, the law, the body, and philosophy, morality, and ethics (to name a few).[19] It is at once a question of materiality and of interpretation, involving both a corpse and a corpus of writing, as articulated here by Derrida:

> there can be an anthropology or a history of death, there can be culturologies of demise, ethnologies of mortuary rites, of ritual sacrifice, of the

work of mourning, of burials, of preparations for death, of the cleansing of the dead, of the languages of death in general, of medicine, and so on. But there is no culture of *death* itself or of *properly dying*. Dying is neither entirely natural (biological) nor cultural. And the question of limits articulated here is also the question of the border between cultures, languages, countries, nations, and religions, as well as that of the limit between a universal (although non-natural) structure and a differential (non-natural but cultural) structure.[20]

Derrida implies that the reticence about purposeful death that we mentioned above follows from its position at the heart of multiple scholarly discourses, or limits. Each of these is inextricably entangled with the others and they, in turn, shape the questions we ask, or do not, after a suicide. If it is true that language constitutes culture, then the ramifications of this cultural aphasia are far-reaching.

The Corpus of Writing

If Derrida[21] argues that death is outside culture, he also theorizes death as constitutive of culture: '[C]ulture itself, culture in general, is essentially, before anything, even a priori, the culture of death. Consequently, then, it is a *history of death*.'[22] In other words, Derrida engages with death in a way that at once foregrounds it as the cornerstone of culture, and effaces it for lack of culture: culture is the history of death, and yet there is no culture of death. Later in this study, I will invoke Derrida in support of my earlier observation that suicide derails even committed anti-humanists. For now it is sufficient to note the self-reflectivity of Derrida's theoretical engagement with death, a quality that permits him to invoke both the presence and the absence of a culture of '*properly dying*,' which is even more apposite in the case of an author's suicide, for whom the silence imposed by death is not casual but intentional, arising not from death's liminality ('neither entirely natural (biological) nor cultural') but from the inextricability of suicide *and writing*:

> How does one give *oneself* death [se donner la mort]? How does one give it to oneself in the sense that putting oneself to death means dying while assuming responsibility for one's own death, committing suicide but also sacrificing oneself for another, *dying for the other*, thus perhaps giving one's life by giving oneself death, accepting the gift of death, such as Socrates, Christ, and others did in so many different ways ... How does one give

oneself death in that other sense in terms of which *se donner la mort* is also
to interpret death, to give oneself a representation of it, a figure, a signification or destination for it?[23]

Secrecy, suicide, and sacrifice each overlie one another both at the point
of writing ('give oneself a representation of it') and at the point of reading (and 'a signification or destination for it'). Of all possible deaths,
suicide, it seems, demands interpretation.

And yet, the people whom I study committed suicide for reasons
that had as much to do with life as they did with writing. *Pace* Derrida, for whom death and writing are inextricably bound up, we might
answer that people have lives and interests outside of their writing.[24]
Scholars have long attempted to get at this differentiation within a living and a writing subject. Borrowing from Durkheim's suicides, Ernst
Kantorowicz's medieval king, and Irina Paperno's anatomical studies
of suicides in the 1800s, the term 'double man' is useful to resolve the
ambiguities embodied by man as both an individual and an institution,
as social and physical, and as immortal and mortal – Christ is perhaps
the most egregious example.[25] Alternatively, Giorgio Manganelli and
Giorgio Agamben employ the term *homopseudonymy*, that is, the use of a
pseudonym that is identical to one's own name, to get at this doubling
of the writing subject.[26] I, too, will attempt to get at the ways the figures
I study are at once individuals with varied interests and needs outside
or independent of the texts they produce, *and* coextensive with their
writing(s).[27] Emile Durkheim's groundbreaking study of suicide[28] theo-
rized the social as an object of inquiry when he took what had hitherto
been considered the most private of acts and turned it into something
quantifiable, chartable, describable – a social phenomenon, not an individual one. In a sense then, I am continuing in his tradition by reading
suicide in its public manifestations but also allowing it to have a private
component as well.

I should clarify, though, that the purposeful organizing and hasten-
ing of death is my object of inquiry. Thus the links between writing and
death will also be significant insofar as they constitute the manifestations of agency on the part of the author. The authoring of one's own
death will be key to conceptualizing the ways suicide acts as a form of
writing or rewriting. Again, as in discussions of motives, which shift
easily from noble to ignoble and back again, we must note the slipperi-
ness of the notion of that agency which, in the case of a suicide, implies
at once autonomy and surrender, victory and defeat, dignity and weakness, sentimentality and stoicism.[29] Such vacillation between the attri-

bution, to the suicide, of positive qualities and of negative ones has two effects. On the one hand, it deprives the suicide of the (perhaps only momentary)[30] decisiveness necessary for suicide, and on the other, it erases from the equation the simple fact that it is difficult to commit suicide – that under any circumstance, it requires an act of will. As Alfred Alvarez, an exceptionally warm, human, and at times poetic narrator of the experiences of the suicidal, puts it, such a deprivation is misguided:

> suicide is, after all, the result of a choice. However impulsive the action and confused the motives, at the moment when a man finally decides to take his own life he achieves a certain temporary clarity. Suicide may be a declaration of bankruptcy which passes judgment on a life as one long history of failures. But it is a history which also amounts at least to this one decision which, by its very finality, is not wholly a failure. Some kind of minimal freedom – the freedom to die in one's own way and in one's own time – has been salvaged from the wreck of all those unwanted necessities.[31]

Similarly, Andrew Solomon describes the *active* quality of suicide, asserting that it is 'really more of an anxiety response than a depression solution: it is not the action of a null mind but of a tortured one. The physical symptoms of anxiety are so acute that they seem to demand a physical response: not simply the mental suicide of silence and of sleep, but the physical one of self-slaughter.'[32] To my mind, the 'certainty' (implicit in Solomon's comments) that one's situation will never improve, however mistaken it may be, supports a reading of suicide as an act of strength, the agony of the suicide's survivors notwithstanding. It is in that spirit that I, too, stake out my position on the matter, for considering how difficult, indeed how impractical suicide is (the amount of planning, forethought, attention to detail often required), it is a short step from malice to deny the suicide, at the very least, the respect due to anyone who follows a path strewn with so many obstacles all the way to its very end. In the more eloquent words of Alvarez, 'To have that last, partial and lop-sided triumph turned, for reasons of decency and bureaucracy, into a malicious accident is to compound failures with final failure.'[33]

The Corpse

It is, in part, that very finality that gives observers (whether intimate or casual) such pause. As an act that can be neither 'denied nor reversed,'[34] suicide makes us look to the artifacts left behind for some sense of the meaning with which the suicidal gesture was imbued. These artifacts may include letters or testaments; they must also include the suicide's corpse.[35] Because the subject of that agency and the object on which it is exerted are one and the same, we must also engage with theories of writing and the body, insofar as the body of the suicide presents a new surface on which to inscribe one's story. Vincent Crapanzano writes,

> The body – more, but not completely, accurately the 'body' – can serve rhetorically to mediate (to give the illusion of mediating), to close (to give the illusion of closing), the split in signification between the signifier and the signified. It is, I believe, precisely the privileged status we grant the body as – How shall I put it? – so intimately bound to us as to be at once object and subject of our (conscious) experience that gives it this mediating role. It permits the confounding of body (as signified) and 'body' (as signifier) and gives to the body a special rhetorical role, one that 'anchors' signification.[36]

This is doubly true for the suicide: observers care what happened to the body of a suicide for reasons that go beyond a simple, covert taste for the macabre or the obscene. We also care about the body because, quite simply, it is often all that is left. In the presence of a suicide note, the body acts in conjunction with the written word as a testament of desire. In the absence of a note explaining or justifying the decision to die, the body serves as the sole 'reliable' relic of the dead, the only indication of proof of will. Thus it is the very site of writing: the suicide writes with her body, literally and metaphorically: he or she writes the final word and rewrites the (real) words. Interpretation, then, can be said to share the lexicon of anatomy; dissection, vivisection, autopsy – these are instances in which the body becomes a legible text. What is more, the corpse of the suicide is the ideal place to understand the relationship between individual and society; for Irina Paperno, anatomy (or the study of the parts to understand the whole) finds its complementary approach in moral statistics (looking at the whole to understand the individual), and together the two represent solutions to the impulse to understand through the processes of dismantling.[37] Put differently, the metaphors linking the body and the text, in the case of suicide, can thus be read both ways. These linkages are visible both in cases of suicide by literary authors and within literature when traced through terms like *madness*[38] (a term now more commonly, and less disparagingly, replaced with *depression*, though that is not always its meaning).[39] And yet the links between depression, suicide, and exceptional creative abilities in men and women alike are strong, particularly among poets.[40]

The material body of the suicide, then, does communicate itself. The body, the thing forces upon us a (re-)turn to the material, to the pragmatic,[41] to forms of inquiry that imply possible resolution, in sharp contradistinction from the self-reflective or purposefully, indeed playfully, indeterminate modes of inquiry characterized by the Derrida passage cited above. At the same time, we are talking about writing which, with Shoshana Felman, 'continues to communicate with madness – with what has been excluded, decreed abnormal, unacceptable, or senseless – by dramatizing a dynamically renewed, revitalized relation between sense and nonsense, between reason and unreason, between the readable and the unreadable.'[42] So we are dealing at once with an aesthetic object, informed by the consciousness of its creator and therefore subject to the same kinds of hermeneutical practices as, say, a poem, and a historical one, whose interpretive practices are susceptible to the potentially fallacious assumption of non-provisionality, totality, and impartiality.

Methodologies

It is my claim that the suicide of an author reinscribes the dyad of writer-reader, instigating a reinterpretation of his or her opus by readers armed with new hermeneutical tools. Insofar as I, too, am part of that dyad, I must make claims (and disclaimers) about the kind of rereading I propose. For if suicide necessitates rereading, then the reading subject is as much up for grabs as the writerly one – perhaps even more so – and must be taken into equal if not greater consideration in any attempt to understand the text anew. Thus it must be clear from the outset that the pages that follow are driven exclusively by my own preferences, biases, and foibles as a reader[43] and, as such, must be approached with a different set of expectations from those one might bring, say, to a scholarly monograph by a card-carrying Marxist critic. Instead, I employ a variety of sources and borrow from a variety of disciplines, including literary theory, history, psychology, philosophy, and theories of suicide, since I cannot allege a less subjective stance without replicating the very postures of critical objectivity, of omniscience, or of 20/20 hindsight that I seek to dispute. It is for that reason, moreover, that throughout the study I will continue to refer to Derrida's concepts of lingering or of haunting (though not necessarily in the ways Derrida intended) in order to invoke the ways the *spectres* (to borrow again) of these suicides inform, i.e. trouble, our readings of their works.[44]

The stakes of this project are literary-historical (in the form of a clearer understanding of four specific authors' lives and works in their respective contexts); social (both in its debt to Emile Durkheim, whose *Suicide: A Study in Sociology* can be said to mark the birth of the field, and insofar as it illuminates the meaning of suicide in a given social context); and theoretical. As I mentioned earlier, my initial premise holds that *prior* to an author's suicide, popular (that is to say, non-scholarly) readings of an author's literature are pro-humanistic and pro-individual subject, and thus popular reading practices are founded on the bedrock of his or her biography. In contrast, scholarly reading practices for the last several generations have striven to do the opposite in accordance with the hegemonic views (following the usual suspects: Mallarmé, Wimsatt and Beardsley, Barthes, Foucault, Derrida) of the author as an entity to be excluded from any and all interpretive approaches to his or her texts. Of these, it is Barthes and his 1968 piece 'The Death of the Author' that really got the ball rolling, although, as Seán Burke cogently notes, Barthes's anti-authorial argument is in fact 'deeply auteurist'[45] in the sense that the deicide for which it calls requires as a prerequisite the conviction that the Author is a kind of God (and indeed Barthes's term is Author-God). Moreover, its injunction is only partial, insofar as it is irrelevant for women authors and for non-white, non-bourgeois male authors, who never enjoyed the privileged status conferred by authorship to begin with. But despite these qualifications (and despite the fact that, as we said, a different view is held by readers *outside* the academy, who might feel that such a proposition is somewhat counter-intuitive), Barthes's assertions have possibly enjoyed a broader influence than any other literary-critical pronouncement of the last forty years.

It is my contention that *after* an author's suicide, the scholarly reading practices to which I refer are discarded. Instead, the scholarly discourse generated by a suicide resembles the pro-individual subject stance taken, say, in reviews and obituaries in the popular press, where the list of considerations runs the gamut from early childhood experiences to personal tragedies, religious beliefs, financial issues, obsessions, compulsions, medications, left- or right-handedness, pet allergies, boxers versus briefs … the list could go on indefinitely. In the case of an author's suicide, scholarly and non-scholarly readers meet on common ground – that is, share similar reading practices – because it is too difficult to maintain the equation author = God in the face of the author's all-too-human demise. Hence the critical mass of theorists who re-eval-uate the role of the author;[46] I contend, instead, that the suicide of an author represents a crisis in critical theory, one that authorizes the tem-porary dismantling of theoretical constructs, with the consequence that after a suicide, the author becomes, effectively, absolutely central to our understanding (or misunderstanding) of the text.

This crisis happens not out of the blue but as the result of long-per-colating conflicts within the critical oeuvres of the two most influential theoreticians of anti-authorialism, Barthes and Derrida. Burke (whose scholarship I oversimplify here) demonstrated that Barthes himself reconsiders the place of biography in interpretation (though never evaluation) in *Sade Fourier Loyola*, as well as *Camera Lucida*;[47] and, simi-larly, Derrida in *Of Grammatology* does away with questions of psycho-biography immediately after making ample use of its methods in his discussion of Rousseau.[48] Indeed, Burke confirms my earlier observa-tion that for Derrida, life and writing were coextensive: 'life itself, in its materiality, even as it was lived, is writing.'[49] This is what Derrida means when he says, 'There is nothing outside the text' in *Of Gramma-tology*: it is a way to have his anti-authorial cake and eat it too.[50] In sum, then, we have Barthes, on the one hand, who in 'Death of the Author' posits an all-powerful Author in order to reduce him more dramati-cally, and then reinstates him in the writings that follow (and we might ask the extent to which he meant any of these pronouncements to be taken seriously, authorial intent being very much of the essence). And on the other hand, we have Derrida disavowing the role of the author by calling him, too, text, so that Derrida can continue to have recourse to the author without having to admit it. So in a sense, then, the return to the popular reading of an author after suicide – a pro-authorial read-ing, that is – represents not a reversal of Barthes's and Derrida's previ-ous critical stances so much as the eruption of those critical tendencies previously present but always repressed, to the surface.

Let me now refine my previous thesis statement. I contend that the question of the author has always represented a site of productive engagement in the theoretical works of Barthes, Foucault, and Derrida, and that this question *appeared* to be largely resolved. Far from it: autho-rial suicide brings to the fore the unresolved nature of critical thinking about authors and authorship. It reveals that this productive engage-ment is in fact a function of a crisis in critical theory, one that has been a long time coming – indeed, at least since 1968 – and that is visible in the temporary dismantling of theoretical constructs that takes place after an author's suicide, after which the author becomes, effectively, absolutely central to our understanding of the text. The rapprochement of popular and scholarly reading practices in the wake of an author's suicide is a direct consequence of the inability of certain kinds of theory to countenance the necessity of an authorial subject constituted not simply as text or exaltedly as God, but built, rather, on a human scale. It is theory coming to terms with its occasionally mystifying tendencies. This is not to say that theories that deal with the author have, like pop music, eaten themselves, but rather, as Greil Marcus demonstrated in *Dead Elvis*, that the dead author has never been busier than since his/her demise.

Thus there are two components to each chapter. The first is an analysis of the effects of an author's suicide on his or her reception. For each author, I initially take a three-pronged approach, examining 1) the critical reception of the author's works by scholars and non-specialists alike before (when possible) and after his or her suicide, 2) obituaries and other commemorative writings that engage issues in the life of the author, and 3) the written artifacts left by the author, usually in the form of letters and diaries, as well as writings of a personal nature *about* the author. The second part of my argument in each chapter takes up my second observation, namely that when an author commits suicide, all critical bets are off. Where previously critical consensus was in command, it abandons ship, leaving a motley crew of readers in uncharted territory. The result is what we might call the 'strange bedfellows' phenomenon, a methodological reorganization such that authors whose works were previously read as aesthetic objects are repositioned with respect to their own personal history, often with unproductive results. The second component of each chapter consists of my own close reading of one of the author's texts. In the spirit of my assertion that the spectres of suicide throw scholarly reading practices – not just of these particular authors' works, but also more generally – into crisis, I propose to enact a new relationship between reader and author, to find a productive middle ground between the two extremes of materialist or biographical reading strategies, which foreground the context of the suicide and events prior to it, and wholly autonomous linguistic readings that draw a *cordon sanitaire* around the works, excising all things extra-textual. I am also interested in interrogating the related question of how collective memories about these authors formed, and which concrete practices serve to maintain or vex them. Thus the theoretical framework within each chapter consists of unorthodox pairings: Morselli with Giuseppe Rensi and Jacques Monod, Rosselli with Sarah Kofman, Pavese with Giorgio Agamben, Gianni Vattimo, and Emanuele Severino, and Levi with Avishai Margalit. Aimed at eliciting readings that are not possible either when the suicide takes centre stage or is suppressed, these pairings work both ways; the theories illuminate the texts and the texts illuminate the theories, and the authors teach us about the theoreticians as much as the reverse.

In chapter 1, we see how suicide creates an author. The chapter is devoted to Guido Morselli (1912–1973), whose suicide caused a scandal in the publishing world not because his death surprised his public, but because until his suicide, he had no public. The simultaneous discoveries of his body and his body of work mean that his discovery as a writer is always in some way a *response* to his suicide. Subsumed under the question of his ill-fated attempts to publish, suicide becomes a secondary or submerged discourse, repackaged as professional failure. Interestingly, Morselli's works (as well as criticism of them) often tell the story of what *might have been,* had individual elements in his protagonists' lives gone differently. The importance of these counter-histories in Morselli's novels seems to corroborate that interpretation, offering a tidy narrative with which to tie his life, death, and writings together. I contend that it is by way of the works on chance, history, and causality of Giuseppe Rensi and Jacques Monod that we may most productively formulate an alternate narrative with which to understand Morselli's suicide. Although they draw upon different bodies of knowledge in their writings – Rensi was a philosopher and Monod a Nobel Prize-winning biologist – their shared scepticism about linear narratives of history and nature, and their preference for a view of life as randomly or arbitrarily governed, argue against the more pragmatic readings about Morselli's professional failure currently in circulation.

The next chapter investigates a case of suicide discounted as madness, in its examination of the poet Amelia Rosselli (1930–1996) and her collection of English-language poems entitled *Sleep*. These poems, considered alongside her suicide on the thirty-third anniversary of Sylvia Plath's suicide, seem to authorize a reading that resituates Rosselli in relation to her genealogical predecessors, specifically her father Carlo Rosselli (an antifascist resistance martyr) and her grandmother (celebrated playwright Amelia Pincherle Rosselli). To understand the complex ways in which issues of genealogy – familial and literary – work themselves out in Rosselli's life and literary opus, I focus on the repositioning of her work in posthumous reviews. After suicide, critics all but ignore kinship ties with her father and grandmother, and they soft-pedal links to those poets with whom she had previously been associated; instead, she is more frequently read alongside Sylvia Plath, who eclipses Rosselli's familial and literary ties. And yet it is philosopher Sarah Kofman, I argue, whose writings (and whose life, the intermittent subject of her writings) better illuminate the ways Rosselli's suicide thwarts attempts at establishing her genealogy. This chapter also asks how the role of mental illness (perceived or real) shapes public views about suicide, and examines the sociological and gender ramifications of Rosselli's case alongside the literary-critical ones.

Chapter 3 is about a successful novelist and suicide, Cesare Pavese (1908–1950), who, unlike Morselli, left behind a highly scrutinized body of works. Pavese's star rose quickly in the years before the Second World War and his writings were firmly inserted into a series of literary-political rubrics (leftist, antifascist, intellectual). Thus with Pavese's suicide, critical revisions of his opus involve not just revising received knowledge about Pavese as an individual, but also reinterpreting his relationship with the Italian left. Since he was supposedly 'at the height of his fame' (the expression itself is already a judgment) when he died, his suicide casts a retroactive pall on the shared history and common values of the generation of readers who previously saw themselves in his writings. Moreover, unlike Morselli's exemplary and sympathetic figure, Pavese's biographical particulars – depression, impotence – lend a whiff of pathos to the scandal of his death. Since then, his suicide has evolved, in the minds of some critics, from an act of modern ideological and/or intimate dissatisfaction to a postmodern one in which bodily death is representative more simply (and infinitely, more openly) of a new kind of writing. This transformation elucidates the political nature of the author's textual remains, which stand in for the authorial body.

Chapter 4 examines the complex figure of Primo Levi, who threatens all previous arguments about the relationship between suicide and literary production. Although Levi's authorial persona was built upon the foundation of a discourse of survivorship, suicide was nonetheless always present in his biography, and death was always present in his writings, whether in the centre, at the sidelines, or as structuring absences. The transformative experience of his suicide on his opus implies, paradoxically, both a continuum of suicidal impulses and their thwarting, by Levi as a historical subject, an author, and a Holocaust survivor. Critics have been very unsuccessful in their dealings with his death, which does not and cannot follow any of the patterns we described in other chapters. We can neither judge it as a function of psychological (or other) instability, as happens with Rosselli and Pavese, because such a move might invalidate his texts; nor can we ignore the suicide, because it was always in some way there. Levi offers in many ways the exception to the rule I have been describing. Where readers and critics would otherwise flatten the distinctions between suicide-writers, drawing conclusions that place them in closer proximity than is possibly warranted by their writings and their lives, Levi is by many accounts understood in stark contrast to them. It is the minority of his biographers (Thomson, Angier) who understand suicide to have been an at least intermittent concern of his throughout his lifetime, the majority preferring to read his life and works as untainted by similar considerations. Thus with Levi we countenance the limitations of our model: the ways both acts of writing such as those of a suicide and the criticism it provokes are also, at times, acts of erasure.

My attempt, in Derrida's words, to 'speak to the specter' is no doubt self-serving, if only because to the extent that we are all haunted by our own ghosts, it gives me a vantage point from which to tangle with my own.[51] From the standpoint of my position as a scholar, such a potentially sensationalist venture (see above for gunshot wound, overdose of sleeping pills, falls from great heights) runs the risk of cloaking its sensationalism under the mantle of condolence. But it is my hope that we as readers, as survivors, may gain some advantage from the practice as well. To that end, the mandate of this study is twofold: first, to clarify our understanding of the relationship of suicide to authorship and reading (and to maintain the validity of both as authorities, in different capacities) and thus to bring greater clarity to the practices of literary criticism; and second, to keep in view the singularity and prerogatives of the authors—not as objects of inquiry so much as points on which to fix, with Wordsworth, our 'inward eye.' Suicide is a special category of death (though a diffuse one, sadly), and so in a certain sense all suicides speak to each other; the trick is to understand their dialogue without losing track of the distinctiveness of their voices. My hope is that such a search for understanding may be beneficial, ultimately, to any endeavour to mourn, to commemorate, and truly to bury our dead.

1 The Posthumous Author: Guido Morselli, Giuseppe Rensi, Jacques Monod

The Life and Death of Guido Morselli

Dispongo che mi si dia sepoltura nel cimitero di Giubiano (Varese), non nella cappella di famiglia, bensì in terra aperta, con una tomba semplicissima, senza alcuna struttura sovrastante, senza ornamenti né simboli ... Una lastra di pietra con il mio nome e nient'altro.

Alla mia morte nessun avviso ne sarà dato sui giornali ... Il funerale avrà luogo nella maniera più semplice e disadorna, senza alcuna solennità o funzione ecclesiastica, senza fiori né 'corone' o simili.

Subito dopo il mio decesso, dispongo che un medico mi pratichi una iniezione al cuore di tal natura da poter determinare di per sé la morte.

Ciò a scongiurare la possibilità di inumazione del vivente – in caso di morte solo apparente, inoltre la salma verrà immessa nel feretro non prima di sessanta ore intere da quella in cui la detta iniezione sarà stata fatta – e ciò anche in deroga di eventuali prescrizioni contrarie di polizia mortuaria.

Autorizzo l'impiego di organi della mia salma a scopo di trapianto. In specie fegato, polmoni e reni – che sin d'ora mi pare di avere in buono stato fisiologico.[1]

I direct that I be buried in the cemetery of Giubiano (Varese), not in the family chapel but rather in open ground, with an extremely simple tomb, without any structure over it, and without ornaments or symbols ... A slab of stone with my name and nothing more.

No announcement of my death is to be made in the newspapers ... The funeral will take place in the simplest and plainest manner possible, without any solemnity or ecclesiastic function, without flowers or 'wreaths' or the like.

Immediately after my death, I direct that a doctor perform an injection to the heart of such nature as could itself provoke death.

This is in order to avoid the possibility of burying the living – in the case of an only apparent death, moreover, the body will not be placed in the coffin until a full sixty hours have passed from the time said injection was performed – and this even in derogation of any possible conflicting regulations by the coroner. I authorize the use of organs from my corpse for purposes of transplant. Liver, lungs, and kidneys in particular – till now these have seemed to me to be in good physiological state.

The life of Guido Morselli (1912–1973) began with a whimper and ended with a bang.[2] With regard to the former, critics are quick to note two facts about his early years. First is the suicide of a family member, Morselli's uncle.[3] Second, Morselli wrote prolifically from childhood, starting with a novel entitled *La mia vita*,[4] begun at eight years of age; he also kept a diary from 1938 until his death.[5] Aside from occasional travels, various lovers, and much horseback riding, Morselli's life was largely devoted to writing. Publications, however, were limited to a tiny handful compared to what he wrote.[6] By the time Morselli died, he had written no fewer than nine novels (plus assorted screenplays and works for theatre), all of which were rejected for publication.[7] It is precisely these rejections that constitute the heart of critical interest in the figure of Guido Morselli. Two weeks before his sixty-first birthday, Morselli shot himself with his Browning. Within a year of his suicide, a major Italian publishing house committed to publishing all of his novels.

How did Morselli's suicide affect his reception as a writer? The simple answer, of course, is it created it: before his suicide, there *was* no reception, unless we consider the letters of regret sent to him by the publishing houses to which he submitted them.[8] We cannot, therefore, engage with his readership and their responses to his literature *before* Morselli committed suicide, and compare it to the criticism that followed. Nor can we expect there to be as *much* criticism of his writings as there is of Cesare Pavese or Amelia Rosselli, authors whose writerly production was more or less immediately commented upon by a waiting public. Instead, we can note, first, that once he was actually (posthumously) published, a different set of data was used to educate readers and to form opinions of his literature; and second, that what criticism there is on Morselli is as often as not meta-criticism, that is, discussion of the ways he has and has not been read. In the absence of pre-suicide reviews of Morselli's literature, the critics turned to Morselli's life.

Morselli's readers seized upon presumed signs of suicidal behaviour both in his literature (as it was made public) and in his diary – a move that differs from responses to Rosselli's or Pavese's deaths in so far as it is concomitant with the development of a readership, not subsequent to it, that his readers were educated, as it were, about his life.

Morselli is, in a sense, not an author or in any case not readable until he commits suicide; suicide is a threshold (following Gérard Genette and Maurice Couturier on *les seuils*, thresholds or paratexts) we must cross to enter into the text proper. Couturier, who sees the reader and the author locked in an economy of mutual, asymmetrical desire, triangulated by the text, wherein the reader continually desires the author's presence and the author desires to differentiate himself, to individuate as something other than that which he has represented, argues that paratexts are a way for the author to distance himself from autobiographical readings or readings that attribute potentially problematic novelistic depictions to their author. These paratexts are construed to include title pages, dedications, epigraphs, author photos, publicity for the book, and so on – all designed (for Couturier) to demonstrate the author's difference from the contents of the actual text. I think we can argue that suicide, then, is an epitext, that is a paratext that is not part of the physical volume of the book, but rather is enacted, like – maudlin thought – a publicity interview or a book tour. As such, in contrast to the differentiation described by Couturier, suicide guarantees the satisfaction of a desiring reader by way of the biographical readings it seems to authorize.

This is evident in the way it is difficult to distinguish Morselli's biographers from his critics. While it is not uncommon for a literary study to begin with a brief biography of the author at hand, it is less frequently the case that the biography is indistinguishable from the criticism. Because his death was contemporaneous with his 'discovery' by publishers and readers, much of what is written about him falls under the rubric of psychobiography, a critical methodology that places weight on certain kinds of phenomena from an author's life. Morselli is thus a useful point of departure in our attempt to understand how we negotiate the knowledge of an author's suicide. Thus in this chapter and the chapters to follow, I will resist the common tendency that takes suicide as the basis for always already overdetermined readings. Instead, I will advocate a different order of operations. Performing an attentive reading of the author's texts – not of his death – seems to me to be the point of departure for any successful engagement with the author if our goal is to make meaning of the work, the life, and the interplay between them.

Wallowing in a Pool of His Own Ink

Si chiamava Guido Morselli, era nato a Bologna nel 1912, è vissuto per anni, strambo e solitario, nella sua tenuta a Gavirate, scrivendo libri su libri che non pubblicò mai. Il 31 luglio si è tolto la vita a Varese. Finis. Finis? No. A parte l'anima, in cui forse questo suicidio credeva disperatamente, resta ora la sua opera, la sua fama. E quelle sono appena all'inizio. Avesse visto come si comincia a battagliare, con la lingua e con la penna, intorno a lui, difendendolo, pesandolo, giudicandolo (c'è chi lo crede addirittura un prete tuttora vivo e vegeto, che si avvale di uno pseudonimo), forse non rimpiangerebbe di essersene andato prima di conoscere di persona che cos'è la 'gloria' letteraria. Ma sarà vera gloria? Nessuno può dirlo oggi nemmeno coloro che scoprono già in lui il nuovo Tomasi di Lampedusa e nel suo libro il nuovo Gattopardo ... E poi, si parla di ben otto – dico otto! – altri romanzi, e parecchi altri testi letterari di ogni tipo. C'è il caso che questo *Roma senza papa* sia solo una delle corde della sua cetra tuttora ignota: magari nemmeno la più sonora e rappresentativa.[9]

His name was Guido Morselli, he was born in Bologna in 1912, he lived for years, eccentric and solitary, in his estate at Gavirate, writing book after book that he never published. On 31 July he took his own life in Varese. The end. The end? No. Apart from the soul, in which perhaps this suicide desperately believed, there remains his work, his fame. And these are only just beginning. Had he seen how they begin to fight about him, with the tongue and with the pen, defending him, weighing him, judging him (there are even those who believe him to be a priest, still living and breathing, who uses a pseudonym), perhaps he would not regret having died before learning the meaning of 'literary glory' firsthand. But is it true glory? No one can say so today, not even those who have already discovered in him the new Tomasi di Lampedusa and in his book the new Leopard ... And then, we are talking about eight – yes, eight! – other novels and several other literary texts of various types. It's possible that this *Roma senza papa* is just one of the strings on his as yet unknown bow – perhaps not even the most resounding and representative.

La prima tentazione è di dire che c'è stato anche un Gattopardo del Nord. Viveva in luoghi profondamente lombardi, tra Gavirate e Varese. Scrisse migliaia di pagine. Sperò a lungo che gli editori si accorgessero di lui. E' morto il 31 luglio dell'anno scorso. Adesso esce un suo romanzo, Roma senza papa, pubblicato dalla Adelphi, e se ne resta attoniti, come davanti a un frutto raro e inimmaginabile.

L'altra tentazione è di dire che questo è il vero caso letterario del'74. Le componenti ci sono tutte: la sorpresa, il sottofondo di una vita ignorata, le carte uscite *post mortem* dai cassetti, l'ombra d'una pena inspiegata e sottile, l'irrompere d'una fantasia profetica. Eppure, come si è trattenuti, dubbiosi. L'etichetta del caso letterario comporta suoni trionfali.[10]

The first temptation is to say that there was also a Leopard from the North. He lived in deep Lombardy, between Gavirate and Varese. He wrote thousands of pages. He long hoped that the editors would take notice of him. He died on 31 July of last year. Now one of his novels is coming out, *Roma senza papa*, published by Adelphi, and they are astonished as though before a rare and unimaginable fruit.

The other temptation is to say that this is the true *caso letterario* of 1974. The pieces are all there: the surprise, the background of a life unknown, the papers that emerged post mortem from drawers, the shadow of an unexplained and subtle pain, the eruption of a prophetic imagination. And yet, they have held back, doubtful. The label of literary case carries with it the sounds of triumph.

Negotiating authorial suicide would imply, presumably, an interplay between materialist and aesthetic readings; it would take into account both the texts as texts and the facts around the suicide and his debut as an author (and any relationships between them). It must also encompass the web of multiple relations in which any book is ensnared, a veritable tangle that includes readers and writers, to be sure, but also the editors, publicists, and critics who have professional (and therefore economic) stakes in the success of the novel. But the introduction of the notion of a *caso Morselli* in the above excerpts (from reviews of *Roma senza papa*, the first novel to be published after his death) illustrates the complexity of the calculus required to achieve that interplay. The first quote, an enthusiastic report on the 'discovery' of Morselli as well as the anticipation of more of his writings to come, ends on a note of regret for the inauthenticity (sarà vera gloria?) of his belated recognition; the second excerpt views the new case with a slightly more jaundiced eye and an ear keen enough to hear the editors popping open bottles of prosecco. Suicide sparks a *caso letterario*: it creates a kind of free-for-all, after which all manner of otherwise unspoken questions are uttered.

Thus questions about the writer's possible motives (is Morselli not a dead writer but a priest, alive and kicking?) as well as those of the publishèr (after all, Tomasi was a real cash cow) are apparently relevant, as are speculations about the contents of his desk drawers. By that token, then, Morselli's suicide represents something rather fiercer than Couturier's triangulated hunt,[11] which now appears as a genteel game of hide and seek. Here, instead, is an ambush – the reader, triumphant, is free to chivvy out the author like a stoat from his hole.

Consider the premise of a book that holds that Morselli is 'uno scrittore amato e stimato dalla critica e dal pubblico per la profondità e l'elevatezza dei messaggi, la verità e l'interiorità dei personaggi, la tristezza e la disperata solitudine della vita, l'ardua dignità del vivere e del soffrire; per avere rappresentato nella sua opera, amplificati dal genio e dalla disperazione, modi di sentire emblematici, nella loro antiteticità, dell'uomo moderno: l'insofferenza e la fragilità, l'esasperazione nel vivere con gli altri, la difficoltà di vivere senza gli altri'[12] (a writer beloved and esteemed by critics and the public for the depth and loftiness of his messages, the truth and inner life of his characters, the sadness and the desperate solitude of his life, the arduous dignity of living and of suffering; for having represented in his works, amplified by genius and by desperation, the emblematic ways of feeling, in their antitheticalness, of modern man: the intolerance and the fragility, the exasperation of living with others, the difficulty of living without others). This assessment of his writing, to my mind, is convincing; it is an acute observation about the concerns of his fiction and the elegance of their exposition. But I am curious about 'the sadness and the desperate solitude of his life, the arduous dignity of living and of suffering.' These seem relevant to his *writings*, and they anticipate what follows about the difficulties of existence and of negotiating life as an anti-social social being. Applying them to his *life*, however, and citing them as justifications for critical and public love and esteem, is arguably motivated exclusively by foreknowledge of his suicide, which is seen as the concrete result of that sadness and desperate solitude. This elision of writerly and personal qualities seems to argue the case for special dispensation toward author-suicides – not toward their writing, but toward their person. For the sake of argument, take the case either of a bad novelist, or of a capable novelist who dies, Methuselah-like, of natural causes: ought we to love them on the basis of their arduous personal dignity as well? If so, on what basis do we determine that dignity – from their diaries? From personal accounts by friends and family? For some, Morselli's suicide seems to authorize jettisoning the conventions of most critical methodologies[13] in favour of an approach that retroactively attributes positive personal qualities to the dead author even as it bestows praise upon his works.

Hence the other tendency we may identify among some of his readers, that of seeking (and claiming to find) one-to-one correspondences between his novels and his diary entries. All roads, it seems, lead to suicide. For example, discussing responses (or their lack) from various intellectual figures with whom Morselli sought to discuss matters philosophical and spiritual, one commentator opined, 'Anche questa è stata una lotta vana durata trent'anni, nella quale colpisce la mancanza di attenzione, la fretta con cui le lettere venivano scorse, senza che nell'interlocutore sorgesse il sospetto di avere a che fare con un gioco intellettuale molto sottile che, come nella roulette russa, aveva ad oggetto di scommessa la vita di un uomo'[14] (This, too, was a vain struggle that lasted thirty years, in which the striking thing is the lack of attention, the haste with which the letters were perceived, without the interlocutor suspecting that he was dealing with a very subtle intellectual game that, as in Russian roulette, had as its wager the life of a man). It is correct to lament the lost opportunities for both Morselli and his would-be interlocutors, but it does not necessarily follow that our author's life was on the line with each rejection; the suicide still might not have happened, or happened at any number of points in his life (an issue to which we will return in our discussion of Giuseppe Rensi and Jacques Monod). Moreover, correlations between his diary and his literature mean that critics need not linger excessively on the actual image of his suicide, because they can subsume it under the question of his ill-fated attempts to publish. Suicide becomes a secondary or submerged discourse, repackaged as professional failure and bad timing. Shifting the emphasis away from multiple or unknowable motives, then, has two advantages. It imposes a logical coherence on Morselli's life, making it easier to package (and market, as sceptics might point out), and it obviates the need for analyses of his life and death that might contradict the dominant narrative. A general tendency among readers is to impose a coherent narrative logic on the life and the writing: this tendency is exacerbated almost to the point of absurdity in the case of authorial suicide. Readings such as these imply that the life before a suicide is a logical, linear construction with an organic, legible motive behind its every component, the sum total of which is a death that stands like the finished product. Arbitrary or contingent elements, indeed all of those 'non-suicidal' moments that like warped planks must be reshaped or discarded, are otherwise irrelevant to the overall construction.[15] Focusing on the professional failure in Morselli's life has the effect of expurgating, bowdlerizing, and prettifying an otherwise messy and discomfiting death.

Or, to put it differently, it reconfigures Morselli's novels as by-products of what Barthes called 'filiation.' Where once there were *texts* (that is, plural, subverting traditional classifications, irreducible, always in production in reaction to sign and not signified, and so on), it seems that suicide reduces them (Barthes might say) to the level of *work*, derived directly from the author, born exclusively of his loins: 'The author is reputed the father and the owner of his work; literary science therefore teaches respect for the manuscript and the author's declared intentions, while society asserts the legality of the relation of the author to work.'[16] According to the commonly held popular view, then, Morselli's professional failures found direct expression in the contents of his novels and, ultimately, in his death, the importance of the latter being precisely in the ways it was foretold in his novels.

Still others viewed the new scandal with the jaded eye of a trend-spotter. This is an equally teleological reading, characterized by the same tight soldering of the writing to the life, but with a different value judgment attached to it. In this reading, the *caso Morselli* is the newest example of the market-driven fashion for dead writers:

Phénomène isolé? Pas exactement si l'on songe, pour en rester au seul éditeur Adelphi, aux fortunes posthumes d'un S. Satta ... de l'italo-américain E. Carnevali ... ou encore de J.-R. Wilcock ... En France, il suffira de nommer l'opération précipitamment menée sur le cadavre de P.P. Pasolini, à la recherche de ses moindres brouillons inachevés alors qu'il n'existe toujours pas de traduction décente de son oeuvre poétique. Et puisque nous voici du côté de la poésie, glissons une dernière allusion aux suicides de E. Alesi, G. Monari, V. Reta (d'autres, moins connus), dans une décennie franchement exceptionnelle pour la 'situation nécrophagique' de l'industrie culturelle ...[17]

Isolated phenomenon? Not exactly, if one considers, to limit ourselves to Adelphi, the posthumous fortunes of S[alvatore] Satta ... of the Italian-American E[manuel] Carnevali ... or again of J[uan] R[odolfo] Wilcock ... In France, one need only mention the operation precipitously conducted on the cadaver of P[ier] P[aolo] Pasolini, in search of his tiniest, least

accomplished scribblings since there does not yet exist a decent translation of his poetry. And while we are talking about poetry, let's make one
last reference to the suicides of E[ros] Alesi, G[astone] Monari, V[ittorio]
Reta (and others less well known), in a decade frankly exceptional for the
'necrophagic situation' of the cultural industry ...

This passage illustrates two of the phenomena I described earlier. First,
we see a metacritical impulse that privileges Morselli's status as a dead
writer before it considers his writings, placing him alongside other
examples of posthumous discovery, though only Satta's case is really
comparable; Carnevali and Wilcock were published during their life-
times. The next reference is to Pasolini, who was enormously visible
when he died and therefore definitely *not* an example of the posthumously discovered writer. And second, the quote's discursive sleight
of hand ('while we are talking about poetry': though not, apparently,
Pasolini's) provides an ambiguous linkage that moves us to a list of suicides, an example of the strange bedfellows phenomenon, which places
Morselli within a catalogue of names whose only point of contact is
their suicides. What's more, this list is juxtaposed with the categorical
denial of the relevance for his suicide of Morselli's inability to publish
his novels: 'Plusieurs éditeurs ... ont refusé ses manuscrits; rien ne per-
met de supposer que ceci ait quelquechose à voir avec son suicide'[18]
(Several editors ... have refused his manuscripts; nothing permits us
to assume that this had anything to do with his suicide). Morselli's
suicide, it seems, would be irrelevant to his writing except for the fact
that he is a suicidal writer. In other words, critical reception is always
within the context of his case. Not simply good, bad, or indifferent as
a writer, Morselli is inevitably weighed against himself, as it were, in a
state of perpetual comparison with the posthumous reputation that sets
the terms for every reading.[19] Take, for example, the review of *Roma senza papa* (in French translation, released in 1979) that implicitly blames
Morselli's suicide on editorial neglect and ends by rather sarcastically
panning the book:

Guido Morselli s'est suicidé en 1973, à l'age de soixante et un ans. De son
vivant, il n'était pas parvenu à faire publier un seul de ses romans. Som-
mes-nous donc passés à côté d'un grand écrivain? ... Las! Le roman de
Morselli, froid, puissant, insidieux et même joliment prophétique, dérape
sur la fin. Le pape n'habite plus Rome et les Suisses débarquent sur la
Lune, ce qui bouleverse le narrateur. Mais pas nous. Dommage.[20]

Guido Morselli committed suicide in 1973 at the age of sixty-one. During his lifetime, he did not succeed in publishing a single novel. Did we then pass up a great writer? ... Alas, Morselli's novel, cold, powerful, insidious, and even nicely prophetic, loses its hold at the end. The pope no longer lives in Rome and the Swiss land on the moon, all of which astonishes the narrator. But not us. Too bad.

The scepticism evident here is meant to function as a corrective to the impulse to paint so many writers with the same brush. But even disregarding the inclination to see *il caso Morselli* as a public relations case in the making, the dominant narrative is nonetheless 1) publishing misfires 2) suicide 3) posthumous triumph, making suicide the grand finale on the virtual tour of his life, death, and miracles. Whether one is a sceptic shuffling dutifully past the grave or a grieving sympathizer, the method and timing of Morselli's death are part and parcel of any discussion of his work. Indeed, his suicide arguably constitutes our most significant received knowledge about them. The question, then, is whether or not that knowledge predetermines our readings by implying in some way that the works might be inferior, and that it took a move as dramatic as suicide (for who would be so heartless as to call it a last-ditch effort for publicity?) to garner critical interest.

The Posthumous Writer

Il caso di Guido Morselli, lo scrittore morto sconosciuto nel '73, è molto più di una disavventura toccata alla nostra editoriale. In dieci mesi sono usciti tre romanzi (*Roma senza papa*, *Contro-passato prossimo*, e, ora, *Divertimento 1889*), e meno che mai si capisce perché Morselli, finché fu vivo, abbia inutilmente bussato a tante porte. Ci sono stati anni di 'boom' in cui si è stampato di tutto: nel bene e nel male, nell'utile e nell'inutile, nel serio e nel poco serio. Per Morselli non ci fu posto. Eppure – e spiace dirlo ora che il riconoscimento può indurre al sospetto d'un tardivo elogio funebre – aveva assai di più delle cosiddette 'carte in regola.' Era, molto semplicemente, un grande e raro scrittore.[21]

The case of Guido Morselli, the unknown writer who died in '73, is much more than a misfortune that befell our publishers. In ten months, three novels have come out (*Roma senza papa*, *Contro-passato prossimo*, and now *Divertimento 1889*) and it is less clear than ever why Morselli, when he was alive, knocked in vain on so many doors. There were 'boom' years in which everything got published, good, bad, useful and useless, serious and less serious. For Morselli there was no place. And yet – and it is unpleasant to say this now that his recognition might provoke the suspicion of a belated funeral elegy – he had much more than his so-called papers in order. He was, very simply, a great and rare writer.

Is this not a more extreme version of the question with which we opened the book, about whether we have ever read Sylvia Plath? For in Plath's case, we might point to a generation of readers who knew her work while she was alive; she was widely published and consistently well received, a prizewinner and a known entity in the rarefied world of poets. For Morselli, however, his 'discovery' was always in some way a response to his suicide. Valentina Fortichiari aptly summarizes the situation thus:

> Sulle vicende editoriali che hanno trasformato il caso di Morselli nel caso Morselli, preferisco non indugiare: non perché non meritino attenzione, ma perché l'hanno avuta. E la prospettiva spesso unilaterale in cui si è affrontato il problema non ha favorito il suo approfondimento. Morselli è diventato una proiezione esemplare dello Scrittore Postumo, respinto in vita dalla incomprensione dei giudici. Come tale è divenuto il centro di quella geografia immaginaria in cui avvengono, o meglio non avvengono, gli incontri tra editori e autori: minaccia incombente per i primi e alibi consolatorie per i secondi, anche se questo non ha purtroppo migliorato, negli uni la professionalità e negli altri lo stile.[22]

> I prefer not to linger on the editorial events that tranformed Morselli's case into the Morselli case: not because they don't merit attention, but because they have already received it. And the often one-sided perspective from which the problem has been confronted has not facilitated its examination. Morselli has become an examplary projection of the Posthumous Writer, rejected in life by the incomprehension of the judges. As such he has become the centre of that imaginary geography in which occur, or rather do not occur, meetings between editors and authors: imminent danger for the former and consolatory alibis for the latter, even this does not improve the professionality of the one or the style of the other.

Fortichiari's observation is an important one – first, because it distinguishes Morselli's situation from Rosselli's and Pavese's and at the same time highlights a commonality between Morselli and another

group of authors ('Posthumous Writers,' who may or may not be suicides); second, because it highlights how speculative (and uncritical)
discussions about these cases tend to be, leading (as she implies) to
highly subjective and therefore unenlightening stances; and third,
because of the way these stances (by writers and editors) spill over or
stain the responses of those readers not otherwise involved. Indeed, an
overwhelming sense of collective guilt emanates from some of the pages of criticism of the dead author, cries of mea culpa that are altogether
absent from the discourse surrounding the cases of other Posthumous
Writers, and indeed of discussions about Rosselli's and Pavese's suicides. Thus think, for example, of Fasano's observation that the *caso
Morselli* stems from literary misrecognition on the part of critics who
failed to see Morselli's talent: 'Scoppiava così il "caso Morselli": ci si
accorgeva con stupore e rammarico che c'era stato uno strano e tragico
episodio di misconoscimento letterario'[23] (This is how the 'Morselli
case' exploded: they understood with shock and regret that there had
been a strange and tragic episode of literary misrecognition). This is
certainly the case: Morselli is by most accounts now considered to have
been an extremely valid novelist unfortunately kept from the public
eye by short-sighted publishers who were afraid to take a risk – and
thus thinking along these lines we might align Morselli with, say, a
Tomasi di Lampedusa (mentioned above) or a Carlo Michelstaedter, to
name two examples of authors whose work saw the light after their
deaths. But the case of Morselli's rejection is more complicated than
the idea of simple oversight implies, because it is bound inextricably
to his suicide (and not, more simply, to his death) and thus to the question of potential cause and effect. Rejection is invariably considered
chief among the complaints that led to Morselli's suicide: 'Un insieme
di circostanze negative giocò imponderabilmente, ma decisivamente,
nell'impedire che questo grande autore riuscisse a comunicare con il
pubblico e affrettò la conclusione della sua parabola esistenziale'[24] (A
collection of negative circumstances played a role, imponderably but
decisively, in preventing this great writer's successful communication
with the public, and hastened the conclusion of his existential rise and
fall).

But if it is the case that readers fixate on Morselli's death, then
what is the precise nature of critical engagement with Morselli's life?
An obligatory stop on the Morselli tour, it is nonetheless a short one,
during which a limited number of personal anecdotes, generally of a
vaguely amusing nature, are highlighted. In the case of Rosselli, we will

note that many of her posthumous critics attributed her suicide to the various psychological and physiological challenges she faced; Pavese's readers, in contrast, attributed his death to largely existential issues. Many critics rightly notice that Morselli was something of an eccentric, and view his quirks with an indulgent eye. Others straddle the fence in their attributions of cause. For example, like Fasano, Fortichiari, too, seems indirectly to support the equation between literary misrecognition (she calls it, echoing Dante, 'il grande rifiuto'[25] – the great refusal) and suicide when she attributes otherwise ambiguous particulars of his personal life to his difficulties in the world of publishing:

> Una scritta, appesa alla libreria, recitava 'Etiam omnes, ego non' (Tutti sì, io no): la frase epitaffia, leggermente diversa ('Etsi omnes, non ego') è incisa sulla tomba di Giuseppe Rensi ... Il significato della frase, citata a memoria e adattato a se stesso, probabilmente alludeva al fatto che Morselli si sentiva incompreso e rifiutato dall'establishment del mondo editoriale, che non gli permise di pubblicare nessun libro in vita.[26]

> A sign, hanging on the bookshelf, declared, 'Etiam omnes, ego non' (Everyone yes, not I): the epitaph, slightly different ('Etsi omnes, non ego') is carved on Giuseppe Rensi's tomb ... The meaning of the sentence, cited from memory and adapted for himself, probably alluded to the fact that Morselli felt misunderstood and rejected by the establishment of the publishing world, which did not permit him to publish a single book during his lifetime.

Also noteworthy is a prurient interest in the minutiae of Morselli's personal life, from his healthy liver, lacto-ovo-vegetarianism, meticulous hygienic practices, and extreme sensibility to sounds (he once wrote a letter to Konrad Lorenz inquiring about how to discourage noisy dormice from infesting his roof) to his prestige as a *tombeur des femmes*, his proto-ecologism, and his natty sartorial style, including a demonstrated preference for elbow patches and pullovers hand-knitted to order.[27] The discursive juxtaposition of Morselli's suicide with an accumulation of personal and professional artifacts points to a larger question about interpretation, specifically about a retroactive necro-hermeneutics.

My use of this term means to question yet again the way suicide throws our previously held methodological conventions into crisis. It has been my contention that in the case of an author's suicide, we observe, first, the decontextualization of the situated subject (the suicide) in the dismantling of critical frameworks constructed around the death of the author, and second, his or her reinsertion within a network of references (chiefly, other suicides). By this I don't mean to imply that the equation Auctor = Auctoritas is reinstated and his or her pronouncements are elevated to the status of Truths. While it is true that the event of suicide serves to stitch the life back on to the work, the effect of the decontextualization and recontextualization I have described in Morselli's case (as a posthumous writer, a wearer of pullover sweaters, a failure) means that the new seam, if you will, is slightly askew. Take, for example, the imaginative fantasy in which one critic projects thoughts and feelings onto the writer:

> Prima della morte, un senso di completa disillusione, di amara sfiducia verso qualsiasi forma di apertura dell'individuo agli altri, deve aver preso Morselli.
>
> Egli deve essere approdato definitivamente alla certezza angosciante di un'impossibile solidarietà fra gli uomini.
>
> E' come se fosse divenuto ormai consapevole che nemmeno la laica solidarietà sociale, sebbene a sfondo egoistico, potrebbe far uscire il singolo individuo dalla sua sfera tutta individuale e soggettiva.
>
> E' soprattutto il romanzo *Dissipatio H.G.* che permette di convalidare una simile, triste ipotesi.[28]

Before death, a sense of total disillusionment, of bitter distrust toward every form of openness of the individual toward others must have overtaken Morselli.

He must have arrived definitively at the anguished certainty of the impossibility of solidarity among men.

It is as though he had become conscious, at this point, that not even secular social solidarity, even of an egotistical nature, could cause single individuals to leave their totally individual and subjective spheres.

Above all it is the novel *Dissipatio H.G.* that permits the validation of such a sad hypothesis.

Stitching the life back on to the work, here, means using rampant speculation about Morselli's state of mind at the time of his death as the starting point for an account of what is going on in his writings. The muddying of discursive genres, the mixing of the disimpassioned scholarly arguments with empathic psychologizing so typical in writ-

ings about suicidal authors, puts a twist on the conventional prohibi-
tion against biographical fallacy. It displaces authorial auctoritas onto
the figure of the biographer or critic, who is no longer beholden to what
the object of study presents for critical consumption. The suicide of an
author provokes a kind of seizure of power by the critics, who speak
for or through him or her as a ventriloquist through a wooden dummy,
often in an apparent effort to justify the choice to die.

In the case of Amelia Rosselli, we will note how the critical processes
of decontextualization and recontextualization will convert her into
something one of a kind, that is, as a poet whose works bear few resemblances to those of other poets. And in the case of Cesare Pavese, these
processes will prompt the re-evaluation of the historical and political
context of his literary production. Morselli's situation is slightly different from both of these, which means that the decontextualization
of which we are speaking is also relevant in the most narrow sense:
his writings were stripped from the context in which they were produced not just as a function of his suicide but also of his publication
history. Consequently, we may note another curious phenomenon in
the case of Morselli's readership; because of the fact that publication
of his novels was not linked temporally to their production – that is,
because the first novels published were not the earliest written; on the
contrary, they were the last – his introduction to the reading public gave
a sense of coherence and specific focus to his novels that they would not
otherwise have enjoyed. Reading *Roma senza papa* (written 1966–7, published in 1974), *Contro-passato prossimo*, and *Divertimento 1889* (written
in 1969–70 and 1970–1, respectively, and both published in 1975), one
might get the sense that his thematic hobby horse was counter-history,
with a penchant for 'what-if' scenarios involving powerful men and
the arbitrariness of history, or, as Michael Caesar elegantly puts it, that
Morselli wrote 'a narrative of the rulers of Italy cast in the subjunctive
mood.'[29] But this supposed coherence, troubled by the publication of
his other works, would have a deleterious effect on his position with
respect to the literary pantheon.

Unlike in Rosselli's situation, readers have not been at a loss to locate
Morselli within the framework of writerly traditions. For example,
there is a strong case to be made for Ennio Flaiano[30] as a point of reference, for reasons both meta-critical and critical – for his status as an
'eccentric' and for his 'posthumous fortune' as well as for his writerly
traits.[31] Similarly, resemblances to Marcel Proust[32] and Robert Musil[33]
have been noted, particularly in the periods when Morselli was work-

ing on critical essays about the two writers. He was also likened to Gide, Broch, and Huxley.[34] For others, he fell comfortably under the rubric of Communist writer – a reasonable placement, as two of his novels are set squarely in the world of Italian Communism in the 1940s and 1950s (*Incontro col comunista* and *Il comunista*, respectively).[35] Politics dominated reviews of *Il comunista*, written 1964–5 and published in 1976.[36] Reviews praised it as a novel of 'ideological dissent' but not an 'ideological novel,'[37] and many critics underscore the realistic recreation[38] of the atmosphere of the years 1956–8 as lucid, dispassionate, and truthful.[39] Reviews of *Incontro col comunista* praise his insightful if indulgent view of the foibles of the young militant Gildo, while lamenting an excessive (and antifeminist) tendency to psychological self-effacement on the part of Gildo's bourgeois intellectual lover, Ilaria.[40] In short, readers came for the politics and stayed for the sex – though for others still, there was not enough of either.[41]

What do these comparisons teach us? The diversity of the references (Musil, Tomasi, Flaiano, Proust, Huxley) and the chicken-or-egg debate about themes (sexy politics or political sex?) supports the observation that as a novelist, he was *not* narrow-but-deep, but rather shallow-and-wide; indeed his interests were arguably as varied as those of many other novelists, and more so than many as well. Indeed it is this perceived eclecticism that became one of the bones of critical contention between supporters and detractors. For the former, Morselli's eclecticism was a function of his mimetic abilities, his ability to function in many registers ('una capacità insolitamente flessibile e duttile di penetrare in mondi diversi'[42] [an unusually flexible and ductile capacity for penetrating different worlds]), an ability that might make him unwieldy in terms of categorization but also bears witness to his elasticity as a writer. This is an ambivalent quality – it lends a kind of internal coherence to each text at the same time that it foils attempts to impose coherence on the author. It also lays Morselli open to a different set of charges, as much political as literary, which, together with his eclecticism, form a kind of circular logic. To his detractors, Morselli's (negative) eclecticism is a sign of his inability to engage with the conventions of the contemporary Italian novel; to his supporters, his (positive) mimeticism is a sign that he is not beholden to convention, rather, that his work is ahead of its time. Whatever the particular value attached to those terms may be, when taken together, epithets such as mimetic and eclectic have the effect of pushing Morselli's writings away from the Italian mainstream:

C'è in Morselli una sorta di sfida nei confronti dei pregiudizi correnti in Italia sul genere 'romanzo' e questo può contribuire a spiegare non solo le incomprensioni incontrate nella vita, ma il particolare carattere di talune riserve (non di tutte, ovviamente) che si intravvedono anche ora ... Si tratta, in non pochi casi, di pregiudizi inconsapevoli ... conosciamo la lentezza con cui scrittori di rilievo sono stati tardivamente accettati dalla nostra cultura, per la ragione, magari inespressa, che si scostano da una tradizione del romanzo italiano più immaginaria che reale e ne eludono certe tacite convenzioni, tipiche di quel circuito ripetitivo in cui finisce per trasformarsi il rapporto autore-critica-pubblico. L'isolamento di Morselli era anche dovuto alla scelta meditata di un atteggiamento espressivo che si poneva fuori sia dai modelli privilegiati in quegli anni sia dalla eversione linguistica dell'avanguardia. Ed è possibile, e forse probabile, che se fosse stato pubblicato dieci anni fa non avrebbe suscitato il consenso di oggi, perché allora mancavano certe condizioni e decantazioni, che invece ora sono venute a maturazione e compimento.[43]

There is in Morselli a kind of challenge to current prejudices in Italy about the novel genre and this might help explain not only the incomprehension he encountered in life, but also the particular nature of some reservations (not all, obviously) that can be perceived even now ... In many cases these are unconscious prejudices ... we know the slowness with which writers of importance have been belatedly accepted by our culture, for the reason, at times unexpressed, that they depart from a tradition of the Italian novel that is more imaginary than real and they elude certain unspoken conventions that are typical of that repetitive circuit in which author-critic-public relations end up transformed. Morselli's isolation was also due to the premeditated choice of an expressive attitude that placed itself outside of both the models privileged in those years and the linguistic subversion of the avant-garde. And it is possible, and perhaps probable, that had he been published ten years ago he would not have provoked the same consensus as today, because at that point certain conditions and decantations were lacking, which today have come to ripeness and completion.

This line of reasoning has ramifications for our understanding of his suicide: mimetic or eclectic, the argument goes, Morselli's inability (or refusal, depending on your view) to pin himself down as an author – to commit, as it were, to a set of thematic interests, or stylistic preferences, or verisimilar temporalities – are indications that he is a man in crisis.[44] I would argue, though, that there is something paradoxical about pathologizing Morselli's supposed refusal to live in the past, present, or future and his preference for setting his novels in a hypothetical, counter-historical or contrary-to-fact limbo, whereby the past is never as it was and the future never as it will be. It turns his fairly consistent interest in mediated temporalities into evidence of his inconsistency; it makes a vice of what was otherwise, for many readers, a virtue. If suicide makes the man, then these debates about eclecticism, political engagement, and the frustrating of generic conventions reveal the foundation on which Morselli's edifice was constructed.

In contrast to this critical stance that sees the author as excavation site, I would argue instead for a more aleatory metaphor: a maze, perhaps, in which the destination is less important than the route taken to get there. The argument advanced here asserts that in Morselli's case, questions of consistency and coherence are of secondary importance when compared to a search for the (inconsistent and incoherent) relations between history, counter-history, and chance, from which emerge not certainties but productive discrepancies. In the reading of Morselli's last novel, *Dissipatio H.G.*, that follows, I will attempt to determine these discrepancies by following some of the many paths that open up onto space in which to engage with Morselli's writerly and historical identities. Specifically, *Divertimento 1889*, *Roma senza papa*, *Contro-passato prossimo*, and *Dissipatio H.G.* each examine the notion that there can exist an infinite number of potential or counter-histories – that is, that at any given moment, one small change of events can lead to a result entirely different from the known outcome – leading to a radical redimensioning of the dominant historical narrative, which becomes merely one of many (infinite) possible narratives.[45] Similarly, far from being confined to detached, apparently objective, and authoritative-sounding narratives, the voice of history varies, to embrace the lunar landscape of *Dissipatio H.G.* as much as 'la musica-champagna di Offenbach' (as the narrator describes *Divertimento 1889* in a postscript to his lady readers)[46] and the grubby, febrile erotic tension of *Un dramma borghese*. Moreover, as we will see, *Dissipatio H.G.* shares with other novels the conviction that history can have various tenses: there are histories of the past (*Divertimento 1889* and *Contro-passato prossimo*), but also of the present (*Incontro col comunista* and *Un dramma borghese*) and the future (*Roma senza papa*). Constructed around an experiential parenthesis or limbo-state, like *Dissipatio H.G.*, these novels deviate from conventional, linear temporalities, preferring to represent a moment outside of time, as it were.

Dissipatio H.G.

Dopo *Dissipatio H.G.*, parlare ancora di un 'caso Morselli' è improprio, se non vagamente iniquo. Ormai sembra giusto riferirsi a un 'miracolo Morselli'. Questo romanzo, col suo inizio di tenebra e di devastazione, potrebbe condurre a un racconto di fantascienza o a una qualche medi-tazione utopica sull'essere che incarna in se stesso il vertiginioso epilogo dei 'formicolanti miliardi' d'altre creature. Morselli rifiuta per altissimo istinto queste soluzioni. Più che al superuomo o al primigenio homuncu-lus d'una Storia nascente dal sepolcro dell'intera umanità, egli sceglie una via simile a quella dell'Arsenio di Montale: si muove tra le scorie di una 'ghiacciata moltitudine di morti', e in esse cerca, come insonne rabdoman-te, un desolato barlume di vita, una parola, un segno, un suono, che possa-no diventare speranze o preghiera. Qualcosa che assomigli a un calore e a un respiro: anche al semplice soffio amaro di una boccata di 'Gauloises.'[47]

After *Dissipatio H.G.* it is inappropriate, if not somewhat unjust, to con-tinue to speak of a 'Morselli case.' At this point it seems fair to refer to a 'Morselli miracle.' This novel, with its opening scene of darkness and devastation, might lead to a science fiction story or to some utopian medi-tation on the being who embodies the vertiginous epilogue to the swarm-ing billions of other creatures. Morselli refuses these solutions by lofty instinct. Rather than a superman or the primitive homunculus of a His-tory born from the tomb of all of humanity, he chooses a route similar to that of Montale's Arsenio: he moves about the slag of a 'frozen multitude of dead,' and in it seeks, like an insomniac diviner, a desolate flash of life, a word, a sign, a sound that might become hope or prayer. Something that resembles warmth and breath: even a simple, bitter puff of Gauloises.

I choose to examine *Dissipatio H.G.* in part because it is my favourite of his works; but it also offers points of contact with the texts by the other authors in this study. It is a first-person narrative, and it deals head on with the subject of suicide, two aspects of the text that allow me to confront more easily the questions posed by the Derrida citation at the beginning of this study: 'How does one give oneself death in that other sense in terms of which *se donner la mort* is also to interpret death, to give oneself a representation of it, a figure, a signification or destina-tion for it?'[48] Morselli's protagonist gives himself death and represents it blow by blow, even analysing its aftermath for us.

What we have seen so far is the predominance in Morselli criticism of one specific epitextual element, namely the concomitant discoveries of Morselli as a successful writer and as a successful suicide. Morselli's writings are read as strongly autobiographical, especially when they deal, directly or indirectly, with issues of death, despair, suffering, or suicide. Whether subsumed under the rubric of a more or less generalized 'failure' (editorial, romantic, etc.) or merely alluded to in broader discussions of editorial cases analogous to his ('un Gattopardo del nord,' for example), Morselli's death stands fixed as the inevitable final destination of the journey of his life. This tendency is exacerbated by the author's enduring interest in what-if scenarios. The temptation is to claim a direct correlation between his penchant for counter-histories and his suicide, perhaps even to claim that Morselli, anticipating his biographers' needs, provided the trope with which to tie his life, death, and writings together: we might imagine something like 'Morselli tells the story, in *Contro-passato prossimo* (or *Roma senza papa*, or *Divertimento 1889*) of what *might have been* had things gone only slightly differently ... a story that corresponds, in retrospect, all too closely with his own' (that is, if individual elements in his life had gone differently, he might not have committed suicide). Such a statement, though satisfyingly pithy, is inadequate as the sole hermeneutical key, but we can, I believe, attribute some significance to Morselli's predilection for narratives of history, counter-history, and chance (for chance, in the end, is the motor that drives a counter-history) nevertheless.

One way to draw productive conclusions about Morselli's interest in alternate outcomes is to take into account two thinkers whose works serve as bookends to Morselli's intellectual development: Giuseppe Rensi and Jacques Monod.[49] These were thinkers whose influence on public discourse was not negligible (though more modest, to be sure, in the case of Rensi). Indeed, we know Morselli read both authors and appreciated them both, judging from the number and depth of direct references in his diary and elsewhere.[50] Although Rensi and Monod draw upon different bodies of knowledge in their writings – Rensi, who wrote in the 1920s and 1930s, was a philosopher and Monod was a Nobel Prize–winning biologist active in the 1960s – they arrive at conclusions that in many ways corroborate each other, conclusions about the arbitrary or random nature of historical and natural life, in contrast to the appearance (one might say, the need) to give form and linearity to the narratives of history and natural or evolutionary events.

Giuseppe Rensi (1871–1941) was a philosopher best known for his 'philosophy of the absurd.' His biography bears a certain resemblance to Morselli's. Rensi's lengthy sojourn in Switzerland starting in 1898, his isolation (both personal and professional: his philosophical thought ran counter to existing trends for its pessimism and for its implied opposition to Fascism), and his somewhat tormented faith all resemble Morselli's personal *iter*. But it is Rensi's 'philosophy of the absurd,' an idea that made its debut in 1924, culminating in his *La filosofia dell'assurdo* (1939), that constitutes his best-known contribution to philosophical thought. The relevance of Rensi for Morselli's novels cannot be underestimated. A study of Morselli's diary is particularly enlightening in this regard, because it throws into high relief the proximity of Rensi's and Morselli's thoughts at various periods throughout Morselli's adult life, a proximity that has bearing in turn on his narrative production in interesting ways.

Jacques Monod's *Chance and Necessity: An Essay on the Natural Philosophy of Modern Biology* (1970) complements Morselli's long-term interest in Rensian historical contingency and chance by transposing it to the field of molecular biology.[51] The importance of Monod for Morselli is that he corroborates, in his discussions of the biological world, what Rensi had already convinced Morselli happens in the realm of human activity. Monod, whose *Chance and Necessity* Morselli read and reviewed upon its publication two years before his death, offers an evolutionary explanation for Rensi's (and Morselli's) conviction that life has no goal, no order, and no plan, but instead is arbitrary, irrational, and therefore blind or absurd (depending on whom you read). For Monod, any discussion of the natural and man-made worlds, which are not always easy to distinguish on the basis of form or function, requires recourse to the concept of teleonomy, which 'implies the idea of an *oriented, coherent*, and *constructive* activity.'[52] Thus we can call teleonomic 'all the structures, all the performances, all the activities contributing to the success of the essential project.'[53] This might include the emergence of the eye among vertebrates, Monod explains, or, equally, it might describe the activities of 'a bashful poet who, prevented by shyness from declaring his passion to the woman he loves, can only express it symbolically, in the poems he dedicates to her,' which, in the event that the beloved responds positively to them, will have 'contributed to the success of his essential project, and the information they contain must therefore be tallied in the sum of the teleonomic performances assuring transmission of genetic invariance.'[54] We may well imagine the appeal of Monod's argument for Morselli, constructing as it does an erudite and highly literary rendering of the scientific bases for a pessimistic worldview analogous in its essence to Rensi's. Turning now to *Dissipatio H.G.*, I will argue that it is by way of the works on chance, history, and causality of these two thinkers that we may most productively formulate an alternate narrative with which to understand Morselli's suicide, beyond the more pragmatic readings about professional failure currently in circulation.

There are a number of immediate observations to be made about this novel in connection to Morselli's death. First, composed in 1972–3, it was the last novel Morselli wrote as well as the last one to be rejected a very short time before he killed himself. Moreover, suicide figures prominently in the novel. As we noted, it is not the only one of his works to address suicide: on the contrary, recall that *Un dramma borghese* has one 'real,' one implied, and one attempted suicide, a minor character kills himself in *Contro-passato prossimo*, and in *Il comunista*, not only does the protagonist's wife try to kill herself, but the novel ends with the expression of passive suicidal desire by the protagonist Walter[55] himself. But suicide lays the very foundation of the action of *Dissipatio H.G.*, beginning with the partially attempted suicide of the anonymous protagonist: 'La notte favolosa fra il I e il II giugno. Quella notte, ero deciso, io mi sarei ammazzato. Perché. Per il prevalere del negativo sul positivo. Nel mio bilancio. Una prevalenza del 70 per cento. Motivazione banale, comune? Non ne sono certo'[56] (That fabulous night between 1 and 2 June. That night, I had decided, I would kill myself. Why. For the prevalence of negative over positive. In my balance sheet. A prevalence of 70 per cent. A banal reason, a common one? I am not so sure). Hence, in part, the tendency to link the novel directly to Morselli's own death. It is considered 'il testamento che precedette la morte volontaria di Morselli'[57] (the testament that preceeded Morselli's voluntary death) or 'un messaggio nella bottiglia'[58] (a message in a bottle). The question of the attempted suicide of the novel's protagonist – a successful, *published* novelist – also seems to authorize analogies to the author. In any case, Morselli's own suicide is a constant presence in readings of this novel, unlike in the reviews of some of his earlier texts such as *Incontro col comunista*, *Il comunista*, *Contro-passato prossimo*, or *Roma senza papa*, where it was at least possible to find the occasional review that did not deploy Morselli's corpse as the vanguard of the hermeneutical regiment.[59]

It *is* correct to point out the many autobiographical references in the novel: as with the historical Morselli, the suicidal tendencies of the fictional protagonist are exacerbated by the threat of building a nearby highway ('Per dirla con Durkheim, ecco l'innesco'[60] [As Durkheim would say, here is the trigger]); and we might try to draw an association between Morselli's death a fortnight before he left sixty for sixty-one, and Morselli's protagonist's plan to die the evening before he turns forty.[61] I would argue, however, that the presence and the number (far more than I have suggested here) of these associations does not authorize so complete an identification between creator and created that, having written a novel about it, Morselli must therefore commit suicide himself. This is so not simply because of the number of writers who pepper their fiction with facts from their own lives (as in the term *autobiografiction*),[62] but also because of the number of writers whose writings function the opposite way, as exorcisms, so to speak, or virtual enactments of that which is desired and feared. Writing can function to forestall or substitute for the enactment of an event by providing an ersatz or proxy. But much more interesting is the way Morselli *plays* with the autobiographical elements of his creation, inverting them in place or ironically deflating them of any hint of self-aggrandizement: interpreting death or giving himself a representation of it does not preclude his having fun with it! So, for example, Morselli's fictional author has successfully published the book on psychology begun by the historical Morselli – indeed, it has even been translated – but copies of it meet an undignified end:

> In casa ho un ripostiglio, che dà sul bosco, per un portoncino sempre socchiuso. Vado di là a prendere una bracciata di legna per la stufa e ci trovo una delle vacche di Giovanni. *Animal bibliophagum*: stava mangiando la mia *Psicologia del Conscio*. I volumi in brochure e con la copertina verde, una trentina di copie che l'editore mi mandò da distribuire agli amici, erano in un palchetto. Lei li brucava di buona voglia, una poltiglia verdastra sgocciolante dal labbrone peloso sul pavimento sparso di pagine a mazzi. Ho riso.[63]

> At home I have a storeroom, that gives out onto the woods through a small door that is always half-closed. I go there to get an armful of wood for the fire and I find one of Giovanni's cows. *Animal bibliophagum*: she was eating my *Psychology of the Conscious*. The volumes with the green soft cover, about thirty copies that my editor sent me to distribute to my friends; they were in a box. She munched them willingly, a greenish glob dripping from her big hairy lip onto the ground scattered with bundles of pages. I laughed.

Morselli's protagonist not only publishes but, more importantly, *doesn't really care* that he has, if the nonchalance with which he views his books' ignominious destruction has any meaning (after all, we know where they will end up). In the same vein, the nocturnal noises and chewing of the dormice that drove the historical Morselli to distraction during his last months are treated in the novel as positive compensation for the protagonist's suffering.[64] Other references in the text are at once autobiographical and intertextual, the close association between author and creation adding another layer of meaning. Like Morselli himself, whose affection for certain of his belongings was well documented by friends and family, both *Dissipatio H.G.* and an earlier novel, *Un dramma borghese*, are concerned with the secret life of things. For the former's protagonist, the precious little items or special objects and possessions (a rifle, record player, typewriter, rug, an Albinoni piano sonata, some of which appear in the other novel as well) practically assault him upon his return home after *not* killing himself, claiming success for his survival.[65] Similarly, Morselli permits his protagonist to make an explicit reference to one of his earlier novels, *Brave borghesi* (written in 1966), and to cite a debate between the real Morselli and the major newspapers, in which the author maintained that the newspapers were the exclusive monopoly of a very few specialists, when they should instead be the voice of public opinion. Along the same lines, at the very end of the novel, the protagonist mockingly discards the previously held hope for *socialidarietà*, social solidarity (a term Morselli introduced in *Roma senza papa*), as an impossible dream. These fictional references to Morselli's own earlier work take place in the section of *Dissipatio H.G.* where the protagonist admits he is losing his mind, the only items under the introductory heading of 'sconnessioni psichiche' (psychic disjunctions) or 'incoerenze' (incoherences), implying if not an outright disavowal of his past production, at the very least, an ironic self-mockery.[66] In sum, the novel wears lightly its self-lampooning *bricolage* of autobiography, auto-referentiality, and literary self-plagiarism.

The novel's premise is the suicide of the protagonist. He had a plan: on the eve of his fortieth birthday, he was to ascend the steep mountain path near his home in Switzerland, and follow it to the mouth of the well that led to the Lake of Solitude. The idea was to slip into the well, cross it in a few quick strokes, then slide into the Lake and drown in relatively short order. The preparations were organized magnificently – he had even allowed time for a final drink. Perched comfortably on the edge of the well, sipping cognac, he found himself engaged in a

long mental excursus on the fallacy of French superiority in the realm
of cognac production:

> Seduto sull'orlo del pozzo, i piedi penzoloni nel buio, mi sono conces-
> so un sorso del cognac. Ne avevo con me una mezza bottiglia. Alle 0 e
> 15 una scivolatina sul sedere, sarei stato dentro; un paio di bracciate per
> risalire il sifone, e il salto definitivo. Ma alle 0 e 30 del mio orologio da
> polso, ero ancora lì. Meditante. Meditavo su questo, che il cognac spag-
> nolo non ha niente da invidiare al prodotto francese. Perché? Perché,
> logico, il distillato dei vini a alto grado zuccherino, prerogativa dei paesi
> del Sud, non può non essere superiore. Gli stessi 'Premiers Bois' francesi,
> sono vitigni che crescono sotto un sole avaro. E ciò neutralizza il vantaggio
> dell'invecchiamento nei fusti troppo famosi della Charente. Sono venute
> le 0 e 40 e io avevo deciso: la gloria dei cognac francesi è effetto di una
> suggestione collettiva, benché secolare. O, tout court, uno dei tanti falsi
> miracoli della réclame.[67]

Seated on the edge of the well, my feet dangling into the darkness, I
allowed myself a sip of cognac. I had half a bottle with me. At a quarter
after twelve, a little slide on my rear, and I would be in; a few strokes to
ascend the siphon, and the definitive plunge. But at half past by my wrist-
watch, I was still there. Pondering. I was pondering this—that French
cognac had nothing over the Spanish kind. Why? Because, it's logical, the
distillate of wines with high sugar content, prerogative of the South, can't
not be superior. Those same French 'Premiers Bois' are species that grow
under a miserly sun. And that neutralizes the advantage of aging in those
famous casks from the Charente. It was 12:40 and I had decided: the glory
of French cognacs is an effect of collective, if centuries-old, influence. Or,
tout court, one of the many false miracles of advertising.

Minutes later, he abandoned his plan. On his way toward the exit, however, he knocked his head hard against a rocky outcropping, just as the
first thunderstorm of the season was heard outside the cave: 'ho dato
a piena testa contro uno spuntone di roccia. Una capata tremenda, da
rintronarmi, e proprio nello stesso attimo un fragore di tuono percuote-
va la valle, nera come la caverna che avevo lasciato. Il primo temporale
della stagione'[68] (I banged my head against a rock spike. A tremendous
blow, and right in the same second a clap of thunder shook the valley,
black as the cave I had left. The first storm of the season). Or is it? For at
the very moment of the supposed thunder, unbeknownst to our hero,
the entire human race disappeared from the face of the earth.

Called, variously, *l'Evento, l'Esodo, Bomba X, Operazione-pulizia, Bomba S (Spopolamento)*, and *Bomba R (rarefazione)*, the connection between the protagonist's blow to the head, the thunder he claims to hear, and the disappearance of humanity remains a mystery throughout the course of the novel.[69] The text's essential narrative aporia of the evaporation of all but one member of the human race may be a scientifically rational (though as yet unexplained) phenomenon, which corresponds to the laws of science and nature in this world, and corresponds closely to the principal element in Todorov's definition of the fantastic: ours is a novel that maintains a consistent indecision about the nature of the events described, both in the reader and in the narrator.[70] In the case of the novel, we would say that the protagonist cannot ever decide whether the inexplicable Event (as I will call the disappearance of all humankind except for the protagonist) takes place exclusively within the experience of the protagonist (in other words, the disappearance of other people is a product of his posthumous imagination – it is all in his dead head), or the disappearance really has taken place, for reasons unbeknownst and unfathomable to our hero, who is the only man alive on Earth. Hence the importance, we might observe, of self-documentation in *Dissipatio H.G.*, such as the protagonist's habit of tape-recording his own sleep. Reminiscent of Morselli's own compulsion to document his weight, diet, and so on, the protagonist's rigorous program of self-observation (like the emphasis he places on hearing and not hearing – recall Morselli's anxieties about noise) seems a legitimate response to a situation created by an event whose causes are profoundly unknowable: he may not be able to know all, but at least he will know what he knows![71]

Key to Todorov's description is that the uncertainty lasts the entirety of the narration.[72] And, in fact, the text offers various hypotheses, ranging from nuclear and chemical disasters to religious rapture, but none, ultimately, is embraced because of the extraordinary circumstances. A nuclear disaster, for example, would have ravaged the countryside – yet the protagonist is surrounded by a lush and healthy landscape, such that the flora and fauna of his region burgeon in ways they never did when humans were alive. Another theory, involving some sort of hypostatic transformation or 'angelification' of human kind, seems more likely, in light of the state of the detritus they left behind, such as beds with the impressions of the recently departed still visible (the 'Event' took place around 2 a.m.), as well as what they did not leave – there are no bodies, dead or alive, whatsoever. Equally uncertain is the question of the protagonist's status: is he alive or dead? And, in the event that he *is* the sole survivor and Universal Heir (in more ways than one) of humankind, is he damned or elect? In either case, the irremediable solitude in which he now exists (once a dearly held dream) is a pyrrhic victory for a man whose wish was to drown in the Lake of Solitude. But true to the nature of a fantastic text, the fundamental phenomenological parameters of the Event are very much up for grabs. Recall Monod's definition of teleonomy, the appearance of coherence and orientation toward a goal. Indeed Monod's examples, like this example of an 'absolute coincidence,' which arises 'from the intersection of two totally independent chains of event,' are apposite:

> Suppose that Dr. Brown sets out on an emergency call to a new patient. In the meantime Jones the contractor's man has started making emergency repairs on the roof of a nearby building. As Dr. Brown walks past the building, Jones inadvertently lets go of his hammer, whose (deterministic) trajectory happens to intercept that of the physician, who dies of a fractured skull. We say he was a victim of chance. What other term fits such an event, by its very nature unforeseeable? Chance is obviously the essential thing here, inherent in the complete independence of two causal chains of events whose convergence produces the accident.[73]

Monod's sweaty-palmed roofer illustrates the arbitrary nature of the relations governing human life. Hence, too, the tone of Monod's summation of this 'natural philosophy': 'Man knows at last that he is alone in the universe's unfeeling immensity, out of which he emerged only by chance. His destiny is nowhere spelled out, nor is his duty. The kingdom above or the darkness below: it is for him to choose.'[74] In other words, the facts of life, as it were, are themselves irremediably random, but insofar as the story we tell about them – the 'essential project' to which we claim to ascribe – can equally exalt or denigrate the teller, it alone carries the burden of meaning. Straight out of Monod, then, does the following passage from *Dissipatio H.G.* seem to arise:

> Io sopravvivo. Dunque sono stato prescelto, o sono stato escluso. Niente caso: volontà. Che spetta a me interpretare, questo sì. Concluderò che sono *il prescelto*, se suppongo che nella notte del 2 giugno l'umanità ha meritato di finire, e la 'dissipatio' è stata un castigo. Concluderò che sono *l'escluso* se suppongo che è stato un mistero glorioso, assunzione all'empireo, angelicazione della Specie, eccetera.
> È un'alternativa assoluta, ma mi si concede di scegliere. Io, l'eletto o il

dannato. Con la curiosa caratteristica che sta in me eleggermi o dannarmi.
E bisognerà che io mi decida.[75]

I survive. Therefore I have been selected, or I have been excluded. Not
by chance: by will. Which is up to me to interpret, that's for sure. I will
conclude that I am *the chosen one*, if I suppose that on the night of 2 June,
humanity deserved to end, and the 'dissipatio' was a punishment. I will
conclude that I am *the excluded one* if I suppose that it was a glorious mystery, the assumption to the Empyrean, the angelification of the Species, etc.
   It's an absolute choice, but I am allowed to choose. I, the elect or the
damned. With the curious characteristic that it is up to me to elect or damn
myself. And I'll have to decide.

These passages weaken the case for basing our interpretation of the
novel on events in the author's life, an interpretation that claims the
certainty of twenty/twenty hindsight. Instead, the proximity of this
novel to a genre with uncertainty, undecidability, and altered states at
its very heart permits us to argue for a different reading, based on a different set of tools, with the goal not of finding correlations, but rather of
productive discrepancies. Thus (to return to our discussion of autobiography in the novel) it seems preferable to me to speak not of presages
or preludes but of wish fulfilment – a conjuring up of the desired situation in order to explore it, live it, weigh it against present reality so that
the death sought and possibly attained by the novel's hero operates not
as a preparation for the real thing but as an apotropaic ritual against
it. After all, almost all of Morselli's novels revolve in some way about
the fulfilment of a fantasy or wish – often a repressed one – that comes
true as a result of the unexpected and unforeseeable collusion of forces
beyond the protagonists' control. This notion of *conjuring up* implies an
economy of desire akin to the one Freud attributes to dreams, in which
one can state the unutterable, which is otherwise censured by the voice
of internal authority, or attain the unattainable, because it is no longer
prohibited.
   Think, for example, of the king's blissfully incognito holiday in
Divertimento 1889, ostensibly for the sale of one of his properties, when
he can travel more or less unescorted, unobserved, and unofficially,
having his cake and eating it too as he indulges his various appetites
and turns a pretty profit to boot. Similar wish-fulfilment is the shooting
accident that may or may not have killed the daughter in *Un dramma
borghese*, the 1961–2 novel in which a middle-aged father finds him-

self entrapped by both his responsibilities and his ambivalent, barely repressed lust for his clinging, regressive, and oversexed eighteen-year-old daughter. Reunited with him after a decade-long separation (Mimmina spent most of her life in a Swiss boarding school after her mother died), and living with him in near total seclusion for over a month in an adjoining hotel room as they recuperate from their respective illnesses, Mimmina has consecrated her life to her new-found father with a filial devotion that nearly suffocates him, standoffish, dispassionate, passive, self-ironic, and highly self-analytical as he is. After a brief affair with Mimmina's best friend Thérèse, he formulates a plan to send Mimmina away instead of keeping her with him as he had promised. It is a plan that is doomed to fail, he later realizes, not least because it provokes in Mimmina a state of near-cataleptic despair. And indeed just as he realizes that there is no solution to his problem, Mimmina herself resolves it, by shooting herself (accidentally? fatally?) with her father's Browning. Here as elsewhere, the fulfilment of prohibited desires always comes at a price.

The other structure that links *Dissipatio* and its predecessors to the notion of wish-fulfilment is that of parentheses, the finite unit of time-in-place in which the protagonist/s can experience some sort of 'altered state,' often involving a change in physical location, such as Mimmina and her father's stay in the hotel, and the king's holiday. We might also mention the protagonist's sojourn to Italy in *Roma senza papa* (1966–7), which allows him to take stock of the states of his personal and religious life in Switzerland, and of Catholicism in general as he observes it at its source, as it were; or Ilaria's 'holiday' from her usual identity as a polished, celibate, upper-class intellectual, a widow and mother of an adult son, to live briefly as the secret lover of her son's friend, a working-class Communist militant, in the 1947–8 novel *Incontro col comunista*.[76] Whether it is a holiday, a period of seclusion, or a more metaphysical parenthesis like Ilaria's change of milieu, we frequently catch Morselli's protagonists in various indeterminate states between two, more definite, ones.[77] The fantastic premise of *Dissipatio H.G.* offers a variation on the parentheses: something more like an open bracket, in the sense that the (again, nameless male) first-person narrator is in a condition whose beginning was clearly demarcated but whose end point cannot be predicted. This limbo (for surely he cannot go on like this forever), complicated by the multiple uncertainties surrounding it – chief among them how and why the rest of humanity disappeared – is one of the book's beauties: we never really figure out what happened or why, unless we return to our observation that one of Morselli's most consistent tropes is that of the wish mysteriously fulfilled. Could our hero's survival not be read as the successful conjuring up of his fondest desire? For here, as in the novels discussed above, we have before us a story whose moral, if you like, can be summed up thus: watch what you wish for, because you just might get it! Indeed, the protagonist himself offers the possibility that the whole thing is but a wish when he recalls lying in the grass high above the valley: 'La grotta del Sifone e il 2 giugno non erano ancora in vista, e io facevo il mio solito giuoco, parentesizzare l'esistenza di miei simili, figurarmi come l'unico pensante in una creazione tutta deserta. Deserta di uomini, s'intende'[78] (The grotto of the Siphon and 2 June were nowhere in sight, and I was playing my usual game, bracketing off the existence of my fellows, imagining myself as the only thinking being in a totally deserted world. Deserted by men, naturally).

This is a moment of pure Rensian absurdity, which allows for a non-causal coincidence between a wish and its fulfilment, throwing into relief a broader affiliation between Rensi's thought and the themes of Morselli's fiction, such as the fantastic, wish-fulfilment or conjuring up of circumstances or events, parentheses in time and/or place, and counter-histories. These are each themes that hinge upon a definitive severing of the relations between coincidence and causality, and a subversion of the notion of history as an unequivocal, *singular* narrative. By way of an illustration, consider Morselli's 13 March 1969 diary entry, which describes how an acquaintance and her children would not have been killed by an errant automobile if they had left home for Sunday Mass one minute earlier than they did. Instead of perceiving in this tragedy the cruel hand of destiny, he argues that in fact this is destiny's true, meek nature, if we take into consideration the number of times people arrive at their destinations unharmed. It is illogical, he continues, to attribute accidents and misfortunes to some sort of cosmic necessity but not to attribute non-events similarly.[79] Morselli's analysis here is consistent with that of Rensi in *La filosofia dell'assurdo*, where Rensi argues, by way of a hypothetical situation similar to Morselli's people on the way to Sunday Mass, that we mistakenly attribute unfortunate events to destiny (thereby imbuing them with some predetermined meaning, identifying a causal relationship with the event and its circumstances) but attribute no such relationship to 'non-events,' that is to events that do not qualify as unfortunate. *Dissipatio H.G.* is organized around precisely this relationship between coincidence and causality, articulated most explicitly thus: '[l]'Inspiegabile si è inaugurato per opera mia. Per lo meno, gli eventi hanno coinciso (all'inizio) con un evento strettamente privato e mio; coincidenza, oso dirlo, non casuale'[80] (The Inexplicable was inaugurated by my own efforts. At least, the events coincided (at first) with a strictly personal, private event: not, I daresay, a casual coincidence). The key, for both Rensi and Morselli, is in the attribution of necessity to events that were governed by chance, as well as the failure to recognize chance in non-events (as opposed to attributing non-events such as the safe passage of the parishioners to Sunday Mass to providence). Moreover this is what History means: the concatenation of some select facts and their investment with a value.[81] History, in other words, involves the foreclosure of all other possibilities in its preference of one narrative over another – hence the definitive and unequivocal (though illusory) sense of finality history brings to bear.[82]

For now it is enough to notice the way the question of perception, that is, of objective versus subjective reality, plays into the protagonist's thinking. As he parses it, the situation is a bit like asserting that Malinowski just invented the Trobriand Islands, since the only other person to confirm their existence is Lévy-Bruhl, for whom they meant something completely different.[83] We might also notice the connection between the ambiguous premise of the novel – am I dead, or is everyone else? – and the fear of being buried alive evident in Morselli's testament. It seems that death is no longer the certainty it once was. Another set of possible rationales behind the Event thus opens up – the protagonist may be dreaming (dreams being the site par excellence of wish fulfilment), he may be hallucinating (perhaps a result of the accidental blow to the head he took when leaving the tunnel), or he may be dead as the result of another kind of blow to the head, this one not from a jutting rock but from his Black-Eyed Girl, the pistol with which he played Russian roulette on the night of the Event. There is ample evidence to support such readings, including the initial blow to the head on the rock, and the blood he later finds on his pillow (though this could be from the same blow to his head).[84] In the event that he *is* dead (and therefore analogous, perhaps, to the deceased protagonist who narrates his own story in *Double Indemnity*), then the story told in the novel takes on a new meaning and, strange to say, a kind of logical coherence. And spending eternity as the last man on Earth takes on the connotations of Dante's contrapasso, in which the nature of one's sin is reflected in the punishment it receives, as the protagonist is well aware: 'Io che coltivavo il vizio raro del solipsismo e avevo per insegna il "vietato l'ingresso" (agli altri), mi trovo vietata l'uscita, indefinitamente'[85] (I who used to cultivate the rare vice of solipsism and had, as my emblem to others, a 'do not enter' sign, found myself denied entry, indefinitely).

There are, in any case, numerous possibilities. Thus to the science-fiction inflected hypotheses in which the protagonist indulges, we may add a new one, in which the narrative impulse is oneiric, unconscious, posthumous, or a combination thereof. In that sense, this novel can be linked to *Un dramma borghese*; their protagonists share – at the macroscopic and microscopic levels, respectively – the conviction that 'l'enfer, c'est les autres.' As *Dissipatio H.G.* proceeds, however, its hero's quest for solitude reverses course, becoming an increasingly urgent attempt to make contact with his friend ('il mio solo amico,' 'my only friend') and former physician, Dr Karpinsky. Karpinsky, the one person he *knows* is dead (and knows how and why he died), is paradoxically the only 'living' human presence the protagonist perceives. This is a more significant feat than might be imagined, if we examine the question of death from a Rensian perspective. For example, Morselli's diary entry from 19 March 1944 offers a glimpse at the associations between Rensi's philosophy of the absurd and Morselli's notion of counter-history,

Il libro 'finito di stampare nelle officine XY, a Varese, il 27 giugno 1933'. Questa data è più che una semplice indicazione cronologica. Rappresenta un giorno ch'io ho vissuto, tutto quell'incommensurabile ciclo di pensieri e di sensazioni che s'inscrive tra un mattino e un tramonto. Il 27 giugno 1933 io ho pensato e goduto con giovanile intensità: quello che ho letto quel giorno, il fastidio di quel caldo, la gioia che mi ha dato assaporare un frutto, sono esperienze che hanno avuto per me un valore profondo, pieno, totale. Non ne rimane una traccia. Tutto è scomparso, morto.

Dunque sono nato ieri, ieri l'altro, due mesi fa?

Cerco invano in che rapporto sia, con me, l'individuo che ha vissuto il giorno 27 giugno del 1933, e che portava, forse abusivamente, lo stesso nome ch'io porto. Di lui ho appena una vaga, remota nozione. Di che si occupasse, quali fossero i suoi gusti pensieri sentimenti, non so. In che cosa egli mi ha 'antecipato'?

Cfr. Rensi, *Aporie*, p. 232.

'... 27 June 1933 ...' This date is more than a simple chronological indication. It represents a day that I lived, that whole incommensurable cycle of thoughts and of sensations that inscribe themselves between morning and evening. On 27 June 1933, I thought and I took pleasure with youthful intensity: what I read that day, the annoyance of the heat, the joy I felt tasting a piece of fruit, these are experiences that had for me a deep, full, and total value. There remains not a trace of them. Everything has disappeared, dead.

Was I then just born yesterday, the other day, two months ago?

Vainly I seek the relations between me and the individual who lived that day, 27 June 1933, and who bore, possibly illicitly, the same name I do. I've only got a vague, faraway notion of him. Of his occupations, his tastes, thoughts, feelings, I know nothing. In what way did he 'anticipate' me?

Cfr. Rensi, *Aporie*, p. 232.

Note that Morselli (here as elsewhere, frequently) provides the text from which his own observations in the diary flow. The page to which Morselli refers (Rensi's *Le aporie della religione: Studio sul problema religioso* (1932)[86] reads as follows:

Se ti dicessero: tu rinascerai, ma perdendo ogni memoria e coscienza della tua vita attuale – vedresti tosto che con ciò non sei più *tu* che rinasci, ma un altro *io*. Cioè, data quell'ipotesi, *tu* rinasci negli altri, *sei* gli altri che nascono.

Occorre dunque tale memoria. Ma come è possibile, se moltissimi fatti della tua vita attuale si sono irreparabilmente perduti fuori della memoria ... ?

... Quindi la scarsa importanza della morte. È pari al fatto che molti eventi o periodi della tua vita tu stesso li hai irreparabilmente dimenticati (ossia sono definitivamente morti). Che te ne importa?[87]

If they said to you: you'll be reborn, but will lose every memory and consciousness of your current life – then you'd see that at that point it is no longer *you* who is reborn, but another *I*. That is, under those circumstances, *you* are reborn in others, *you are* the others who are born.

Therefore memory is necessary. But how is that possible, if so very many facts from your current life are irreparably lost to your memory ... ?

... Hence the slight importance of death. It is on a par with the fact that you yourself have irreparably forgotten many events or periods from your life (or rather they are definitively dead.) What does it matter?

The passages read together cover a lot of territory. Morselli's inspiration comes from a discussion by Rensi about the necessary fallacy of memory – necessary because without it, the subject is comprised of a series of distinct figures whose only coherence lies in the way they are viewed by others; and fallacy, because of its unavoidably fragmented nature. Rensi concludes that this inevitable, inexorable forgetting, tantamount to the partial loss of identity, is equivalent to death itself – we experience, unknowingly, so many small deaths that final death is of 'slight importance.' Morselli's response is a meditation on the nature of the subject divided from itself across time, but viewed exclusively from within (unlike Rensi's emphasis on coherence from without), so that the I who existed in the past is irrecoverable by the I of today; indeed, far from being one subject viewed diachronically, they are a series of subjects viewed in perpetual synchrony. As separate and distinct entities, then, neither holds sway as predominant or authentic. Where does the I reside, Morselli seems to ask, if it cannot be identified outside the moment of its enunciation? This is the question Morselli takes up again in his fiction. The dialogue mid-way through *Dissipatio H.G.* between the protagonist and his friend Mylius, the radical pessimist (he is recollected by the protagonist, having disappeared with the rest of humankind), summarizes the novel's principal existential position:

> Occorre partire dalla premessa realistica di ciò che significa per noi 'essere morti'. Impartecipazione al mondo esterno, insensibilità, indifferenza. Stabilito che la morte è questo, si conclude che la vita le assomiglia, il divario essendo puramente quantitativo[88] ... Siamo morti a tutto ciò che non ci tocca o non c'interessa. Non dico a ciò che succede sulla Luna, ma a ciò che succede a loro che stanno di casa dirimpetto a noi.[89]

> We must begin with a realistic notion of what it means for us 'to be dead.' Abstention from the outside world, insensibility, indifference. Having established that this is death, we conclude that life resembles it, that the gap is purely quantitative ... We are dead to all that does not touch or interest us. I don't mean what's happening on the moon, but what's happening to the people who live in the house opposite.

Death and life are so indistinguishable that there is nothing anomalous about the situation in which the novel's protagonist finds himself. After all, this is the author whose testament requested an extra sixty hours for death to be confirmed, and even then he wanted the extra assurance of a lethal injection. The source of this position can be traced back decades, to 14 May 1944, indicating a decided continuity in his thoughts:

Tutti siamo condannati a morte quanti siamo uomini. Secondo Pascal, 'l'image de la condition des hommes' è quella stessa di un gruppo d'uomini in catena e dannati alla pena capitale, di cui ogni giorno alcuni siano sgozzati sotto gli occhi degli altri che rimangono. Se non avvertiamo che tra noi e quegli uomini non c'è differenza, gli è perché non è vero che noi uomini sappiamo, a differenza degli animali, che morremo. (Rensi, *Aporie*, 71).[90] Il pensiero della morte è in noi esterno, saltuario e superficiale: non è mai attuale coscienza. (Forse, provvidenzialmente.) E la morte, secondo osserva Simmel, 'è sempre un venir uccisi, tanto che ciò si operi mediante il coltello o il veleno, quanto mediante i microbi della tubercolosi o il cardiopalma.' (Rensi, *ibid*.)

Nota Leopardi, che quando si rivede una persona dopo molto tempo, guardando il suo viso si ha l'impressione che gli sia accaduta una sciagura (citato da Rensi, ibid) ... [91]

We are all condemned to death insofar as we are men. According to Pascal, 'the image of man's condition' is that of a group of men in chains and condemned to capital punishment, for which every day some of them are slaughtered before the eyes of those who remain. If we don't recognize that between us and those men there is no difference, it is because it is not true that we men know, unlike animals, that we will die. (Rensi, *Aporie*, 71). The thought of death is external to us, intermittent and superficial; it is never actual consciousness. (Providentially, perhaps.) And death, according to Simmel, 'is always a getting killed, as much when it is enacted by a knife or by poison as by way of the microbes of tuberculosis or cardiopalmus. (Rensi, ibid.)

Leopardi notes that when we see a person after a long time, looking at his face we have the impression that a misfortune has befallen him (cited by Rensi, ibid.)

The themes of this passage are at the heart of *Dissipatio H.G.*: death as condemnation and visitation (a 'getting killed'); man's ignorance or denial of death; death as always already in process; life as misfortune; postponement of pleasure to beguile the time (not because it is fleeting but because the zenith of joy has already passed); and finally, history as a chronicle of misdeeds. It is the final stop on the existential itinerary that took us from meditations on the indeterminacy of one's position (am I elect or damned?), to the realization that the I on which that question hinges is in fact not an organic or recuperable entity but exists, rather, only in its enunciation, to the final realization that both questions (which am I, and what am I) are always already mooted since, actually, there was no choice to begin with: we are already essentially dead. Hardly a cheery little litany, particularly when, in the novel, the equivalence of life as death, as well as the fallacy of a unified and unequivocal historical narrative, extends from the protagonist's own unique (or so we must assume) history to the collective history of mankind.

> E con questa si chiude la cronaca esterna dell'evento, si apre quella interna … Ormai la mia storia interiore è la Storia, la storia dell'Umanità. Io sono ormai l'Umanità, io sono la Società (U e S maiuscole). Potrei, senza enfasi, parlare in terza persona: 'L'Uomo ha detto così, ha fatto così …' A parte che, dal 2 giugno, la terza persona e qualunque altra persona, esistenziale o grammaticale, s'identificano necessariamente con la mia. Non c'è più che l'Io, e l'Io non è più che il mio. Sono io.[92]

> And with this the external chronicle of the event closes, and the internal one opens … Now my interior history is History, the history of Humanity. I have become Humanity, I am Society (with capital H and capital S). I could, without exaggerating, speak in the third person: 'The Man said this, did that …' Except for the fact that, since 2 June, the third person and any other person, existential or grammatical, must be identified with me. There is nothing left but this I, and this I is none other than mine. It is I.

In other words, after the Event, history is precisely that: his story, the story of the living dead.

Let us briefly abandon the living dead, and take as an alternate hypothesis the notion that the story narrated takes place inside the narrator's head – that we are reading of some form of afterlife, a posthumous vision exclusive to the narrator, or in any case of a subjective vision entirely internal to the narrator – because it allows the various possibilities (scientific, religious, fantastic) behind this doomsday scenario to coexist without privileging one over the others, thus overturning, in a sense, the observation by the protagonist that there is no third route for the *suicide manqué*, 'tertium non datur: il tuffo nel sifone, o il rituffo nel quotidiano'[93] (tertium non datur: I dive into the Siphon, or back into the everyday). We are thus in the realm of desire production, of the enactment of a fantasy scenario that did not/could not happen 'in real life,' that is, during the narrator's biological life. As a subjective vision, it is, precisely, a-historical (outside the temporal world and outside or against tradition) but not anti-historical. Morselli's narrator rewrites reality,[94] not in order to replace one master narrative with another, but to supplement it, as it were: to rehearse other, possible realities whose narration would not otherwise occur.

It is certainly not by chance, then, that the Event takes place in a fictionalized Switzerland, which is depicted, typically, as the heart of civilized stability[95] – that is, as a place where the contingent or arbitrary elements of a life are reduced to the bare minimum, by virtue of the strength of Swiss cultural norms. Instead, this place that privileges causality over coincidence, in which actions lead predictably to reactions, is the perfect site for a phenomenon with neither precedent nor repeatability. Moreover, the Event's location mirrors, at the national level, the individual contrapasso experienced by the protagonist: just as his fate was to suffer eternally for the solitude he so fervently desired, so has the stringency with which the Swiss adhere to collective cultural norms, according to the novel, obliterated the very identity upon which those norms were founded.

Individual and national interests become further imbricated during the narrator's perambulations through the deserted Zurich (which he disdainfully calls Crisopoli: City of Gold) and its hinterland – which are all the narrator can access in this post-apocalyptic scene. His wanderings occasion lengthy (and sometimes hilarious) meditations on life and death, on nature and culture, and on the vicissitudes of chance, to be sure, but here the narrator grafts these concepts onto a specifically, stereotypically Swiss[96] body politic, whose cleanliness, godliness, and excellent fiscal infrastructure – each in clear evidence[97] – are unexpectedly useful. Switzerland's vaunted efficiency, for example, permits the protagonist to live in comfortably heated and well-lit surroundings, because the generators are so well maintained that they can run indefinitely without need for human operators.[98] And the abundance of cheese, particularly neufchâtel, is handy not because it provides sustenance – the protagonist satisfies that need by eating large quantities of Swiss chocolate – but rather because the cheese can be used to gauge the passage of time by measuring the height of the mould layer that forms on top of it.[99] Recall Rensi's and Monod's notion of the arbitrary or random nature of historical and natural life, which is opposed to the appearance (one might say, the need) to give form and linearity to the narratives of history and natural or evolutionary events. The protagonist's creative reassignment of function signals an alignment on the part of the text with Rensi's critique of the privileging of single, unequivocal narratives over multiple, indeterminate ones when he points out that after 'limit events' like the Exodus, all bets are off – far from cuckoo clocks and vaunted Swiss efficiency, it's the cheese that really matters.

Thus Zurich's storied preponderance of banks and financial institutions (our hero counts the headquarters of no fewer than fifty-six banks), which are comparable in variety and function but nearly double in number to its places of worship (thirty-one),[100] are of little use after the Event except insofar as they afford the protagonist the opportunity to wax ironic:

> Santa Plutocrazia. Potrei aggiungerle un nuovo nome, Crisopoli-Cristopoli, e un qualunque Max Weber medierebbe l'antinomia. Ma non me la sento d'ironizzare ... Guido meditativamente la mia vetturetta apocalittica, su asfalti silenti, inodori, asfalti dell'eternità.[101]

> Holy Plutocracy. I could call [this city] by a new name, Crisopoli-Cristopoli, and any Max Weber could mediate the antinomy. But I don't feel like being ironic ... I meditatively drive my apocalyptic little jalopy on silent, odourless asphalt, the asphalt of eternity.

He remains similarly unmoved by the sight of the city's most recognizable landmarks, evacuated of all human life.

> [N]on si sono portati via nulla. Non hanno subìto violenze i tavolini fuori del Café Odeon, né la facciata Jugendstil. I cristalli, dietro i quali un millennio fa si sono seduti Trotzky, con sua moglie, e Lenin.
> Rimane anche quello che è organico e vivente, ma non umano. La geometria dei tulipani davanti all'Hôtel Esplanade, e le acacie che si piegano al peso dei loro fiori. Il famoso gelsomino, o gimnospermo, che gronda dalla centralissima villa del barone Aaron.[102]

> [They] did not take anything with them. The little tables outside the Café Odeon submitted to no violence, nor did its Jugendstil façade. Or the glass, behind which Trotsky, with his wife, and Lenin sat a thousand years ago.
> That which is organic and living, but not human, remains. The geometry of the tulips in front of the Hôtel Esplanade, and the acacias that bend under the weight of their flowers. The famous jasmine or gymnosperm, that pours from the very central villa of the Baron Aaron.

In other words, those hallmarks of Zurich's venerable history (Trotsky and Lenin), and distinguished culture (elaborate gardens and architecture), are admirable precisely as *natural* elements, not as artifacts of a disappeared civilization.

Ultimately, the protagonist moves to Zurich, abandoning his rural home, which, before the Event, had been chosen for its isolation – it was fifty minutes' walk from the nearest town, straight uphill on a path between larches and spruce trees, their tops hidden in the dense fog. 'Dovevi rintanarti a millequattrocento metri d'altezza'[103] ('You had to build a burrow at 1400 meters above sea-level,' his ex-lover complained.) But although it is the remoteness of human life from his mountain aerie that the protagonist proclaims as its appeal, it is precisely this quality from which he eventually flees. Having previously shunned urban life as a dedicated 'anthrophobe,' after the Event he abandons the countryside in order to inhabit – haunt, we might say – the formerly populous spots of the city (which, not by chance, are also the vital organs of Western urban capitalism – grand hotels, banks, and the stock exchange chief among them).[104] Indeed, he decides to live in the city because the silence of the countryside has swelled to a deafening roar. The protagonist's wishes are fulfilled: and then some! The tidy city was purged of those elements that threaten disorder, and the very firmament of culture need no longer act as a bulwark against oblivion – the apocalypse is now. As the alpha and omega of mankind, his historic position is as uncertain as Zurich's, which now represents either the apex of civilization or the ground zero of its annihilation, especially insofar as the very ontological existence of its only denizen is debatable – after all, he may be dead. His philosophical musings on a culture that is understood to be distinctly – and mythically – Swiss (as lived, however, by an Italian) foreground that uncertainty: Zurich is as privileged and damned as he himself is.

And yet, at novel's end there are two bright spots, if that is possible in a novel like this one. First, the protagonist concludes that suicide is no longer among the options left open to him, insofar as suicide requires an interlocutor of some sort and he has none. Second, the death of (almost) all people has brought about an intense burgeoning of the animal and vegetable world. This alone, within the novel's meagre economy of joy, justifies calling it an optimistic ending. We may not understand what has happened or what it means, the text seems to conclude, but there are at least some benefits to this great new unknown world, benefits we would not have predicted. Indeed, at the novel's end, this cradle (and grave) of civilization has been invaded by animal life: There are 'corvi sul frontone del Teatro Nazionale, [e] i gatti, a frotte, sulle gradinate

del Crédit Financier e della Diskonto'[105] (crows on the pediment of the
National Theatre, [and] the cats, in swarms, on the steps of the Crédit
Financier and of the Diskonto). Chickens rummage on the grounds of
the Stock Exchange. The City of Gold, once the centre of culture, has
been given over to nature: contraria per contraria expiantur. Switzerland is no longer the heart of Europe but rather the very world itself,
and Zurich is no longer a pious burg with fifty-six banks and thirty-one
churches, but rather a new Eden, where chamois graze in the streets
and wildflowers spring forth from the cracks in the sidewalk.

At the same time, the deconstruction in a fantastic key in this novel
of counter-history of the city and its last human inhabitant undermines
the optimism this vision might imply, in spite of the newly flourish-
ing fauna. At the heart of the existential order of his narrative is the
protagonist's overarching concern with knowledge – specifically, with
making meaning out of sensory phenomena – and fundamental questions about what is real, what is dream, and what the difference might
be outweigh any pleasure that might be taken in the phenomena themselves. Thus, for example, in search of a theory to explain the Event, he
discards a number of hypotheses, including genocide by death-rays,
biological warfare by disgruntled Venusians, remote nuclear clouds.
He concludes, eventually, with the observation that his own experience
is the best guide:

> Mi succede, invece, di chiedermi se non sia un sogno … Mi ripasso (a
> memoria perché non ho libri: a suo tempo non ho voluto portarne nemme-
> no uno, quassù) la polemica di Pascal con Cartesio. Questi scusandosi di
> non saper giustificare la realtà che attribuiamo all'esperienza e neghiamo
> ai sogni, quello rispondendo trionfale: ma se basta il nostro senso imme-
> diato e infallibile (*notre coeur*, dice Pascal) a provarci che l'esperienza è una
> cosa, e che i sogni sono un'altra cosa, la non-cosa. Tasto il mio cranio, ci
> trovo la cicatrice, la bella testata contro la roccia nella grotta del Sifone, la
> notte fatidica sul 2 giugno. E do ragione a Pascal.[106]

> It occurs to me to ask myself if it is not a dream … I review (from memory
> because I have no books: at the time I didn't want to bring a single one
> up here) Pascal's polemic with Descartes. The one excuses himself for not
> knowing how to justify the reality we attribute to experience but deny to
> dreams, the other responds triumphantly: but our immediate and infalli-
> ble sense (*notre coeur*, says Pascal) suffices to prove to us that experience is
> one thing, and dreams another thing, a non-thing. I feel my skull and find

the scar there, the nice whack against the rock in the grotto of the Siphon, that prophetic night of 2 June. And I agree with Pascal.

After a brief reflection on the corpulence of his neighbours, he reaches the preliminary conclusion that they have been vaporized. It is a conclusion that stems less from his own experience than it does from his predilection for dialectical thought: 'Un mondo tutto corpo, credente solo nella tangibilità, viene scorporato. Contraria per contraria expiantur'[107] (a world of pure body, that believes only in the tangible, is disembodied. Contraria per contraria expiantur). With this discovery (never fully embraced as an explanation except as a kind of contingent), the protagonist becomes agonizingly aware of the ramifications of the Event for his future. It is also at this point that the protagonist has the first of several of what he defines as hallucinations. They are variously auditory and visual, and revolve around the appearance or promised future appearance of Dr Karpinsky, who, although dead, will become our hero's final hope – not for salvation, redemption, or any other similar deliverance, but rather for simple, unvarnished human friendship. The promise of his arrival (*en attendant Karpinsky*) staves off total despair in the protagonist, his days structured by the search for clues to the doctor's whereabouts (the details of the rendezvous were not specified). Such a search is consonant with what we noted was the protagonist's penchant for dialectical thought, in the sense that it renders him, too, a participant in the Event by way of the metaphor. For we may understand the disappearance of humanity as metaphor for failed contact: after spending most of his life attempting to exclude the rest of humanity – to prevent them from contacting him – now he must make the effort by calling, writing, and seeking the Others out in places he had previously enjoyed the privilege of avoiding. Even attempts to hear a radio transmission fail miserably: 'L'apparecchio funziona a meraviglia, le diverse stazioni hanno ciascuna il suo diverso mugolio, miagolio, scoppiettamento, fischio. Ma non una voce. Non una nota musicale. Dall'etere universo neppure una canzonetta'[108] (The apparatus worked like a dream, the various stations each have a different moan, meow, crackling, whistle. But not one voice. Not one musical note. From the universal ether, not even a pop song). This metaphor is underscored in an art exhibit (*Arte-comportamento*, Art-behaviour) into which our hero wanders: the installation by the Italian representative, entitled *Spazio* (Space), consists of a glass table, a telephone connected to the rest of Europe, and a pile of telephone books, and all calls in

Europe up to ten seconds long are free! Needless to say, however, no one answers at any of the many numbers attempted.[109]

The search for human contact devolves eventually into its artificial manufacturing. Our hero erects a series of monuments to the departed, the first of which is best described as an orgy of symbols from the world of Western capitalist excess: cars, television sets, bottles of Coca-cola, and a huge photo advertisement, taken from a travel agency window, of the Bahamas with the apposite inscription: 'Let's fly down there, where life is better.'[110] Then there is the monument in the piazza and one in the communal swimming pool, fabricated with department store manne-quins weighted at the foot with bricks such that they bob upright in the water, moving with the breeze.[111] He also decides to try an experiment: he will repopulate the world like Deucalion, but instead of scattering pebbles, he will use sleeping pills sprinkled on the tennis court so that the new generations will be born beautiful of body and fair of spirit.[112] We may even read his eventual preference for cross-dressing as a form of manufactured contact (justified in terms of comfort, to be sure, but with a distinct hint of sartorial pleasure).[113] Finally, we must see a con-nection between the problem of failed communication and our hero's occasional tendency to talk to absent friends (such as his former lover Tuti) and his acute awareness of auditory stimuli and their absence, which is as oppressive and overwhelming as the live burial so feared by Morselli: 'E il silenzio da assenza umana, mi accorgevo, è un silen-zio che non scorre. Si accumula'[114] (And the silence of human absence, I realized, is a silence that does not flow. It accumulates). Conjuring up what was previously an impossible dream of total sensory isolation, Morselli's protagonist has wedded Rensi and Monod's logic of perpet-ual contingency to Freudian economy of desire. The narrative resolves not on a note of delight at this dream-come- true, but rather on one of horror: the final illustration of the primacy of chance.

History, Counter-History, Chance

Nel paradiso a cui dopo morte approda lo storico di professione c'è l'Ar-chivio delle possibilità non realizzate.[115]

In the paradise at which the professional historian arrives after death stands the Archive of unrealized possibilities.

Rensi's *Aporie* makes its last direct appearance in Morselli's *Diary* in a discussion of negative theology and its relationship to mysticism.[116] Again, we note the coherence of Morselli's interests, which appear to broaden the question of identity and subjectivity to include issues of faith and reason. The themes of history as chance, of identity as a function of memory (and the loss of both across time), and of the inevitability of death, which were introduced earlier, are embedded here in an equivalence between the artist's creation of his work (poem, painting, musical composition) and the mystic's creation of God, so that the divine is less an Absolute Essence than an individual essence. Here we see that Rensi has taken Morselli to the end of the line of reasoning taken up by *Dissipatio*: our identities are illusions, life is actually death, past human endeavour is tragic (when it has any meaning at all), and to top it off, God is but a projection of our foibles and hence is implicated in the questions of chance and of evil (*male*), which Morselli very closely associates with suffering.[117] After reading Rensi,[118] Morselli concludes that religious faith is insufficient as the guiding force behind life's 'essential project': that is, as a narrative capable of embracing the contradiction of a just and loving God, on the one hand, and the surfeit of suffering, on the other.[119] This is one way to read the continued exploration of questions of illegibility and inexplicability in novels such as *Dissipatio H.G.*, in which Morselli presents a situation that by definition resists interpretation. Finally, Rensi provides Morselli with explicit arguments for the kinship between history and novel:

[T]utto procede assolutamente *senza ragione*, senza che ci sia la menoma ragione perché così anziché altrimenti … cioè in modo assolutamente cieco.

Cieco. Ma che vuol dire? – Il maggior interesse che ricaviamo dalla lettura d'un libro di storia (e così d'un romanzo ben fatto) è quello che deriva dalla pungente sensazione, ad ogni momento incombente, che vi erano varie altre possibilità, che le cose avrebbero potuto andare altrimenti, che a ciascun passo dobbiamo esclamare con passione e sconforto: guarda che disdetta, che fortuna, che caso! Muore in un momento decisivo questo personaggio, che se avesse fatto un passo più lungo o più corto o se il cavallo del suo medico non fosse stato in quel giorno troppo stanco, avrebbe potuto salvarsi; viene perduta questa battaglia che alcuni gradi di più o di meno di temperatura, lo scioglimento della neve, l'ingrossamento d'un fiume sarebbe bastato a far vincere! Questo è l'elemento veramente drammatico, che c'è in ogni libro di storia.[120]

Everything procedes absolutely without reason, without there being the smallest reason for things to happen one way instead of otherwise ... that is, absolutely blindly.

Blind. But what does that mean? – The greatest interest we extract from reading a history book (and likewise a well-made novel) is that which derives from the intense sensation, imminent at every moment, that there were various other possibilities, that things could have gone differently, that at every step we must exclaim with passion and discomfort: what a misfotune, what bad luck, what chance! In a decisive moment a character dies who, had he taken longer or shorter strides or had his doctor's horse not been too tired that day, might have been saved; a battle is lost when a few degrees more or less in the temperature, the melting of the snow, the swelling of the river would have sufficed for victory! This is the truly dramatic element that exists in every history book.

History, in other words, reads like a novel precisely for the ways it imposes a narrative; it makes meaning, a meaning that *might have been made differently* under minimally different circumstances (a variation, then, on what Rensi was arguing elsewhere, namely that history is one story recounted out of an infinite number of potential stories feasible within a single set of circumstances). The assertion that history is a construction analogous to a novel not only calls into question what seems to be among the fundamental characteristics of history (its claims to neutrality, non-partisanship, and transparency) but it also allows us to reconsider the status of the novel. Such a declaration exalts the novel, permitting it, too, to make claims to truth that obfuscate its status as *fiction*. The modernity of Rensi's argument about history as construction is surprising – he anticipates key debates in late twentieth-century historiography – but it is the implication of his collapsing of history and literature that has importance for us here. For if we *can* equally ascribe to literature the qualities of history (neutrality, non-partisanship, and transparency, and so on), what is to stop us from these kinds of elisions between a first-person narrator and his/her creator? What is the truth value of literature, whether of texts that lend themselves to such readings (the realist novel, say, or the memoir) or of texts that subvert any such claim (as in surrealist poetry, or avant-garde theatre)?

Morselli seems to ask that very question not only in those novels that present counter-histories (*Contro-passato prossimo*, *Roma senza papa*) but also in those whose actions constitute a historical hapax or one-time, parenthetical event (such as the king's holiday in *Divertimento 1889*, or the hotel stay in *Un dramma borghese*, both mentioned earlier). In both of these cases, regardless of the presence or quantity of structural similarities to historical writings, we are dealing with novels that, when read with a Rensian eye for the contingency of each of their events, become exercises in what might have happened. Indeed, the premises of these texts mean that the movements and states of each element in the texts (not just the protagonists but also the minor characters, the geography in which characters move, even the weather) are perpetually fraught with peril because the stakes are so great. At any given turn, after all, the king might be unmasked, incest might be committed, suicide might be attempted. Far from a dry exercise in philosophical abstractions, Morselli's interpretation of Rensi demonstrates the dramatic, flesh and blood consequences of such a contingent notion of history.

After all, is not the entire premise of his last novel an illustration of the arbitrariness of all of human action, expanded to universal (and parapsychological?) proportions? Is not the suicide attempt of the protagonist, including its motivation – a subjectively determined percentage of suffering over joy, *and* an eleventh-hour failure due, precisely, to the unexpected reversal of that ratio when he tasted the cognac – a prime example of the infinite number of crossroads in the path of destiny? And is not the inexplicability of the Event an illustration of the blindness, irrationality, indeed the absurdity (to use Rensi's word) of Nature, which for neither Rensi nor Morselli is ruled by a sympathetic, loving or even coherent God? Nowhere is Morselli more clearly staking out a position of the hermeneutics of suicide – giving himself death, giving himself a representation of it – than when he stands at the crossroads of Rensi's and Monod's philosophies, extending their respective bailiwicks (history and the natural world) to encompass each other's. Reading the *caso Morselli* in the context of these two thinkers means understanding human history as a history of chance: that is, as a history of the unknowable, which constitutes the fundamental and (paradoxically) defining feature of any life. In my reading, Morselli's death is the last event – at once accidental and willed – in a narrative determined by absurdities, but not by failure.

2 The Corpus and the Corpse: Amelia Rosselli, Jacques Derrida, Sylvia Plath, Sarah Kofman

Genealogies

What woke those tender heavy fat hands
Said the executioner as the hatchet fell
down upon their bodily stripped souls
fermenting in the dust. You are a stranger here
and have no place among us. We would have you off our list
of potent able men
were it not that you've never belonged to it. Smell
the cool sweet fragrance of the incense burnt, in honour
of some secret soul gone off to enjoy an hour's agony
with our saintly Maker. Pray be away
sang the hatchet as it cut slittingly
purpled with blood. The earth is made nearly
round, and fuel is burnt every day of our lives.[1]

To speak of Amelia Rosselli's life, it is conventional to begin with a death, that of her father Carlo Rosselli. Co-founder and principal theoretician of the Italian antifascist resistance group *Giustizia e Libertà*, he and his brother Nello were assassinated on 10 June 1937 by French *cagoulards* sent by Mussolini in order to quash their influence as antifascist leaders. The practical and symbolic importance of their deaths, and the public nature of their lives and legacy – over 150,000 people attended Carlo's funeral – must not be underestimated if we are to have any sense of Rosselli's position as the daughter of one of the brightest stars in the firmament of Italian Resistance heroes.[2] To a generation of Italians, Rosselli is inseparable from her father's legacy.[3] By way of a comparison, think, perhaps, of the photos of young John-John at John F. Kennedy's funeral, which are similarly indelible images in the American popular imagination: as much *la figlia di Carlo* as a writer,[4] Rosselli was the daughter of 'the very incarnation of the Resistance'[5] long before she was a poet. Later, her familial and literary identities merged when she became custodian of her father's memory as the editor of his personal correspondence.[6]

Rosselli was also a poet in her own right. Initially she moved on the fringe of a fairly exalted poetic circle, the influential and daring Gruppo '63. She gained a wide audience in 1966 when selections of her poems were published in the journal *Menabò*, with an introduction by Pier Paolo Pasolini. Although her works were never particularly popular with the general public, among the cognoscenti she was considered a formidable and innovative poetic voice from early in her writing career. Neither her creative successes nor her illustrious parentage, however, brought Rosselli much in the way of fame during her lifetime. Rather, it was after she jumped to her death, on 11 February 1996 – that is, the thirty-third anniversary of Sylvia Plath's suicide – that her readership broadened and inspired a deeper engagement with her work.

Movement, Memory, Commemoration[7]

>   at the corner the dew
> on the corpse awaits stiff
> unaware of the many purposeless
> strings it holds in its hand. Awaits
> a greater danger yet a greater
> shiver in the dusk slips the sleeper
> down the foaming steps of hell and the garage
> holds wide
> its hoary cavern mouth.[8]

Rosselli is a good example of the strange bedfellows phenomenon to which I referred earlier in this study. When Rosselli committed suicide on the anniversary of Plath's suicide, her readership reassigned her a new 'genealogy,' so that previous associations such as with other neo-avantgarde poets, beginning with the Gruppo '63, that were motivated by facets of her writings – radically innovative, and frequently opaque almost to the point of illegibility – were supplemented with references to her 'suicide sisters,' real and fictional female figures from the world of literature, including (besides Plath) Antigone, Electra, Sappho, Ophelia, Emily Dickinson, Virginia Woolf, and Ingeborg Bachmann (a possible suicide).[9] This is not to say that these comparisons are necessarily untenable or that they result from shoddy scholarship. But my point here is that after a suicide, there is a tendency among critics to enact paradigm shifts that bring their readings closer to those more typical of the popular press, which engages an author's biography before her writings. As another example, consider fellow poet and contemporary Andrea Zanzotto's praise for 'l'immensa generosità dell'atto poetico di Amelia'[10] (the immense generosity of Amelia's poetic act). This is a kind of posthumous cheerleading, a fear of speaking ill of the dead that is at once insulting and counterproductive: Zanzotto's Rosselli sounds not like an accomplished poet but rather like the splendid hostess at a dinner party. What's more, remarks like these actually obscure her poetry within the white noise of good intentions, making it hard for readers to form their own impressions, whether good, bad, or indifferent. They aim, instead, to rehabilitate the woman ('Amelia') behind the work.[11]

Hence the prevalence, after 1996, of readings that emphasize female filiation. Among these women, it is no surprise that (the anniversary aside) Sylvia Plath, who is arguably the most accessible of the bunch, looms large.[12] There are, in fact, numerous associations between Rosselli and Plath. Critics are quick to note, for example, that they share certain biographical data (both women lost their fathers as young girls; both women underwent electroshock therapy), and Rosselli was very familiar with Plath's life and works: she translated Plath, she frequently named Plath as one of the greatest American poets,[13] and she argued for a close study of Plath's poetry as a way to understand Plath's suicide.[14] The superficial resemblances between the lives of Rosselli and Plath (as well, as we will see, as Sarah Kofman) are admittedly trivial. Turning the poets' lives into socks to be matched, these minutiae discount the gravity of their deaths, of the losses they suffered and our loss of them. And yet Rosselli's engagement at multiple levels with these women and their legacies is irreducible proof of the life outside Rosselli's texts. These similarities, taken with the suicide date, mean that according to the canonical reading, Rosselli's suicide was deliberately enacted on the anniversary of Plath's as a gesture of identification and of commemoration. Thus, in contrast to the genealogical formation she entered at birth, critics pointed to a new one established at her death. Moreover, it was a decidedly matrilineal inheritance: after suicide, she was not so much the *figlia di Carlo* as a second Lady Lazarus, following Plath's eloquently mortuary poem about suicide attempts.[15]

We need not assume that Rosselli intended to die on Plath's anniversary, since, for my purposes, whether it was by accident or design is unknowable. But to the extent that intention has been attributed to the date of her death, then we must understand what that date entails. As a poet, a woman, and a suicide, Plath's figure contrasts so strongly with Rosselli's almost mythic father that it rivals, in a perverse way, his death, if not for symbolic or ideological impact, then for the spectacle it created. Like her father's death almost sixty years earlier, Rosselli's death similarly functioned as both a sight to behold and a historical event. And as her father's death became an act to be commemorated, Rosselli's *is* an act of commemoration – but not for him.[16] The symbolic role of Plath, then, is twofold. First, Plath threatens to eclipse Carlo Rosselli's position in Amelia Rosselli's posthumous biography. And second, Plath reframes Rosselli's relationship with her mother, Marion Cave: the gendering female of Plath as Rosselli's antecedent reflects a substitution of the maternal body analogous to the substitution of her father. It claims to disavow Cave's influence by redoubling her absence. Thus Rosselli's death produces distinct tensions around the questions of both gender and ancestry.

This same irresolution between her role in life, as Carlo's daughter, and, in death, as Plath's sister, plays out with respect to her poetry as a vacillation between two conflicting readings. The two standard tropes are located at opposite ends of the historicist-aesthetic continuum. On the one hand, she is all history, a pure product of Western Europe in the late twentieth century, such that everything from her ability to write in three languages to her penchant for plosives and her confessional style is a symptom of the historical trauma visited upon her tragic generation.[17] On the other hand is a pathologizing concern with her aesthetics. For many critics, she was unique in her interiority – her writings are from a kind of psychic sidereal space, fascinating and beautiful but ultimately cold and unreachable. Though discourses of biological, literary, and linguistic engenderment abound in her writings, after suicide, apart from Sylvia Plath, her writerly identity was understood to be nearly devoid of literary antecedents. Indeed, basing their posthumous perceptions of Rosselli as biographically and emotionally *déracinée*, some of her most important critics essentially severed all ties between her opus and the work of her contemporaries, reassessing her work as resolutely *sui generis* in its dogged disavowal of any possible literary kinship.[18]

Note, too, that although these two interpretive tendencies are often in conflict, their effects in the context of discussions of her suicide are similar: as we saw in the case of Guido Morselli, whose 'story' was reduced by some to a simple question of professional failure, these, too, justify her death by reducing its motives to a single, impersonal master narrative. In the case of an interpretive framework organized around Rosselli's aesthetics of singularity, her death is justified by her status as an anomaly (and a psychologically unstable one at that), while, in the case of the historicizing reading, her mental illness and suicide are seen as collateral damage from the war, subsumed under the rubric of collective tragedy (for who could survive it?). The pages that follow will take into consideration the complex ways in which issues of progenitors – both familial and literary – work themselves out in Rosselli's life and literary opus in order to understand the ramifications of her suicide for her readership. Specifically, I would like to argue that if we set aside the questions of mental illness and suicide (and thereby read Rosselli beyond the historicist-aesthetic continuum), what emerges is in fact a poetic redimensioning of the twin traumas of violence and loss, and, ultimately, their successful working through.

History of an Illness: Maternal Bodies and Writing

> The King and Queen sat beheaded firmly
> embraced, enlaced in a fit of action troublesome
> to their fitsome senses. A fire to my dandy
> lover! responded the Queen to her lover's
> embraces, a fire to the wind which scurries
> in the veins of my beheaded head! The King
> sat a-mused while he played with her hand,
> dripping with the juice of his head. Her
> head lay despondently on the rim of the
> throne fit for a King to sit on, lest he
> lose his Grace on the matrimonial day which
> was granted by the Divinity on her losing
> her socket which joined the bones of man
> and women as they sat firmly embraced under
> the pine-tree a-pining for the tree of love
> soul-less as an apple. Joined by the knitted

> brow of God, the Queen embraced her Courtly
> lover and enlaced his firm pocket with gold
> handkerchiefs with which to pine on. Weeping
> for her primordial sin she whipped a bite
> off the old pine-tree, and fell a-nursing
> her teeth, troublesome to her mannered
> head a-squinting in the foam of her death
> grinned smile of a face, courtly notwithstanding
> all. All sat and smiled and there was the
> end of the travail she had undergone to
> save her Master's soul under the pine-wood
> tree of action.[19]

Important as Rosselli's father's legacy was, it pales in comparison to that of her grandmother, Amelia Pincherle Moravia (1870–1954). She poses a triple threat: as a celebrated playwright and essayist, as the formative ideological force behind the development of her two sons, and as a no-nonsense stand-in for Rosselli's mother. Thus her overlapping spheres of influence are literary, political, and familial, in contrast to Rosselli's mother, whose influence on her daughter's writing, perceptible first and foremost at the linguistic level (she was a native English speaker), is predominantly private.[20] What are the ramifications of these writing women (if we include her mother's sizeable correspondence) for Rosselli? Let us start by noting Rosselli's intermittent choice to write in English, most significantly in the collection of poems entitled *Sleep* (though the great majority of her published works are in Italian). For literary scholar Shoshana Felman, the question of language is bound up with the questions of strangeness, indeed of madness, when she writes, 'what is at stake in the passage from one language to another is less translation in itself than the translation *of oneself* – into the otherness of languages. To speak about madness is to speak about the difference between languages: to import into one language the strangeness of another; to unsettle the decisions language has prescribed to us so that, somewhere between languages, will emerge the freedom to speak.'[21] Otherness, unsettling, somewhere between: these terms are analogous to the ones we will find useful to describe Rosselli's early history (slippery, shifting). If we want to take into account both the life and the text, can we not argue that writing in English means, for Rosselli, writing not only her own strangeness ('somewhere between languages') but also the strangeness, conceived as simultaneous sameness and difference, of her mother? To give an idea of the intensity of the symbolic subjective overlap between the two, consider that in the years immediately after her mother's death in 1949, Rosselli signed her published articles with her mother's married name (not her maiden name).[22] Similarly, in contrast to her more widely known Italian poetry, we might call her English writings a private language, one that perhaps declares its kinship with the private writings of her mother and, at the same time, distances Rosselli from her namesake, the other Amelia Rosselli, who achieved fame as a writer in Italian. We might therefore add to our list of questions about the relationship between the younger Amelia Rosselli and the two generations of women before her what the effects of that shared or in any case ambiguous identification were. Like her father, these two women manifest themselves in *Sleep* both as presences and as structuring absences: that is, as clear antecedents and as models to be rejected. Linguistically, Rosselli's collection, too, is both entrenched and deracinated, in the strangeness that is writing in English as well as the strangeness of not writing in Italian. (After all, she could have chosen not to write in Italian and still not chosen her mother's language – why not French, for example?)[23]

The relations between writing, language, and madness are perhaps most explicitly addressed by Rosselli herself in *Storia di una malattia* (*History of an Illness*), ten dense pages about her years-long experiences of a persecution complex. She described how from 1969 until early 1977 (when the *Storia* was written), she was victim of a political persecution and terror campaign that manifested itself, among other things, in deliberately tainted food, and in the use of electromagnetic devices in her apartment both to hear her thoughts and to transmit messages to her, and to inflict harm on her muscular-skeletal system. In order to combat her tormentors she denounced them on various occasions to different government officials in Italy and in the United Kingdom, only to be told that there were no longer any Fascists in Italy:

Seguirono incidenti vari con macchine chiaramente d'origine fascista. Ebbi diverse cadute dal motorino, con traumi cranici relativi. La casa era precedentemente stata messa sottosopra in cerca di droghe, che ovviamente non ho mai comprato né consumato di mia volontà.

Essendo chiarita parzialmente la mia reputazione nel quartiere, ed essendo diminuite in intensità le 'voci' maschili udibili in casa pensai di avere finalmente un periodo di tranquillità. Per contenuto il parlottare tra di loro di queste voci maschili, che a questo punto supponevo dell'Ufficio

Politico o di derivazione simile, era nell'insieme non minaccioso. Pensavo addirittura si trattasse d'una forma di protezione, dati i tempi e a causa del mio cognome Rosselli.

Ma attorno al 1973 subentrarono nuove voci, alcune maschili alcune femminili, di cui il parlato era americano anche se gli accenti non tipici, ma d'un inglese neutro. Iniziò un dialogo a dir poco assurdo se non grottesco: speravo che si trattasse di scienziati, sociologi o psichiatri o comunque aspettando di determinarne l'origine. Cominciarono con commenti per metà apparentemente umoristici, tanto da fare poi pensare che si trattasse d'una compagnia d'attori disoccupati. Questo frammisto però a minacce. Al mio chiedere 'cosa fate qui' ebbi risposta 'non siamo qui per farti piacere.' Notte e giorno veniva ripetuta la parola *good* (bene), in maniera che a me da prima pareva soltanto ridicola ma che in realtà serviva ad interrompere ogni mia forma di pensiero continuato, e che secondo me era una specie di parodia di una parola d'ordine forse d'uso tra i servizi segreti in genere. Tra le sei-sette voci distinguibili in quanto sempre eguali a se stesse ne spiccavano all'inizio due di donne, una delle quali piuttosto giovane. Compresi più tardi che si trattava di persone drogate: pare che tramite l'uso di certe droghe pesanti sia possibile la lettura del pensiero, abbastanza esatta anche se si tratta di lettura degli strati consci, superiori, del pensiero immediato. Queste due donne si davano un daffare impressionante nel ripetermi, già prima ch'io finissi di 'pensare' una frase, le sue prime parole in modo da rendere una qualsiasi interiorità o *privacy* di opinioni o analisi impossibile. Anche quando mi svegliavo di notte udivo commenti ironici, continuava ossessivamente la lettura del pensiero ripetuta. Si credeva in questa maniera di rendermi o incapace o non autonoma e di comunque ridurmi a specie di manichino ai loro ordini. Ad alta voce però esprimevo le mie opinioni politiche abbastanza chiaramente, e accusai loro d'essere della 'Goodyear Co.' ossia delle Sette Sorelle. Finsero d'essere offesissimi.[24]

Various accidents with cars of clearly fascist origin followed. I had several falls from my scooter, with related cranial traumas. The house had previously been turned upside down in search of drugs, which obviously I had never bought nor taken of my own will.

Once my reputation in the neighbourhood partially cleared up, and once the male 'voices' audible in the house diminished, I thought I might finally have a period of tranquillity. As for the content of the mutterings of these masculine voices, whom I supposed to be from the Political Office or of some other similar derivation, it was by and large not threatening.

Indeed I thought it had to do with some form of protection, given the times and my last name Rosselli.

But around 1973, new voices took over, some male some female, whose way of speaking was American, though the accents were not typical, but more of a neutral English. I began a dialogue that was absurd, to say the least, if not grotesque: I was hoping they were scientists, sociologists, or psychiatrists, in any case I was waiting to determine their origin. They began with comments that were apparently half-humorous, to the extent that I thought I was dealing with a company of unemployed actors. This, however, was mixed up with threats. When I asked, 'What are you doing here?' I got the response, 'We are not here to make you happy.' Night and day, the word *good* [in English] was repeated, in a way that at first just seemed ridiculous but that in reality served to interrupt any form of continuous thought for me, and which in my opinion was a kind of parody of a password perhaps in use in the secret service in general. Among the six or seven voices that were distinguishable because always the same, two women's voices, one of them quite young, were distinctive. I understood later that these were people on drugs: it seems that with the use of certain heavy drugs it is possible to read others' thoughts fairly exactly, though it is only a reading of the conscious layers, the uppermost ones of immediate thought. These two women went to impressive lengths to repeat to me, even before I had finished 'thinking' a sentence, the sentence's first words in such a way as to make any sort of interiority or *privacy* of opinions impossible. Even when I woke up at night I heard ironic comments, the repeated thought-reading continued obsessively. They thought that this way they could either incapacitate me or take away my autonomy and in any case reduce me to a kind of mannequin at their service. But I expressed my political opinions fairly clearly out loud, and I accused them of being from the Goodyear Company, that is, from the Seven Sisters. They pretended to be extremely offended.

Several aspects of these distressing episodes are of interest to us. First, we cannot fail to notice the highly political motivation of her supposed persecutors, which seems to support the reading of Rosselli as the embodiment of historical circumstances. Rosselli clearly and continually associates her tormentors with the Fascists, who slide in and out of American bodies, and assumes it is her last name that sparks their interest, though initially she interprets this interest in a positive light: they are there for her protection. She claims that high-ranking public officials ordered her surveillance, called it off, intervened or pretended to. Their nationality seems to vary with the episodes, but her hallucinations are most frequently peopled with Americans who don't sound American because of their 'neutral English' accent – later, the Welsh actor Richard Burton makes recurring appearances. Thus we see yet another manifestation of the imbrications of the intimate and the political: she is ostensibly subjected to this hounding because of her father, but it takes place not in the actual political world but in the inmost sanctum of her psyche. She has incorporated, as it were, her father – he is inside her head, apparently to the extent that her private political views, like his public ones before her, could be perceived as a threat to national, indeed international, interests. It should not surprise us, then, that her tormentors would use tactics that smack of political torture. The code words, mind control, absolute lack of privacy, and covert drug operations of which she writes take on the contours of a political thriller (*The Manchurian Candidate* comes to mind, though I am not prepared to posit Amelia Pincherle Rosselli in the Angela Lansbury role), or in any event of a wartime drama.

But it is the two women who figure prominently in these visions who interest me here, because of the ways they become significant in the light of our previous discussion about Rosselli's mother and grandmother. It is not my claim that they are directly represented in her hallucinations: such a claim would be untenable and unproductive. It is useful, however, to point out the analogous structural positions of these hallucinatory female figures with the historic ones in their relation to language. In the hallucinations, for example, the two women have the ability to anticipate Rosselli's thoughts: they predict them before Rosselli has even had the chance to articulate them fully in her mind, and thereby succeed in robbing Rosselli not only of her privacy but of her *language*. For the goal of those predictions, she claims, is an act of disruption, that is, a stunting of the thought process, so that Rosselli returns to a state of dependence (incapacitate me or take away my autonomy). The women of the hallucination want to preclude the possibility of independent thought at the level of its conception, that is, at the linguistic level, reducing her to some kind of mannequin designed for their needs. This is further accomplished with the mantra-like repetition of the code-word *good*, which sets off the response (perhaps akin to the *Manchurian Candidate*'s playing card). She is not, in other words, a tailor's dummy so much as a ventriloquist's, talking through them and at their command. My point, of course, is *not* that Cave and Pincherle Rosselli had similarly nefarious designs on Rosselli's brain, but rather that they, too, were intimately involved in the formation and organization of Rosselli's linguistic and ideational development at the level of its production and its reception (by which I mean both interception, like the Americans' voices and Rosselli's thoughts, and reaction or response). The bilingualism of these hallucinations, too, recalls Cave, in particular. Alongside the repetition of *good*, in English, we read a page later of a group of Italian voices that repeat the word *brava*:

> Da quel punto in poi s'accentuarono i 'trattamenti' psicologici e fisici del gruppo Americano: le poche voci italiane che udivo sembravano anzi appoggiare un mio resistere alla fatica, con incitamenti tramite la parola 'brava' usata ripetutamente anche se non a vanvera. Macchine scalcagnate di marca americana con tipi un po' loschi dal fisico infatti americano a volte m'attendevano al portone o infastidivano per strada. Ma a ciò ero ormai abituata.[25]

> From that point on the psychological and physical 'treatments' of the American group heightened: the few Italian voices that I heard seemed to support my withstanding the strain, by inciting me with the word 'brava' used repeatedly, but not haphazardly. Run-down American cars with shady looking guys with American physiques sometimes waited for me at the street door or bothered me on the street. But by then, I was used to it.

Although we might interpret all of these *good*s and *brava*s as a form of encouragement, a bilingual cheerleading squad inside Rosselli's head, we must recall that the use of the English word *good* had deleterious effects on Rosselli's ability to think and to speak. The two women talking in Rosselli's head wreak psychological havoc even as they appear to give praise. So there are three observations to be made here with respect to the voices. First, they instill a conditioned response that tyrannizes the relationship between language and thought. Second, they create a disjuncture between what words say and what they mean. And third, they pit one language against another, since the effective meanings of *good* and *brava* conflict. Authentic encouragement, apparently, comes only in Italian. But the Italians, it seems, are in the minority, since even the cars and their lurid inhabitants are American. We may also point to the political component of the hallucinations, which are explicitly tied to her family history ('a causa del mio cognome Rosselli'), and the contemporary political scene between the years 1973–5 to which these passages refer. Political and emotional conflicts thus work themselves out as linguistic ones, in hallucinations as in real life.

Rosselli's torment became so acute that she repeatedly sought the protection of hospitalization, where she knew her food would be safe to eat and she would be well looked after. To gain entry she threatened suicide, but when, to remedy her depression, she was offered electroshock therapy (and here we might invoke Sylvia Plath's experiences), she initially declined and was released from hospital. After her release, however, the hallucinations returned with such vehemence that she in fact became suicidal. She subsequently agreed to undergo the therapy, which left her with irresolvable head pain. The episodes eventually diminished in strength in March of 1977, coinciding, she said, with the election of Jimmy Carter to the presidency of the United States.

What do Rosselli's experiences teach us about reading her work? Evidently, Rosselli's first move after her persecution ended was to write about it. *Storia di una malattia* was written on 16 September 1977 and published soon thereafter. Despite the apparent immediacy of the writing, however, her cousin Aldo gives the impression that it was an old story, told on many occasions, with the goal of persuasion:

> Più implausibile, atroce, inaccettabile era il suo racconto, più poteva sembrare che il visitatore di turno stesse inoltrandosi in un giallo dai contorni circonvoluti, nel nero di un congegno horror dove però persistevano spezzoni di quotidianità, addirittura familiarità. E nello svolgersi del suo interminabile plot esistenziale, presentato ora còme una confessione affannosa, indicibile, ora come un soffocato grido d'incredulità pure da parte di chi dipana terrificanti momenti di implausibilità, blocchi di pura sofferenza presentati come i racconti di un orrore quotidiano, minimale (non dissimili, ad esempio, dalla prosa ingannatrice ... [di] Patricia Highsmith), Amelia coinvolgeva l'ascoltatore ignaro o renitente in una forzata ma anche soave accettazione. [26]

> The more implausible, atrocious, and unacceptable her story was, the more it seemed that the visitor on duty was immersing himself in a mystery novel of convoluted contours, into the blackness of a mechanism of horror in which, however, bits of daily life and the familiar persisted. And in the development of its interminabile existential plot, presented either as a breathless, unspeakable confession or as a stifled cry of incredulity on the part of the very person who unravels terrifying, implausible moments, blocks of pure suffering presented as the tales of a daily, minimal horror (not unlike, for example, the deceptive prose ... [of] Patricia Highsmith),

Amelia co-opted the unknowing or unwilling listener in[to] forced and yet mild acceptance.

Important here is the idea of the literary quality of Rosselli's narration, which complicates both terms of the piece's title: at the moment that we associate the contours of these experiences with literature, they take on a new status beyond history and illness. Thus they change our relationship to it as well as hers, ironizing both the implication of pathology and of therapy. Aldo Rosselli's observations thus raise the question: whose incredulity is more shocking, hers or ours? His is a comment on the nature of madness, so to speak, in readership as much as in authorship, for as literary as her descent appears, so does he posit our willing suspension of disbelief as a gesture perhaps worth questioning. In other words, this is a text that asks to be taken at face value and, on the surface of it, supports the reading of Rosselli as a victim of historical forces. It is surprising, then, that of all of her writings this one is read for its literary value, and her much more tightly hermeneutically sealed poetry is read as history.

In 1978, a year after *Storia* was published, Rosselli told her interviewer, Sandra Petrignani, that she felt during the period of persecution (the five previous years) that she had lost her talent as a poet, comparing it to the loss of language itself: 'Non sento di avere talento, ora. E' come non riuscire a parlare una lingua. E' terribile'[27] ('I don't feel that I have talent, now. It is like not being able to speak a language. It is terrible'). So the women and men who haunted Rosselli *were* successful: they did cause her temporarily to 'lose her talent,' her ability to think and to speak: to lose, precisely, her language. Considering the conflicts between public and private life, and between the history and the illness, at odds with each other in this text, the impulse to read this through the key of Rosselli's death requires understanding this loss of language as a function of historical trauma as it is inscribed upon and introjected by Rosselli. But this position that Rosselli's suicide is evidence of the failure of writing as a form of *Trauerarbeit* is given the lie by both the fact of her writing, and the use to which she puts it: if she can make hay from these experiences, the sun must still be shining. She turns her losses (of language, of autonomy within the genealogical and more broadly historical networks in which she is caught) into writing. Recall Felman's madness ('the translation *of oneself* – into the otherness of languages') – here, the transformation of trauma into text – is thus also its own antidote. I would argue, then, that when we bracket, however temporarily, the suicide and tend carefully to the writings, Rosselli's literal and figurative embodiment of historical trauma becomes, too, the embodiment of recovery. And the 'strangeness' of writing in a different language for Rosselli (even if English, too, is her language) is by this logic born not from an exigency of illness but of identity – the translation *of oneself* into a form with which to establish kinships of preference (the *anima* of which her grandmother wrote?), and not necessarily of birth. Here the terms slippage, shifting, and deracination seem applicable, both to Rosselli in historical perspective and to the haunting ground of writing. It comprises her genealogy even more than the historical players themselves, if we consider that the writings last long after their creators have ceased to exist. Thus Rosselli's writing – its places and people, its overt and covert goals, its secret and stated agendas – challenges the critical urge to reconstitute Rosselli as a victim of the forces of history, even while it recognizes the roots of a history that is both of, and from, the dead.

Suicide and *Sleep*

A soft sonnet is all the strength i have
To create, full easy life have i ever and ever
again and again destroyed, but it was god crying
within me turn out all
lights! No love be granted to he who
hates all love save life
writ on paper there goes my
seed wild into
death.[28]

Let us move now to the other end of the interpretive spectrum, dominated by aesthetic readings of Rosselli's poetry. We will take as our object of inquiry her collection of English-language poems, entitled *Sleep*. Written between 1953 and 1966, it is considered a precursor to Rosselli's 'more mature' Italian-language poetry, a kind of poetic calisthenics in preparation for the main event.[29] But we may also read *Sleep* as a metapoetics, a text to run parallel to her Italian poetry and thereby to present observations on the ways her poetry has been understood, or misunderstood, by her Italian critics: the voice of *Sleep* is that of a poet commenting on how her poetry has been and might in future be received. Thus her poetic interlocutors are not necessarily or exclusively the standard ones – a lover, or God, for example – instead, they also address the reader him- or herself and double back to engage the poet. This assertion has relevance for much of Rosselli's work, as well as for our understanding of her construction as a public persona, because much of that persona is made visible by way of her poetics of self-examination. In my reading, Rosselli's English-language poetry elucidates a presumptive relationship with her readers, her critics, and a series of other poets, whose works and (equally importantly) whose lives function as touchstones for Rosselli. Put in different terms, the text of *Sleep* represents Rosselli's move to the other side of the page. By writing a poetic commentary on her critical reception, Rosselli establishes herself not only as someone to be read, identified with, and/or gazed upon, but also as herself part of the gaze.[30]

Indeed, visual metaphors comprise an integral part of the collection. It is precisely this identification of I and eye, of poetic subject and object, that has 'pathologized' Rosselli's writings (and the poet herself, by extension), stripping them bare of their genealogical roots and imposing a discourse of disease alongside that of irreducible alterity.[31] It is this conflation of life, text, and authorship that I now aim to explore from two distinct directions. First, following the program laid out in the introduction, I address the critical interventions of two of Rosselli's readers, to understand the ways her work has been untethered from the poet as a writing subject, and I offer as a counter-argument the connections between Rosselli's poetic techniques and those of the French Surrealists. Second, I examine visual metaphors in *Sleep* in order to elucidate the forces that conspire to confirm her supposed 'illegibility' on the grounds that the hermeneutical challenge she seems to pose stems not so much from the difficulty of her writings as from the subject position that produced them.

Rosselli's works were first introduced to the public in the 1963 edition of the journal *Menabò*, directed by Italo Calvino and Elio Vittorini.[32] In an introductory essay that would become the touchstone for Rosselli criticism for years to come, Pier Paolo Pasolini identified the 'lapsus' or slip as the primary linguistic phenomenon in her poetry: 'è dominata da qualcosa di meccanico: emulsione che prende forma per suo conto, imposseduta, come si ha l'impressione che succeda per gli esperimenti di laboratorio più terribili, tumori, scoppi atomici'[33] (it is dominated by something mechanical: an emulsion that takes shape of its own accord, possessed, as one has the impression occurs in the most terrible laboratory experiments, tumours, atomic explosions). His introduction provides two of the tropes that will become commonplace when describing Rosselli's poetry: first, Pasolini uses images from the realms of disease and catastrophe,[34] and second, he employs those images in such a way as to deny all agency on the part of the thirty-three-year old poet. According to Pasolini's formulation, Rosselli is on the one hand relegated to the position of passive bystander, an observer in the laboratory recording events as they unfold without her intervention; on the other hand, she is the Petri dish herself, the medium in which the tumours can metastasize. Pasolini offers two readings of her work that 'naturalize' her poetic production by defining her as the site and subject – and consequently not as the agent or author – of the creative process. The founding gesture of Rosselli as a poet, in other words, is not only highly gendered but gendered in such a way that even that which is exclusively female (the potential to bear children) is evacuated of its agency – she is not so much the woman who labours but the egg from which the poetry hatches. Note too that her suicide will take on the same rhetorical contours – her association with mental illness signifies the gendering of her terminal act, as well, insofar as depression and hysteria have been associated with women (in the same way that male madness is associated with genius). Not understandable as an act of courage or deliberation, her suicide seen in this light becomes the inevitable result of her disease just as the monstrous birth of the lapsus followed mechanical possession. (In contrast, as we will see, Rosselli's poetic voice genders her reader male – we will return to that in our discussion of the poems.)

It is a surprising move, then, when Pasolini attempts to insert Rosselli's use of the lapsus into a broader poetic framework as a point of contiguity with both her predecessors and her contemporaries; the lapsus, Pasolini writes, is 'l'unico fatto che rende questa lingua storicamente o almeno correntemente determinata'[35] (the only fact that renders this language historically or at least currently determined). In other words, it is for Pasolini both idiopathic, i.e. spontaneous or of unknown origin, *and* historically situated. Indeed, Pasolini himself seems at a loss to countenance the contradiction; as soon as he articulates a connection between Rosselli and other poets, he disclaims it in a series of parenthetical disavowals, among them that Rosselli's lapsus is characteristic of the linguistic poets (though she is not one), or that it also appears frequently in works by French Surrealists (to whom, for Pasolini, she bears no relation).[36] In broad strokes, Pasolini's otherwise insightful introduction to her work runs aground when confronted with her etiological indeterminacy.[37] His coupling of scientific and ideological discourses effectively equates the defining feature of Rosselli's poetry with both excess and lack; if the lapsus is the place where the pen slips, it is also a slip of the chromosome producing a tumour, a slip where the chain of historical cause and effect breaks. Rosselli's poetry, in other words, is like a tomb, which functions to contain the now superfluous body in the absence of a soul.

Writing thirty-two years after Pasolini, Stefano Agosti reaches related conclusions regarding Rosselli's poetry. In his 1995 collection of essays on contemporary Italian poetry[38] Agosti convincingly argues for the primacy of the associative over syntagmatic competence, by which he means that the actual framework of a text is deformed by features such as vacillating accord, anagram rhymes, and alliteration, rather than the proposition or terms of the text. He cites the lapsus as the pre-eminent example of associative competence, focusing in particular on the 'semantic short circuit' created by combining new words to create indeterminate but highly suggestive new ones, such as *deglutare* to suggest both *deglutire* (to swallow) and *degustare* (to taste or sample).[39] Similarly, lexical iteration and analepsis function to create a sort of snowball effect as the same phrase is repeated and built upon. With *Sleep* we may extend his observations beyond the economy of the individual poems, since one of Rosselli's poetic techniques involves intermittently reiterating phrases or series of phrases that interlink with one another across the collection. For example, one poem consists simply of the words, 'hell, loomed out / with perfect hands,'[40] words that will reappear in the first line of a longer piece almost sixty pages later.

The effect of such a technique is twofold. The polysemic, stratified construction of sound, word, and imagery within and across the poems creates a tight network of multiple meanings, a hypertext if you will, of meanings superimposed one upon the other in such a way that on the one hand, interpretation is potentially infinite, and perpetually indeterminate on the other. For Agosti, meanings are so various that in the end we cannot decide upon any as a result of the framework of the poems – associative, not syntagmatic. Here Agosti confronts a challenge analogous to Pasolini's, of making meaning at the site in which excess and lack coexist. Recall Pasolini's formulation, which appropriates the very technique it describes: Rosselli's language is 'imposseduta,' that is, not grasped, possessed, or mastered.[41] But by whom? For Pasolini's lapsus is meaningful in two ways, one positive and one negative. With his Rosselli-inspired combination of two words to create a richer, more

suggestive one ('imposseduta'), he is arguably paying a sort of trib-
ute to Rosselli. But he plays at the same time on the broader context
of his remarks to create ambiguity in their attribution of agency. Put
more simply, there are two implications for Rosselli's poetry: that the
reader is doomed to fail to grasp the multiple meanings of the poems,
and, more problematic, that Rosselli herself cannot master them. What
do these implications suggest? When coupled with Agosti's observation about the associative framework of her poems, they suggest that
Rosselli's poetry eludes mastery (both hers and ours) precisely because
of the site from which it was produced. We cannot point to a locus of
enunciation, whether of flesh and blood or bodied forth in a text, except
in the form of a movement. Rosselli's poetry cannot be mastered, possessed, grasped because it was written in transit, on the fly, on the way
from nowhere to nowhere. But is the lapsus really the root cause of
her difficulty? Unlikely, since after all techniques such as that are not
unique to her poetry; indeed the generation of Italian-language poets
with whom she is often, if only tangentially, associated – I Novissimi,
la Nuova Avanguardia, later il Gruppo Sessantatrè – is known in large
part for its predilection for the 'poetry of non-meaning': in terms that
sound similar to Pasolini's, Franco Fortini describes the work of the
Neoavanguardisti, for example, as 'impersonal, arbitrarily organized'
and engaged in a 'radical denial of communication' in order to 'destroy
the 'normal' linguistic universe.'[42] At issue then is arguably not Rosselli's technique but rather something more nebulous.

The Slip and Surrealism

> You might as well think one thing or another
> of me; I am not at mercy's chance, nor do
> I want your interpretation, having none
> myself to overpower me. You withdraw into
> your fevered cell, like a microscopic angel
> do engage battle with my thoughts, as if
> they were to my revolutionary heart, a
> promiscuous bell. Hell itself is what you
> want: a needle into necessity, foreseeing
> I shall not do better than you want.[43]

It is here that we may return to Pasolini's observation about the
French Surrealists' predilection for the lapsus. My objective here is

not to make major claims about Rosselli's relationship to the Surrealists (I will do so later about her relationship with Sarah Kofman's work) but rather to support my observation that critics are reluctant to draw too many connections between her work and the work of other poets beyond her association with the Gruppo '63. Rosselli's familiarity with the works of the Surrealists can be established from her writings, though it should also be added that she more frequently acknowledged links between other poets' works and those of the Surrealists than with her own.[44] (And perhaps this too is significant: her earliest assignment in journalism was to deal with André Breton; Rosselli demurred, suggesting that she write instead about Boris Pasternak.)[45] The similarities between the Surrealists' works and Rosselli's are more structural, or perhaps procedural, than they are political, either in the broader sense or in the specific terms of, say, the *Second Surrealist Manifesto* of 1930;[46] and it should also be said that in spite of the subset of shared techniques, the outcomes are radically divergent. But these techniques are significant to my argument insofar as they locate Rosselli's works in relation to identifiable literary predecessors (I will discuss Leopardi later as well), thus calling into question the notion that her work is somehow aberrant or without genealogical antecedents (except in her use of the lapsus, itself an aberration); equally importantly, they offer a further gloss on Pasolini's and Agosti's observations about agency and authorship. The points of contact between Rosselli and the French Surrealists help elucidate the role of the reading I/eye in *Sleep*, insofar as it is identified both with the poet herself, and in relation to the readership the poems address.[47] Agosti's discussion of the semantic short circuit, for example, is evocative of the hermetic rebus characteristic of the Surrealists. The hermetic rebus consists of the 'mediation of disparate entities,'[48] which is visible in Rosselli at various levels: in the semantic short circuit, a word or words that embrace multiple meanings, and, by extension, at the level of the text itself in the form of repetition across the opus. The imbrication across the length of *Sleep* of images, lines of text, and texts in their entirety similarly finds its correlative in Breton, in his formulation of a poetics of 'l'un dans l'autre' (the one in the other), that is, the network of relations between poetic objects.[49] Agosti's characterization of these as both excessive and lacking, while not inaccurate, obscures the depth and breadth of Rosselli's poetic kinship relations, emphasizing instead her singularity.[50]

More complicated, perhaps, are Pasolini's discussions of the origins of the lapsus in conjunction with Surrealist concepts such as 'automatic writing.'[51] As we saw earlier, Pasolini invokes the Surrealists in order to disavow any connection to them. While the move itself is curious (though not wholly unjustified, particularly in light of Rosselli's predilection in *Sleep* for poetic reversals), the effects are enlightening, because Pasolini's ambivalent invocation of the Surrealists nonetheless serves a secondary purpose beyond shoring up his argument about the 'mechanical' or 'spontaneous' quality of Rosselli's writing. The bridge that links Rosselli with a specific poetic tradition, it can only be crossed by way of the discourse of pathology, for Pasolini's recourse to the images of disease and catastrophe[52] in Rosselli's poetry can be traced (in a rather less apocalyptic way) to Breton by way of Pierre Janet, professor of psychiatric medicine and teacher of Carl Gustav Jung. Obligatory reading for Breton and his cohort at medical school,[53] Janet's *L'automatisme psychologique*[54] inspired Breton's interest in automatism, that is, providing access to the most deeply hidden recesses of the mind by way of a kind of purposeful inattention (not unrelated to the channelling of seers or psychic mediums), and particularly automatic writing, which is meant to assist the patient (or poet) to unveil repressed emotions: if s/he 'cannot lift the self-censuring mechanism of reason that bars access to automatic thought,' automatic writing can 'squeeze out the data.'[55] Thus it is 'orphan language,' language that 'denies' the presence of a writing subject in favour of a kind of transcendental transcriber. Janet (like Freud) saw automatic writing as a therapeutic tool for patients with psychological disturbances. Perhaps the pathological is unavoidable in any discussion about Rosselli: not because of any inherent organic defect of hers (or in any case any that could be considered relevant) but more simply because of her abiding interest in psychoanalysis, especially the theories of Freud, and because of their ramifications for the study of poetry: after all, part and parcel of repression takes place through condensation and displacement, which are structural qualities common both to dreams and poems. Indeed, if Rosselli's and the Surrealists' works are based on 'simulated states of mental alteration' (as Franco Fortini asserts), might we not also claim the same for all poets?[56] In other words, there is a way in which reading *Sleep* through Breton problematizes Pasolini's and Agosti's assertions about the idiopathic nature of her poetry: paradoxically, it is precisely the way her writings give the impression of having come from nowhere that situates them, that grounds them in a poetic tradition. It is Rosselli's 'orphan' language that permits us to identify her poetic forebears.

Sleep and the Gaze

> Hell, loomed out with perfect hands, wrapped
> our glare with a fierce shudder of fright into
> the night exchanged for a pair of rubies. Fright
> Desdemona's petticure, was all-afrantic he
> might come off rushing on the last bus, but
> we were ready to admire his creative genius
> and let nothing disturb us save the chime at
> the door-bell when it rang off at its best.
> Necessarily our gun-drop dropped off at hell's
> timing: loomed out again into a wrapped parcel
> containing all of our bodily food. Soul discomposed
> watched from afar but no regard of angels enwrapped
> his studious regard with love.[57]

Let us turn now to a poem mentioned earlier (reproduced above) which to my mind both illuminates and problematizes Pasolini's and Agosti's interpretive dilemmas. Here we can count four instances of 'semantic short circuits' (petticure, gun-drop, enwrapped, and, you could argue, discomposed as well, both because of its uncommonness and because it seems to point to the more frequently used elements decomposed and discomfort). We might also note the lexical iterations: the words fright, hell, regard, and loomed appear two times each, and 'wrapped' appears twice in addition to its presence in 'enwrapped.' *Loomed* is a particularly pregnant term, since it is associated with both the semantic field of weaving (an active, creative, productive process) and the visual field (we say that things loom in the distance, for example). In this case the usage seems to be drawn from the field of weaving, at first blush – 'perfect hands' are responsible for the looming, hands that produce an object (hell) that 'wraps.' But that is only a partial meaning, for it is the 'glare' that is wrapped in line 2, which must in turn be linked to its related terms – admire, watch, and regard. Compare the 'glare' that is 'wrapped' by hell in the first lines with the visual terms of the last lines: 'Soul discomposed / watched from afar but no regard of angels enwrapped / his studious regard with love.' The terminology of watching that frames the poem contains within it four distinct vantage points: our glare, Soul watched, regard of angels, and his studious regard. The consistent use of the first person plural throughout the poem locates our visual allegiance, as it were, on the side of the speaking subject in sharp contrast to the third person singular of 'his studious regard.' We may look, the poem implies, but when *he* looks, he looks alone (no regard of angels enwrapped his studious regard with love). That is to say that the speaking subject and we readers by extension maintain sole possession of the gaze (or I should say the glare), unlike the male subject whose regard is nullified by the absence of angelic observers.

More explicit in their indictment of the male gendered reader is the pair of poems that begin 'Do come see my poetry':[58]

> Do come see my poetry
> sit for a portrait, it
> hangs in dimples, by the
> light bay window, and pronounces
> no shape of word, but that
> you find it imperative.
>
> Do come see me writhe, in
> the shadows of lust, as
> if the sun had cleared
> it from all narrow doubt.
>
> Do see it shake off all
> posts with a stick, hitting
> the air, in long shadows.
> It never made better claim
> before, than to turn you
> loose upon my sorrows.

Similar structures appear in another poem ten pages later:[59]

> Do come see my poetry
> demand it sit for a portrait
> in silence recalling
> all past experiences
> with no boredom enslaving
> its cheeks which wait.
> Do come see my poetry

be forceful and desperate
(if ever desperation were ever
a nest in the mind). In kind
it is suave almost, but rather
uncertain as to its premises
and as to its finalities
it avoids gaps, principles,
rests on unconscious decision
while you paint.

With a stroke of the brush you
empower it, with a bliss which
was not there, before we talked.
With a slip of the pen you
endow it, with thoughts which
were never there at all, save
that you lurked in the shadows
finding out its message.

And now the sitting is at end
your new principle stares
you in the eyes, and with dread
it surmises, you were never
born before you wrote
of tender surmises.

The invitation to observe (do come see) and interpret (be forceful and desperate) the poetry is coextensive with an invitation to gaze upon the body of the writing subject (do come see me writhe), an invitation whose inevitable outcome is the undoing of both the poet and the product (it never made better claim / before, than to turn you / loose upon my sorrows).[60]

The second poem is noteworthy for its combination of self-referentiality and the introduction of writing imagery and painted imagery ('it is suave almost, but rather / uncertain as to its premises / and as to its finalities / it avoids gaps, principles, / rests on unconscious decision / while you paint' and the next stanza). Note here that the 'it' to which the poem ostensibly refers – Rosselli's poetry itself – could as well refer to her interlocutor's written or painted product, so that the object of interpretation is ambiguously attributed and thus, presumably, faulty in its execution. The conclusion of the poem supports this reading ('you were never / born before you wrote / of tender surmises') insofar as it simultaneously provides motive for the interlocutor's act, and denies him all subjectivity outside the act of writing about her work. Note the shift in ownership of the gaze – where at the beginning of the poem it was the interlocutor who could 'come see' the poetry, at the end of the poem the roles have reversed: 'now the sitting is at end / your new principle / stares you in the eyes.' Finally, note the recurrence of the theme of lurking (similar to looming in the first poem), here connected explicitly with the lapsus that is attributed to the interlocutor this time: 'With a slip of the pen you / endow it, with thoughts which / were never there at all, save / that you lurked in the shadows / finding out its message.' Such an attribution puts a new spin on our initial observation that Rosselli's poetry is *imposseduta*, unable to be possessed or grasped, because of the site from which it is produced. Perhaps more accurate would be to say that the source of the challenge is not the site but the sight – that is, the vacillating origin of the gaze, first attributed to the reader then to the poet, with one all the time aware of the other – resulting in a simultaneous expansion and foreclosure, not just of possible meanings but of visual perspectives.

Here again we may invoke Plath, who looms over Rosselli as the latter evokes Plath's famous manifesto of suicide, 'Lady Lazarus.' Compare Rosselli's poem to this excerpt from Plath's poem:

Dying
Is an art, like everything else.
I do it exceptionally well.

I do it so it feels like hell.
I do it so it feels real.
I guess you could say I've a call.

It's easy enough to do it in a cell.
It's easy enough to do it and stay put.
It's the theatrical

Comeback in broad day
To the same place, the same face, the same brute
Amused shout:

'A miracle!'

That knocks me out.
There is a charge

For the eyeing of my scars, there is a charge
For the hearing of my heart –
It really goes.

And there is a charge, a very large charge,
For a word or a touch
Or a bit of blood

Or a piece of my hair or my clothes.
So, so, Herr Doktor.
So, Herr Enemy.

I am your opus,
I am your valuable,
The pure gold baby

That melts to a shriek.
I turn and burn.
Do not think I underestimate your great concern. ....[61]

Both poems invite the reader to observe the spectacle of a female body
at once identified with the poets and with their works; or, to borrow
from Derrida, the corpus and the corpse.[62] Plath's invitation to observe
the spectacle of the resuscitated woman (the Lady Lazarus) concludes
with an ironic recognition of the observer's pain. Rosselli, in contrast,
takes full cognizance of the damage of the spectator's gaze ('It never
made better claim / before, than to turn you / loose upon my sorrows'). Privileging Plath and not her blood relations as a corpus and
a corpse thus serves a double function. It reinscribes Rosselli's genealogy in a horizontal, non-consanguinary line, so that we might more
properly speak of affiliation than of deracination, and, perhaps more
importantly, it reasserts her poetics as a translation of *herself* 'into the
otherness of language' (Felman) without denying its autonomy. In my
reading, hers is no longer the disavowal of genealogy but one (however
hellish) loomed out with *her own* perfect hands.

The question of the spectacle is illuminated by Kaja Silverman's distinction, following Lacan, between the gaze and the look. She states

that the gaze is not 'coterminous with any individual viewer, or group of viewers. It issues "from all sides", whereas the [look] (sees) only from one point.'[63] For Lacan, the gaze, which 'exceeds' or 'triumphs' over the look, is 'unapprehensible.'[64] The look, in contradistinction, 'foregrounds the desiring subjectivity of the figure from which it issues, a subjectivity which pivots upon lack, whether or not that lack is acknowledged.'[65] Thus for Lacan the gaze is comparable 'not to the male look, but to woman-as-spectacle.' He writes, 'At the level of the phenomenal experience of contemplation, this all-seeing aspect is to be found in the satisfaction of a woman who knows that she is being looked at, on condition that one does not show her that one knows what she knows. The world is all seeing, but it is not exhibitionistic, does not provoke our gaze. When it begins to provoke it, the feeling of strangeness begins too.'[66] So there are two issues at stake here – the issue of desiring lack, on the one hand, associated with the look; and the more phenomenological issue of awareness. With a word choice that uncannily recalls Pasolini's 'imposseduta,' Lacan's description of the gaze as 'unapprehensible' reaffirms what we have already observed in the poems. Amelia Rosselli's poetry is 'unapprehensible' too, we might say, because of its alignment not with the look (*le regard*, for Lacan – no regard of angels enwrapped his studious regard with love) but with the gaze. Moreover, if we continue in this vein we must conclude that Pasolini and Agosti and their talk of the lapsus are really talk about lack, about desiring subjectivity constituted by their unacknowledged hermeneutical lack; hence, to return to Lacan, the 'feeling of strangeness' that ensues.

In a short poem at the end of the collection Rosselli makes oblique reference to Leopardi's celebrated poem 'L'infinito.'[67] But where Leopardi, seated upon the hill, has the view blocked and so vividly imagines it, Rosselli's vantage point seems to be lower – she, gazing up at the hill, cannot apprehend it by virtue both of her (faulty) vision and the block created not by a hedge, as for Leopardi, but by the interlocutor. Compare 'L'infinito' and Rosselli's poem (both quoted in their entirety):

L'INFINITO

Sempre caro mi fu quest'ermo colle,
E questa siepe, che da tanta parte
Dell'ultimo orizzonte il guardo esclude.
Ma sedendo e mirando, interminati
Spazi di là da quella, e sovrumani
Silenzi, e profondissima quiete

Io nel pensiero mi fingo; ove per poco
Il cor non si spaura. E come il vento
Odo stormir tra queste piante, io quello
Infinito silenzio a questa voce
Vo comparando; e mi sovvien l'eterno,
E le morte stagioni, e la presente
E viva, e il suon di lei. Così tra questa
Immensità s'annega il pensier mio:
E il naufragar m'è dolce in questo mare.

THE INFINITE

Always dear to me was this lonely hill
Ay, and this hedge that from so broad a sweep
Of the ultimate horizon screens the view.
But, as I sit and gaze, my fancy feigns
Space beyond space upon the further side,
And silence within silence past all thought,
Immeasurable calm; whereat well nigh
Groweth the heart afraid. And as I hear
The wind sough thro' these thickets, then between
That everlasting silence and this voice
I make comparison; and call to mind
The Eternal, and the ages dead, and this
The living present, and its clamour. So
In this immensity my thought is drowned:
And sweet to me is shipwreck in this sea.[68]

This is Rosselli's poem:

too vast a promontory for my sight
is this hill of belief: too vast
a thought you hide from my sight
this hill which slopes.
too strange a coincidence, your hand
on mine.[69]

Located at the end of the collection, Rosselli's response to Leopardi functions in two significant ways – one, it cements the relationship between the primacy of the gaze and any potential understanding of her poetic project (it is her interlocutor who blocks the view); and two, it aligns her readership with the lapsus, with the excess and desiring lack of which she herself is accused, not only because of the shifting vantage point from which the poetic gaze is produced, but also because of the active, ambiguous, unacknowledged occult role of the interlocutor – 'too strange a coincidence, your hand / on mine.' Consequently, we must note our own readerly collusion in that threat, discernible within the texts themselves as a kind of insistent triumvirate; *Sleep* is structured, in part, around the repeated assertion that 'we are three,' though their identities (the poet, a lover, father, reader, critic, alter ego, God, the panoptic gaze?) are never specified.[70]

Put differently, in *Sleep*, Rosselli's commentary on the relationship between the gaze and the look problematizes the attribution of agency in the conventional Poet/Reader dichotomy. In doing so (in Lacanian terms, by calling attention to the presence of the gaze), her writings provoke the feelings of strangeness that could be summed up not with that synthetic disavowal 'Je sais bien mais quand même ...'[71] but rather, simply, 'je sais bien.' In other words, with Rosselli we are confronted by the suggestion of a text that rejects the fundamental disavowal upon which all subjectivity is constituted; moreover, Rosselli's is thus a text that unbinds or calls into question the coherence of the ego (here identified with the poem's male interlocutor – God, Lover, Reader) not in order to supplant it with a feminine subject fortified by her own constituting disavowal, but in order to point out its utter, potentially devastating precariousness, thus articulated by Rosselli: 'nor do I want your interpretation, having none myself.' The founding gesture for you and me, too, is the lapsus.

Rosselli and Sarah Kofman

SLEEP

Slightly nauseated with all cry I fell
into bemused sleep, oh the tender dangerous
virgins on the mountain top watch a sleep
which is not mine since the radiant bed
of earth covered me moss like. I am a
broken fellow cried the fish monger, and
belayed his true nature. I am the bemused
man on the tree top cried the arch duke
pleased he had slept with divinity. I am

the cry in the night exclaimed the author
as his book fell. The sun slept into a douche of cloud like sun drop, the
   earth
rounded the point. All cry is a massacre
when sleep is the virgin; the reason is
lost when all impatience is neglected.

The banality of all superiors is a danger
for the host. The intricacies of court
life is the danger. I am the danger of
a court massacre, exclaimed the virgin
on the tree top as the tree fell, swarmed
down to putritude. Sleep fell on, the reason
went, and the host remembered he had forgotten
the power and the glory.[72]

In our examination of Guido Morselli, I suggested that responses to
his suicide complicate some of the fundamental and long-held critical
tenets of which Barthes's 'Death of the Author' is representative. Now I
want to examine the ways the figure of Rosselli leads us to draw similar
conclusions about Jacques Derrida's stance toward suicide as it emerges in *The Work of Mourning*, a text of commemorative speeches, letters,
and essays that he wrote after the death of friends and colleagues, all
of whom were luminaries in the world of literary criticism, philosophy,
and critical theory. I arrive at Derrida indirectly, by parthenogenetical-
ly positing another 'sister' in the family created by Rosselli's suicide:
the French philosopher Sarah Kofman (1934–1994). Here, as was the
case with Sylvia Plath, we may catalogue the biographical similarities
between Kofman and Rosselli. Kofman's father, like Rosselli's, was
killed when Kofman was eight years old, after which Kofman's childhood, like Rosselli's, was characterized by frequent moves. Both women
were deeply, publicly ambivalent toward their biological mothers, who
either suffered from poor health (Rosselli) or were ascribed it (Kofman).
Both women were raised, at least in part, by strong maternal substi-
tutes. Recall Rosselli's mother, Marion Cave, whose frequent absences
and poor physical health meant that she played an only intermittent
role in Rosselli's life, and Amelia Pincherle Rosselli, the paternal grandmother whose strong presence in the Rosselli household made her into
a kind of substitute mother-figure for Rosselli and her siblings. While
Kofman's mother was (according to Kofman in *Rue Ordener, Rue Labat*)

not actually ill, she came to be *associated with* ill health, bad habits, and shameful behaviours as a result of inculcation by the woman (called Mémé) who rescued Kofman and passed herself off as her mother, as a precaution against Kofman's possible arrest during the war.[73] In their writings, Rosselli and Kofman moved with ease between languages (French, English, and Italian for Rosselli; and French, Yiddish, and Polish for Kofman). Both women were physically unwell for substantial portions of their lives. And finally, both women committed suicide (at sixty-six and sixty years of age, respectively). Like Rosselli's death on the anniversary of Plath's, Kofman took her own life on a day that is significant in light of her enduring interest in Nietzsche – her suicide was enacted on the 150th anniversary of his birth.

But aside from these similarities, which are striking but not particularly uncanny, is a less apparent, less teleological kinship that stems from their shared interest in the twin topics of the body and writing. In the remainder of this chapter, I will juxtapose two Rosselli texts – *Storia di una malattia* and *Sleep* – with two of Kofman's texts: *Rue Ordener, Rue Labat* and her piece on Rembrandt's 'The Anatomy Lesson of Doctor Nicolaes Tulp, 1632.' I read these texts alongside Sylvia Plath's poem 'Lady Lazarus' in order to refine Jacques Derrida's assertions in *The Work of Mourning* about the relationships between the corpse and the corpus, that is, between the finite body and the infinite text.[74] He says, 'a book always comes to take the place of the body, insofar as it has always tended to replace the proper body, and the sexed body, to become its name even, and occupy its place, to serve in place of its occupant, and insofar as we collaborate with this substitution, lending or giving ourselves over to it, for this is all we ever really do, we are this, we like this, and each word speaks volumes for lending itself from the very first moment to this spiriting away of the proper body, as if already at the behest of the proper body in question, following its paradoxical desire, its impossible desire, the desire to interrupt itself, to interrupt itself in sexual difference, interrupt itself as sexual difference.'[75] Kofman herself seems to authorize such a reading, insofar as Derrida is borrowing terms she already put into circulation. For Derrida, in other words, the relations between book and body are theoretically those of interchangeability, relations in which we readers are complicit ('we collaborate in this substitution'). And indeed he seems to enact these relations in *The Work of Mourning* when he re-collects commemorative letters, speeches, remembrances public and private. But in doing so, he exceeds the limits of what he describes in general or theoretical terms to summon forth, very precisely, the specific ('singular,' to use his word) case of a specific individual: 'For me too, of course, Sarah was unique.'[76] Derrida is thus a prime example of my thesis that theoretical constructs crumble in the face of a suicide, so that those hermeneutics built on the exclusion of the subject are supplanted by romantic pro-subject views of the dead author. Furthermore, Derrida observes that the body after death is *not* finite – it is subject to the same opening up as the textual body, the same examination, scrutiny, or autopsy, to which other texts are subject. Thus I will also argue that it does not necessarily follow that those examinations result in the production of knowledge, the revelation of truths, or the dissemination of meanings. On the contrary: the juxtaposition of Plath, Rosselli, and Kofman indicates to me instead that those examinations, with their emphasis on documentation, serve rather to consolidate the always already-formed power relations between origin and object of the gaze.

Writing about bodies, and the invasion of uninvited Authorities who peer at their inner workings, Kofman and Rosselli (in *Sleep*) come together with Sylvia Plath in the triangle writing–suicidal body–gaze; Plath's 'Lady Lazarus' in particular shares concerns similar to those of the two Rosselli texts and to Kofman's *Anatomy Lesson*. Somewhere between autopsy and freak show, Plath's Lady occupies an intermediate space, not along the usual continuum (living body–dying body–cadaver) but rather in an uncertain dimension of return from the dead. Thus to her poetics I adjoin a variation to Rosselli's and Kofman's bodily spectacles and to the invasive gaze of the doctor: though, not precisely an *invitation* to gaze upon the female body, Plath's Lady charges admission:

> There is a charge
>
> For the eyeing of my scars, there is a charge
> For the hearing of my heart –
> It really goes.
>
> And there is a charge, a very large charge,
> For a word or a touch
> Or a bit of blood
>
> Or a piece of my hair or my clothes.
> So, so, Herr Doktor.

In each of these texts, doctors are at once engaged in intellectual inquiry and its repression (Rembrandt), in acts of commerce (Plath), and in acts of violence (Rosselli's *Storia* and *Sleep*). (Complicating the play of gazes emanating from the doctors in Rembrandt's painting is the flesh-and-blood doctor to whom Kofman first recounts the story that becomes *Rue Ordener, Rue Labat*.) In this way, *Storia di una malattia* differs radically from the poetry of *Sleep*; in the former text, the prying gaze of her unidentified observers is a violent one, imposed forcefully and against the subject's will, whereas in *Sleep* the unnamed interlocutor is explicitly invited to observe the violent spectacle:

> Do come see my poetry
> demand it sit for a portrait
> in silence recalling
> all past experiences
> with no boredom enslaving
> its cheeks which wait.
> Do come see my poetry
> be forceful and desperate
> (if ever desperation were ever
> a nest in the mind). In kind
> it is suave almost, but rather
> uncertain as to its premises
> and as to its finalities
> it avoids gaps, principles,
> rests on unconscious decision
> while you paint.

The juxtaposition of these two poems conveys Plath's and Rosselli's shared concern with documenting the relations between the suicidal female's body and some gaze-bearing Authority. With Rosselli's characterization of Plath's poetic gaze as inward (thereby embracing the latter's meditations on the temptations of suicide), we are thus confronted with a discomfiting spectacle: Rosselli contemplating Plath contemplating suicide. Thus to return to my earlier formulation, the *Sleep* of Rosselli's poetry is a proleptic slip, a slip into the big sleep. The slip or the lapsus is suicide, not because she 'slipped' to her death but because the slip is only visible as a movement. Rosselli's gaze, retrospectively identified with Plath's, shifts the site of Rosselli's writing to a place outside the poet, drawing in yet another interlocutor to engage with, and possibly obstruct, her poetic gaze: 'we are three.'[77]

Sarah Kofman's memoir of her eighth to eighteenth years, *Rue Ordener, Rue Labat*, documents an analogous series of moving bodies. The book opens with a description of her father's fountain pen, one of the few remaining articles in her possession and the very thing that makes her 'write, write,' followed by a description of her father's arrest and deportation (he was arrested in front of his wife and six children).[78] The next movement involved Kofman's being dragged from pillar to post by her mother in various (and variously successful) attempts to find new identities for her children so that they might be safe from persecution as Jews, an operation which resulted in Kofman's repudiation of her mother, her Judaism, and her class origins. Then, her mother attempted to wrest Sarah (now called Suzanne) back from the loving grip of Mémé, Kofman's 'new' mother, to cancel out Mémé's traces and to reassert Kofman's Jewish identity. Like Rosselli, Kofman, too, can be reductively read as all history, as collateral damage from the trauma of war. These shifts and transpositions of Kofman's body (and her father's) in physical space are coterminous with the contestation of Kofman's identities and allegiances as Sarah or Suzanne, Jewish or gentile, Polish or French, Mémé's or her biological mother's (Kofman never names her mother in *Rue Ordener, Rue Labat*), philosopher or writer of memoirs. Though it was actually the penultimate of her writings, Kofman proclaimed that this book was the culmination – the one to which all others were leading ('Maybe all my books have been the detours required to bring me to write about "that"').[79] A lifetime of writing on Freud and Nietzsche – that is, on some of the foundational narratives of modernity – does not culminate in a scholarly magnum opus, but rather in a memoir about her childhood.

The importance for our argument of these shifts, and shifts of allegiance, is twofold. First, while her earlier book, entitled *Paroles suffoquées*, was dedicated to Robert Antelme, Maurice Blanchot, and, most importantly, perhaps, her father, *this* book is dedicated to her physician, Philippe Cros. Kofman's translator Ann Smock describes the dedication thus: 'Unexpectedly, she found that she could tell the story to a physician whom she consulted regularly (she was often ill), and she dedicated *Rue Ordener, Rue Labat* to him. So whereas in *Paroles suffoquées* she had to make a mute voice heard – a voice that was not just bereft of, but also preserved from, all ability and capability – in this more recent book it became possible to break an old silence.'[80] No longer writing to other writers (Antelme and Blanchot) but rather to a *silent* interlocutor signifies Kofman is speaking for herself and also, essentially, *to* herself, since her chosen recipient of the message is mute (think of doctor-patient confidence) and merely absorbs hers, rather like Rosselli: 'nor do I want your interpretation, having none myself.'

The second quality of these shifts of allegiance about which she writes is that they organize the narrative, giving shape to the series of memories whose logical connection resides solely in the vacillation between Kofman's identities expressed from chapter to chapter. That is, in spite of the text's appearance of relative chronological coherence – after the brief initial description of her father's fountain pen, the narrative begins on 16 July 1942 and ends when Kofman begins university – within this framework, there is a fair amount of jumping around in time. Consequently, in spite of the plethora of dates, the events described seem almost ahistorical – they take place in an alternate or parallel historical period whose landmark events (with some notable exceptions) originate in and are reckoned by Kofman herself. Rosselli's *Storia di una malattia* functions in similar fashion, embedding historical events in the matrix of her own experiences instead of the other way around. History, or collective experience writ large, provides the punctuation for a narrative whose grammar is otherwise utterly individual in both texts, which we might call the intimist provenance of these micro-historical narratives. *Rue Ordener, Rue Labat* shares with Rosselli's *Storia di una malattia* the quality of 'lucidity unclouded by insight'[81] – that is, Rosselli and Kofman are both astoundingly clear-eyed in their depictions of the traumatic occurrences that befell them; and yet, in spite of the clarity of their expositions, in neither case do they subject these events to analysis, either of motives or of affect. Just as we never really learn the reasons Rosselli attributes to for being gaslighted (as in the Ingrid Bergman movie by the same name) beyond the vague possibility of a resurgence of Fascism, we are never privy to an analysis of the dynamics between Kofman, her mother, and Mémé. The writings of Kofman and Rosselli, in other words, seem to have as their raison d'être the mere object of recording events and sensations, not of perspicacity about them. Thus, as Rosselli's did with her unidentified persecutors in *Storia di una malattia*, Kofman's penultimate text imbricates the colonization of the female body within a writing that, insofar as it stops short of analysis, accepts the contestation of that space.

The other relevant Kofman text is her piece on Rembrandt's painting, 'The Anatomy Lesson of Doctor Nicolaes Tulp, 1632' (an essay that

Derrida particularly privileges in his commemoration of Kofman in *The Work of Mourning*), a text in which Kofman articulates this imbrication of reading, writing, and bodily regimes (to borrow a phrase from Karen Pinkus). She describes the painting in this way:

> They have before them not a subject but an object, a purely technical instrument that one of them manipulates in order to get a hold on the truth of life. The dead man and the opening of his body are seen only insofar as they provide an opening onto life, whose secret they would hold. The fascination is displaced and, with this displacement, the anxiety repressed, the intolerable made tolerable, from the sight of the cadaver to that of the book wide open at the foot of the deceased, who might now serve as a lectern.
>
> This opening of the book in all its light points back to the opening of the body. For the book alone allows the body to be deciphered and invites the passage from the exterior to the interior. It is this book (and the opening it provides onto the science of life and its mastery) that attracts the gazes, much more even than the point of the scissors that has begun to peel away the skin from the body stretched out there.[82]

The points of contact with Rosselli are multiple, and build upon the observations we made about reading, writing, and the body in *Rue Ordener, Rue Labat*. Kofman here could just as well be talking about the quandary of suicidal poets as Rembrandt's painting, and she even seems to gesture, albeit obliquely, toward the Plath of *The Bell-Jar* or of 'Lady Lazarus' mentioned earlier. In all three cases, the body is the focal point for some Other(s) who seek knowledge therein; indeed, the body is conceived as an instrument of knowledge destined exclusively for another. For both Rosselli in *Storia di una malattia* and Kofman in the *Anatomy Lesson*, the possibility of *self*-knowledge, however, seems remote, insofar as these bodies-as-texts provoke no analysis – Rosselli registers her experiences but does not provide insight into their motives, and Rembrandt's cadaver is all mute materialism. Moreover, these bodies (Rosselli's own and the cadaver in the painting) are legible only from the outside by a reader whose gaze is *imposed*, not invited.

Kofman writes that the shift of the gaze from the body to the book signifies 'the intolerable made tolerable.' But as Plath has shown, the price to be paid for this comfort is exacted not as money but as knowledge, in the form of the repression of anxiety. Looking, then, really means looking away – looking away from the subject herself. This is equally true of individual works by Rosselli as it is of her opus taken in its entirety. Critical modesty may be maintained – that is, we need not look at Rosselli's invaded body (or mention the madness – and here recall the barely repressed discourse of failure we noted in discussion about Morselli) – if we can simply point to the illegibility of the texts that that body produced. Hence the semantic fields from which earlier critical discourses arose. Recall Pasolini's introduction to Rosselli's poetry: 'è dominata da qualcosa di meccanico: emulsione che prende forma per suo conto, imposseduta, come si ha l'impressione che succeda per gli esperimenti di laboratorio più terribili, tumori, scoppi atomici' (it is dominated by something mechanical: an emulsion that takes shape of its own accord, possessed, as one has the impression occurs in the most terrible laboratory experiments, tumours, atomic explosions). The substitution for an ailing body of an ailing poetry (itself comprised of tumours, monstrosities of nature, atomic explosions) means that the reader can avert her eyes from that which is unsightly: the intolerable made tolerable. Hence the body is, yes, a source of writing much like a book – and therefore a text to be read, but it is also itself an act of 'writing, writing' that represses and obfuscates – and therefore a text to be written. The question, then, is by whom? If we identify the subject inhabiting the body as the agent of this kind of writing, then we may attribute a kind of therapeutic quality to it. As the notion of the 'talking cure' seems to indicate, rendering one's story in narrative form is among the surest strategies for surviving it, by detaching from it and observing it more objectively. (It was conceivably for this reason that *Rue Ordener, Rue Labat* was the book to which the others were leading ['Maybe all my books have been the detours required to bring me to write about "that"'], or that for some readers, the experiences recounted in *Storia di una malattia* read like a mystery novel.) On the other hand, such an identification (between the poetic I and the agent of repressive writing) inscribes the subject in her own observation, as it were – it implies that the invasive gaze of the doctor, the reader, the oppressors is in some way already accounted for in the writing. Indeed, they are the target audience, ironic spectral projections of the presumptive threat posed by the lapsus to the coherence of the ego.

And yet, asserting with Kofman that the book alone allows us access to the body without the need for its examination, we must nevertheless admit to a continued fascination with the body, with these suicidal bodies, in ways that we are not by the 'regular' dead. The fact that the book is only a partial substitution – that we continue to be obsessed with the body – is an indication of the only partial success of that substitution. Seen in this light, coming to grips with our suicidal authors means coming to terms with them as bodies and as bodies of works. For Derrida, Kofman's substitution of the book for the body must not be seen as 'a simple negativity of distraction (negation, denegation, lie, occultation, dissimulation)' but instead, 'in a no doubt very Nietzschean fashion, a cunning affirmation of life, its irrepressible movement to survive, to live on.'[83] Derrida's is a surprisingly affirmative response to Kofman's death; in it, he sees a kind of apotropaic ritual or a conjuring act (to use Kofman's own word – and here again, recall Morselli), a calling forth of death in order to ward it off.[84] And writing these bodies, whether anatomical cadavers, dead fathers, or figures risen from the grave or hurtling toward it, salvages Kofman's, Rosselli's, and Plath's own suicidal bodies from being written into oblivion. Returning to the flight of Rosselli's suicide, then, does not mean trying to catch her, it means watching the transient beauty of the moves: 'Do come see my poetry.'

We have seen how Kofman is relevant to our discussion of Rosselli, not because of her suicide but because of her abiding interest in the imbrication of reading and writing bodies, of female genealogies, of knowledge and death. But beyond those connections, the self-induced death of Kofman – as a writer, as an intellectual, as a subject caught in a web of conflicting historical forces (like Rosselli's *figlia di Carlo*, Kofman is *fille de ... qui?*) – also raises questions that have repercussions on our understanding of theories of authorship. In Derrida's consideration of Kofman's opus in light of her status as a scholar of Nietzsche, the fact of Kofman's suicide is a conspicuous absence, one that belies its status as the source of the humanist fallacy that characterizes Derrida's *The Work of Mourning* ('For me, too, Sarah was unique'). This is evident in the urge, cited throughout the work, to reread the works of his dead colleagues and friends as a way of postponing the impasse (to speak of them versus to speak for them?) that their death has caused. Reading Kofman and Derrida alongside Rosselli, I have argued, teaches us something about Derrida: namely, that that probing posthumous gaze to which Derrida makes continual reference in *The Work of Mourning* was, in fact, already taken into account by Rosselli and by Kofman. Their writings reckon – playfully, at times – with the voices that speak through them (Rosselli), the looks that size them up (Plath), and the forces that impel their bodies and identities to shift position (Kofman). It is perhaps in part for this reason that Derrida's summation of Kofman's suicide as an enactment of nihilism and therefore as a gesture of liberation is not entirely satisfactory, insofar as the imposition of whatever forms of Authority from which she might have sought liberation continues, unabated, opening up the infinite next hermeneutical world.

Suicide as Text

you seem to hear angels mocking you,
you seem to cry out look to the stars!
and run out rapid against a fence of spine.[85]

If we reflect back on the various modalities of discourse about suicide, which ranged from scientific (Jameson's correlations between suicide and high-level creative ability, and genetic predisposition) to sociological (Durkheim's anomie) to moral-ethical (Campbell and Collinson's good and bad suicides) to practical (Camus's *Myth of Sisyphus* talks about the problem that simply can't be solved) – and all of these are contingent upon the very definition of suicide being used – it becomes clear that Rosselli's suicide exceeds them all.[86] Each of these categories is relevant to her suicide, and yet none can be said to explain it sufficiently, least of all for those who mourn her. It is precisely because of the excess of a suicide, the way it spills over the borders of any attempt to contain it – the very inadequacy of any possible *explanations*, however well-conceived or convincingly demonstrated – that we may and indeed must take the reader (also in a sense a survivor) into consideration. Thus I believe that we may put to good use these various modalities of discourse, just not for the purposes for which they are intended. Rather than apply the categories to the suicide him/herself, we can ask which ones of them have the most resonance for us. That is, the ways we as readers apply these categories may be the only objects of examination that will yield an explanation of a suicide. Hence the goal of this chapter: to come to grips with my own responses to Rosselli's suicide as a reader, to get at the heart of what has struck me as relevant to my engagement with her works and life. Thus I have not mentioned events that may be of greater interest to, say, a biographer (her brief but intense friendship with Rocco Scotellaro, for example, or her extensive musical training), or texts that might be considered more representative of her thought, writ large (other of her many poetry collections, for example, or her essays and journalistic writings). Mine is thus an idiosyncratic narrative, whose plot revolves, broadly speaking, around her complex family history, her ambivalent critical reception and its causes, her invocation of the notion of madness, the questions of the body, subjectivities, and identity made visible, at the most fundamental level, as *language*, and the paradox of illegible language. I have not funnelled this narrative through any one specific critical discourse, but have found it useful instead to conceive of its moments as movements: as shifts, slides, flights, and displacements, applicable both to Rosselli the historical subject and to the body of her works. Rosselli as a *corps* and as a corpse (to borrow again from Derrida) makes her mark most visibly when she is in flight, like a firefly, perhaps, or a bolt of lightning. Using flight, shifts, and movement as the overarching metaphors of my reading also embraces the threat of her suicide, of its excesses, avoids imposing coherence upon some of the major historical events and the minor disparate elements of her life – the places and times she inhabited – where there otherwise would be none. Conceived in this way, these shifts were already part of the writing before the writing occurred: not as a series of signs that were already present but only interpretable after the fact, but as the very gesture upon which the writing was founded. The shifts and slides, and the places where an author like Rosselli defies interpretation to become illegible, are, of course, the project of Derridean deconstruction, whether or not we are reading the works of a suicide. Amelia Rosselli, I have argued, demonstrates that it is precisely in the realm of the suicidal author that deconstruction stumbles on its own ideal, turning a text always already open to rereading into one indelibly marked by events external to it.

3 The Post-Biological Author: Cesare Pavese, Gianni Vattimo, Emanuele Severino

Torino 28 agosto

Ieri sera una cameriera dell'albergo Roma, in piazza Carlo Felice, passando davanti alla stanza occupata da due giorni dallo scrittore Cesare Pavese, si sovvenne che la porta della stanza non era mai stata aperta in tutto il giorno. Bussò. Non ottenne risposta. La porta fu poco dopo forzata e fu fatta la triste scoperta: lo scrittore giaceva riverso sul letto e non dava segni di vita. Secondo il medico legale la morte risale a sabato sera.

Accanto a lui, sul tavolino da notte, era aperta una delle sue ultime opere *Dialoghi con Leucò*; sul frontespizio del libro egli aveva scritto con mano ferma le parole: 'Perdono a tutti e a tutti chiedo perdono. Va bene? Non fate molti pettegolezzi.' Su una mensola dell'attigua stanza da bagno si trovarono ventotto cartine aperte con tracce di una polverina bianca.[1]

Turin 28 August

Yesterday evening a chambermaid at the Hotel Roma in Piazza Carlo Felice, passing by the room that for two days had been occupied by the writer Cesare Pavese, recalled that the door to the room had not been opened all day. She knocked. She got no response. The door was forced soon thereafter and the sad discovery was made: the writer lay supine on the bed and gave no signs of life. According to the medical examiner, the death occurred Saturday evening.

Near him, on the nightstand, lay open one of his last works, *Dialogues with Leocò*; on the title page, he had written with firm hand the words, 'I forgive everyone and of all I ask forgiveness. All right? Don't gossip a lot.'

On the counter of the bathroom next door, twenty-eight open packets with traces of white powder were found.

The suicide note of Cesare Pavese (1908–1950) doesn't clarify much about his death. Earlier we saw that the conventional story about Guido Morselli's suicide is that it remedied the failure to publish that motivated it, and this professional failure was viewed against the backdrop of his quirky but otherwise sympathetic personal life. We also noted how Amelia Rosselli's posthumous claim to fame as a poet stemmed either from her historical position or from the difficulties she presented to her readers, who were often concerned with pointing out the distinctiveness of her work. As a consequence, her poetry and her death were broadly assumed to be manifestations of her psychological instability, which, in turn, was exacerbated by the trauma of her father's death. It is much more difficult to encapsulate the general consensus about Pavese's suicide in such reductive and pedestrian terms.

This is in part because more time has passed since his death, but there are other reasons as well. First, unlike in the other cases, Pavese left an ample, already highly scrutinized body of works (there were no books lying about in drawers awaiting discovery, except perhaps his notebook, the *taccuino*).[2] Though we can identify trends among his readers over the last sixty years, there is nothing like the general critical consensus among Morselli's and Rosselli's respective readers. Instead, scholarly responses to Pavese's death are comparatively heterogeneous, and readers are quick to disparage critical approaches that differ from their own, so much so that his works function as a kind of methodological shibboleth. And second, Pavese's critics don't find common ground in a desire to make allowances for lives well lived or hard-fought, as they do for Morselli and Rosselli.[3] By and large, Morselli's biographers tend to view his eccentricities as benign, and Rosselli's emotional vicissitudes frequently inspire more pity than censure. Pavese, in contrast, has not been painted in similarly cheerful colours.[4] If the perceptibly condescending tones with which his life is discussed are an indication, Pavese's biography makes for a deeply ambivalent and not desperately inspiring story, and his personal characteristics are generally either passed over without comment or described in the unflattering clinical jargon (preferably in Latin) of the sexologist.[5] It is conventional to say that Pavese provides an occasion for other polemics; I contend, in contrast, that other polemics are very much an occasion to discuss Pavese.

This is not to say that his works are not widely – and justly – praised; but in my reading, critics conjure the spectre of Pavese *l'uomo* even when they claim exclusive concern with his works.

Critical Trends: Vacillation

> Digging out Pavese is like trying to find someone in Pompeii while the lava is still hot.[6]

Like that of our other authors, the account of Pavese's suicide is founded on assumptions about links between writing and living. Reactions to his death evince characteristics both of Morselli's and of Rosselli's, depending on which way the political winds are blowing and which literary trends are dominant. But unlike the other cases I examine, in which writings about the author after his or her suicide studiously avoid passing moral judgment on the act itself, Pavese's suicide provoked something of a scandal, visible in the ambivalence that doubles back to reflect (largely negatively) upon his literature. Giuditta Isotti Rosowsky describes it like this: 'Di fronte ad un gesto definitivo come il suicidio, la reazione fu duplice: stupore e rispetto, ma anche incomprensione e l'immediata interpretazione che faceva del suicidio un'implicita conferma dell'incapacità dell'uomo Pavese di confrontarsi con la realtà'[7] (Facing a definitive gesture like suicide, the reaction was double: stupor and respect, but also incomprehension and the immediate interpretation that made his suicide into an implicit confirmation of the man Pavese's inability to deal with reality). I use the word ambivalence to mean the vacillation between historical approaches (including psychobiography) and literary approaches we have noted in the other cases of authorial suicide. I also mean to point to the strategic deployment of a discourse of ambivalence about Pavese's life, death, and miracles, as the Italian saying goes. Besides being exemplary of the kinds of shifting thresholds that characterize the critical crisis that ensues after a suicide, these discourses also maintain the 'implicit confirmation of the man Pavese's inability to deal with reality' cited above.[8] Thus a standard survey of Pavese scholarship might note that there was ideological criticism in the 1950s; psychological and psychoanalytical criticism in the 1960s (plus the first generation of proponents of a 'return to the text' in the 1964 *Sigma* group); linguistic and myth studies in the 1970s; recontextualizations and rediscoveries (e.g., Pavese and the cinema; his poetry) in the 1980s and 1990s; and lately, thematic studies (cities; women and work). These shifts in focus are usually put down to changes in the predominant hermeneutical methodology. While that is certainly the case, I would argue that there is also an undercurrent of antagonism not accounted for by the simple invocation of trends. With Pavese, it's almost always personal.

Mountains of material were written about the ideological positions held by Pavese's characters, including those that placed them firmly on the fence.[9] Posthumous critical revisions of his opus involved not just revising received knowledge about Pavese as an individual, but also reinterpreting his and his characters' ambivalent relationship with the Italian left. It was not the case, however, that his readers were unanimous in their assessment of his political engagement. The 1950s, which was the decade in which the Italian left was best able to consolidate its cultural and political hegemony in post-Fascist Italy, is the decade when Pavese's legacy was most hotly debated.[10] Previously, his contributions to *Cultura e realtà*, a new magazine founded in 1949 for the Christian left, had been very poorly received by the PCI and particularly by Togliatti, then director of the Communist journal *Rinascita*.[11] The following year, 1950, saw a number of attacks on Pavese's grasp of both ideology and engaged literature, which contributed to the lingering rancour of the left long after his death.[12] Then it was found that the protagonists of his works of fiction were profoundly and unconscionably politically passive. Indeed, the contents of the whole bourgeois kitbag (his literature, his lifestyle, and in particular the contents of his private journal, published in 1952, two years after his suicide) were roundly condemned by many for their proof of his fundamental 'decadence': anathema in Communist circles, if by decadent we mean concern with the individual and not the group, with the inner life and not life's material conditions, or with narcissistic issues of romantic love and sexuality. No less important a figure than Alberto Moravia contributed to that image when, in 1954, he dropped a veritable bomb, not only calling Pavese 'decadent' but also characterizing him most uncharitably as a failure in all ways:

> Ho letto in questi giorni per la prima volta *Il mestiere di vivere* di Cesare Pavese. È un libro penoso: e questa pena, a ben guardar, viene soprattutto dalla combinazione singolare di un dolore costante, profondo e acerbo con i caratteri meschini, solitari e quasi deliranti di un letterato di mestiere. Da un lato questo dolore che in Pavese aveva motivi concreti e purtroppo irremediabili; dall'altro una vanità infantile, smisurata, megalomane ...

un'invidia anch'essa infantile ... una mancanza stizzosa di generosità e di carità verso amici e sodali ... una credenza ingenua, inspiegabile nella letteratura come società, come fatto sociale, pur con l'aria di disprezzarla.[13]

In these last few days, I read *Il mestiere di vivere* by Cesare Pavese for the first time. It is a painful book and this pain, upon careful scrutiny, derives above all from the singular combination of a constant, deep, and bitter sorrow with the wretched, solitary and almost delirious character of a professional man of letters. On the one hand, [there is] this pain that had concrete and unfortunately irremediable motives in Pavese; on the other, a immeasurable, infantile, megalomaniacal vanity ... an envy that, too, was infantile ... a peevish lack of generosity and of charity toward friends and fellows ... an ingenuous, inexplicable belief in literature as society, as a social fact, though with the air of someone who despises it.

This is a good example of the kind of discursive sliding that took place – deeply personal and, in this case, mean-spirited assaults emerged from behind their ideological cover. By the end of the decade, it was Pavese's greatest supporters who seemed to be fanning the flames of his public roasting. First, in 1960, an important biography was published by one of Pavese's close friends, Davide Lajolo. His *Il vizio assurdo: Vita di Cesare Pavese* depicted Pavese as a kind of tragic hero whose fatal personal and family circumstances prevented him, despite his best efforts, from participating more fully in civic life, in large part because of the obsession with suicide (the 'absurd vice' of the biography's title) that occupied much of his time.[14] With the publication of another seminal biography, Dominique Fernandez's significantly titled *L'échec de Pavese* (*Pavese's Failure*, 1967), readers were privy to an even less rosy portrait of Pavese than the one offered by his friend Lajolo in 1960: here, Pavese's 'absurd vice' had less to do with his obsession with suicide than it did with his obsessions with masturbation and *ejaculatio praecox*.[15] Sandwiched in the years between the biographies is the publication of an edition of the magazine *Sigma*[16] devoted exclusively to Pavese, which argued for dispensing with his biography altogether, in order to focus on less fraught questions such as the nature of Pavese's poetics, his interest in myths, or the function of recurring themes such as the hills and the city in his novels, thus averting the eyes, so to speak, from the spectacle of his intimate life. But Fernandez had let the horse escape, and there was no longer any point in closing the barn door. Forgotten was the accusation of decadence that had plagued his memory in the 1950s. The Scylla of political engagement having been navigated, it was time for the Charybdis of sex, with readers no longer busy with attempts to reinsert Pavese's literary opus into a more firmly leftist rubric,[17] but rather with inserting minutiae from his childhood and adolescence, like his detached and distant mother, into a psychoanalytical narrative about his adult difficulties with women.[18] Thus Pavese's heroes were now deemed remarkable for the way they bared themselves to an unstinting, unflattering view, no longer to be censured for their inactivity but praised for the rigours of their self-analysis.

This constituted a decisive turn toward a camouflaged form of autobiographical reading that would hold sway for the years to follow. For example, studies ostensibly about Pavese's abiding interest in myth prevailed in the 1970s. Far from a value-neutral intellectual interest, Pavese's literary myths were viewed as a function of his psychological fabric, representative of some regressive need to retreat from reality. This is visible in the discursive sliding that takes place between subject and object: myths in Pavese and Pavese as myth.[19] Critics reckoned with, on the one hand, his professional interest in anthropology (one of his areas of specialization at Einaudi)[20] and his insertion of mythical elements into his own literature (*Dialoghi con Leucò* and *La luna e i falò* being the most obvious examples) and, on the other hand, the attribution of a mythical status to Pavese himself. Together, they provided a protective covering behind which to continue to dig out Pavese while seeming to avoid the lava. Investigating Pavese's association of the ancients with the childhood of culture became a vehicle with which to argue, through more or less explicit use of psychoanalytic theory, that Pavese himself yearned for a child-like state (i.e. a state in which we view things for the first time) but, Leopardi-like, recognized the impossibility of such a return. At the same time, Pavese's creation of his own mythicized symbolic vocabulary (fire, hills, vineyards, the moon, and sex chief among them) was catalogued, analysed, and found to corroborate this reading, as were themes present in Pavese's fiction, such as the discovery that the pursuit of sexual, socio-economic, and professional ambitions is doomed to disappoint when satisfied (think of Rosetta in *Tra donne sole*, or Anguilla in *La luna e i falò*). Pavese's characters reach adulthood reluctantly, they lose their innocence, or, as Gian Paolo Biasin puts it, the ability to commit fully or without half-measures (visible, for example, in the contrast between Corrado and Dino in *La casa in collina*).

But adulthood is in no way coterminous with maturity (or ripeness, to borrow from *Lear* and *La luna e i falò*), and it is precisely the lack of maturity that forms the central psychological dilemma in so many of Pavese's characters. Maturity too, then, is a myth, often staged in the novels as a voyage of return characterized not by triumph but by disillusionment (Clelia, Corrado, Anguilla). From here, it is a short step to posit that Pavese's suicide, too, was inextricably bound up in these mythical states.[21] Without the potential for resolution, whether in the form of movement backwards to the epoch of innocence or forwards to maturity, there was simply no point in continuing.

Myth, in other words, like impotence and political engagement, is more grist for the mill that produces Pavese from his fiction. Like M.C. Escher's *Drawing Hands*, the man and his writings are perceived as locked in a gesture of reciprocal creation: life is writing and writing is life, and neither can stand in isolation from the other. Indeed, Pavese's life is viewed as perfectly coterminous with his writings,[22] as he himself implies when he inscribes his suicide note *in one of his novels*. Elio Gioanola provides an elegant example of this view:

> [L]'esplorazione del rapporto sofferenza-scrittura rappresenta un momento ineludibile della comprensione dell'opera di qualsiasi scrittore contemporaneo; tanto più per uno scrittore come Pavese, che nella scrittura ha attuato un'autentica strategia dello scampo ... Dunque non si può non prendere sul serio il nesso che Pavese immediatamente propone tra vocazione allo scrivere e vocazione al morire: dalle prime lettere del diciottenne alle ultime note di diario dello scrittore famoso si pone a fondamento di un destino l'aut-aut tra scrittura e suicidio. Non c'è niente di 'assurdo' in questa alternativa drammaticamente assoluta: il 'vizio' di voler morire, ben lungi dal rappresentare una deprecabile debolezza personale che malauguratamente interviene a minare la carriera di uno scrittore, è semplicemente l'altra faccia della scrittura.[23]

> [T]he exploration of the relationship between suffering and writing represents an inescapable moment in the understanding of the work of any contemporary writer; all the more for a writer like Pavese, who in his writing has carried out an authentic strategy of escape ... Therefore one is obliged to take seriously the connection that Pavese immediately proposes between the vocation of writing and the vocation of dying: from the first letters of the eighteen-year-old to the last notes in the famous writer's diary the obligation to choose between writing and suicide is placed at the

foundation of destiny. There is nothing 'absurd' in this dramatically absolute alternative: the 'vice' of wanting to die, far from representing a dis-
graceful personal weakness that unfortunately intervenes to undermine a
writer's career, is simply the other side of writing.

Gioanola is not arguing that Pavese is unique in this way; on the
contrary, his point is that Pavese is subject to the same social, cultural,
and ideological pressures that have plagued Europe from before the
beginning of the long Novecento. Leopardi, Pirandello, Svevo, Proust,
Kafka: each gives evidence of suffering from an analogous tension
between life and writing.[24] But Gioanola makes the case for identifying writing as the sole, exclusive motivation for Pavese's existence
based on Pavese's own assertions.[25] He offers half a dozen examples
from Pavese's personal correspondence in which Pavese makes crystal
clear 'la propria incapacità di consistere, e persino di darsi un'identità,
al di fuori della scrittura'[26] (his incapacity to consist, and even create an identity, outside of his writing). What I want to note here,
though, is that unlike in the case of Leopardi, Pirandello, and company, Gioanola requires Pavese's presence as a *dead* author. Gioanola's
seemingly simple assertion about Pavese's unexceptionality is not an
example of biographical fallacy, by which events from the author's life
are assumed to stand in close correspondence to textual ones, so much
as it is a necrological fallacy: Pavese's suicide stands as the founding
event of his writing career and, by extension, of his life. Gioanola's
reading of Pavese's suicide offers a variation on the popular reading
strategy that assumes the Author as guarantor of textual meaning, by
requiring him as a spectral presence. He furthers my earlier observation that we never read suicidal authors free of or untainted by our
knowledge of their ends: for the critic, Pavese is actually constituted
precisely by that knowledge.

The Business of Living

> Pavese guardò Morselli e disse: 'Vedi, Guido, noi due messi assieme fac-
> ciamo un Hemingway. Tu con le tue donne, io col mio successo.' Morselli
> non rispose.[27]

> Pavese looked at Morselli and said, 'You see, Guido, we two put together
> make a Hemingway. You with your women, me with my success.' Morselli
> didn't answer.

Even Pavese's definitive declarations do not preclude the possibility that there is more to the story of his death than the simple equation writing = life. As he himself points out, 'Non ci si uccide per *una* donna. Ci si uccide perché un amore, qualunque amore, ci rivela nella nostra nudità, miseria, inerzia, inermità, nulla'[28] (One doesn't kill oneself over *one* woman. One kills oneself because a love, any love, reveals us in our nudity, misery, inertia, defencelessness, nothingness). The saying goes that 'a suicide's excuses are mostly by the way,'[29] which is to say that while the motives for suicide are too complicated to be reducible to any sort of simple cause, suicides and survivors alike are quick to find them, with art and love topping the list. We might also observe, concerning the question of motives, that there is something strategic about concluding that Pavese killed himself when he was good and ready,[30] because he had nothing left to say (and in a later chapter, we will see a version of this reasoning with respect to Levi).[31] It is a defence mechanism masked as sympathy: it mitigates the crime of passivity of which he had already been found guilty, because it reinscribes him as active, as the agent of his own destiny. At the same time, reviewers speak of his suicide 'at the height of his creative power,'[32] an assessment that seems to contain the promise of more excellent work, unless it implies that there is nowhere to go but downhill from here. For some readers, this was borne out by the 1966 release of his letters edited by Italo Calvino and Lorenzo Mondo.[33] The letters, which vacillate between extreme beauty and mawkish masochism, did not so much change the discourse about his suicide very significantly as provide confirmation of old theories via a new set of data to analyse. As one editor puts it, 'every shoddy line of Pavese's that is recuperated is a gain,' implying that like the goose that laid the golden eggs, everything created by Pavese is self-evidently valuable.[34]

The relative intensity of such interest is evident in the debates sparked by the publication of *Il mestiere di vivere* in 1952, which played out on the culture pages of the Italian newspapers for the remainder of the decade and evolved along two lines: the political and the extremely personal. On the one hand, Pavese could be read as the novelist of *failed* political engagement – that is, of detachment from the political arena – just as easily as that detachment might constitute the very proof of his engagement. And on the other hand, the principal interest of Pavese's diary for many readers consists in its unflinching sexual self-examination. As the saying goes, the personal really is political, and vice versa. It is fitting that it is in a diary – that most

hybrid of texts – that the clash of interpretive keys gets played out;
in a text written for personal consumption but possibly also approved
for public viewing, the status of Pavese's authorial persona is nowhere
else as contested.[35] As readers seeking insight into an author's life, one
methodologically valid sleight of hand we can perform is to note the
structural similarities between author and protagonist. But a journal
or diary is something quite different, insofar as we can never determine at what point, if ever, the diarist wrote with an eye toward future
readers, whether authorized or not. Thus the very ontological status
of *Il mestiere di vivere* poses certain problems for readers, regardless
of their specific interests. But remarkable to me is the way this very
unstable textual form causes the pot of conflicting interpretations,
already simmering by the time of Pavese's suicide, to spill over.[36] It is
precisely a diary, private and yet not,[37] that we privilege for its unvarnished glimpses of the author. We read it because it was written by a
famous novelist ('ogni riga ricuperata'), but also because of what we
expect it to contain about his suicide.[38] The instability of the textual or
generic form carries over, in the case of this suicide, as an instability or
vacillation among mutually reinforcing hermeneutical codes. Indeed,
one critic identifies it as a *womb* book ('libro matrice') as well as a *tomb*
book ('libro-tomba'), and calls Pavese the *book man* ('l'uomo libro').[39]
The fate of *Il mestiere di vivere*, in other words, recapitulates the fate
of Pavese himself as a historical figure. In a chiastic move, the author
is read as the bodily enactment of textual failure, and the opus as the
textual enactment of bodily failure.

My goal in these last pages was not to perform yet another survey
of Pavese's works but rather to question the doxy about his chang-
ing critical fortune. Emphasizing the methodological variability in
the scholarship serves as a screen with which to obscure two things.
First, we must note the strong undercurrent of *schadenfreude*, visible in
slights about supposed psychological (and occasionally physiological)
shortcomings that we cannot infer in Morselli's or Rosselli's reception. And second, there is an attendant paradigm shift whereby the
hierarchy of the physical life (and death) of the author and his texts
has become inverted. Pavese readers have moved from veneration
of the author behind the text (visible in the Pavese case in the 1950s)
to a poststructuralist *dis*-interest in him (1970s), finally to a reading
space wherein we venerate the text behind the author in a manner
reminiscent of the particular discursive status granted by Foucault's
author function.[40] If it is true, as our parsing of the pre- and post-Bar-

thes positions implied, that the author's body, previously the guarantor of textual authenticity, has traded places with the text, such that
now literature guarantees the author, then our obsession with even
the shoddiest signs of him is a logical, if not necessary, consequence.
And Pavese's bodily death has not bibliographical implications but
hermeneutical ones: the termination of his writing. Hence Gioanola's assertion that the vocation of writing and the vocation of dying
are co-terminous. Suicide is thus the moment of supreme rapprochement between the body and body of work, after which what was once
twinned but distinct becomes permanently, ambiguously entwined.

The Endless Body of Writing

Tutto questo fa schifo.
Non parole. Un gesto. Non scriverò più.[41]

All this is sickening.
Not words. An act. I won't write any more.

Bearing in mind this idea of the co-terminality of the life and the writing, let us return to the discussion we began in chapter 2 of Derrida's
The Work of Mourning, in which the philosopher uses the words of the
dead to elaborate memorial discourses that speak both to the singularity of his relationship with them, and to the multiple relations between
them and their readers. Borrowing terms already put into circulation by
Sarah Kofman, we said, Derrida affirms that the relationship between
the finite body and the infinite text is one of interchangeability, in which
the text replaces the body as the site for investigation, and, further, he
avows complicity in these relations ('we collaborate in this substitution'). This is not without some discomfort. The rub is that in Kofman's case, to speak *of* Kofman in this way is to enact precisely what he
observes *in* Kofman. It is not just that Kofman provides the language
with which to memorialize herself: she also provides the body! And
this is where Derrida runs aground, because despite his assertion, he
nonetheless requires recourse to Kofman's necessarily infinite corpus
(womb-book? tomb-book?) in order to access the specific (or 'singular')
case of that specific individual.[42] That is, one replaces the other in the
same moment that it serves as a necessary antecedent.

Derrida remarks on the piece by Kofman mentioned above, 'The
Anatomy Lesson of Doctor Nicolaes Tulp, 1632,' in such a way that we

understand how uneven the discourse of substitution is, that is, the extent to which it privileges the book over the body it replaces:

> It is a lesson, she says ... Sarah interprets in this painting the strange historical relationship between the book and the body, between the book and the proper or lived body of the mortal, to be sure, but also between the book and the body of the body or corporation of doctors gathered there, a body whose gaze is completely occupied by the book rather than the body ... It is, in the first place, the story or history of a *preference* for the book. We can there follow the narrative of historical fascination with the book when it comes to occupy the place of the dead, of the body-cadaver ... For what does Sarah Kofman tell us of this *corpse* in *The Anatomy Lesson*? That this image of the *corpse* is *replaced* or *displaced*, its *place taken* by the book (as seems to be happening at this very instant), replaced by 'a book wide open at the foot of the deceased' ... This book ... stands up to, and stands in for, the body: a *corpse* replaced by a corpus, a *corpse* yielding its place to the bookish thing, the doctors having eyes only for the book facing them, as if, by reading, by observing the signs on the drawn sheet of paper, they were trying to forget, repress, deny, or conjure away death – and the anxiety before death.[43]

As we observed in the case of Pavese, where his death – inscribed in a book – was parsed as the text of failure (failure of text?), Derrida here is *reading* Kofman's death. Moreover, he is caught between two conflicting impulses. On the one hand, he seems to inscribe her *suicide* within the category of philosophical ones (specifically, to attribute Nietzschean undertones to her death, ascribing to it a positive – because active – motive). Hence his assertion that for Kofman (herself an accomplished scholar of Nietzsche) the conjuring of death enacts Nietzsche's affirmation in *Will to Power* about suicide; it is in fact an

> affirmation of life, its irrepressible movement to survive ... to affirm this truth of life through the symptom of repression, to express the irrepressible as it is put to the test of repression, to get, in a word, the better of life, that is to say, of death, giving an account of life.[44]

On the other hand, he seems intent to hunt for ways her *writings* communicate ambivalence about the substitution of the text for the body. He seems to argue, in other words, that the death of the body itself is a fine enough thing but the inevitable replacement of that body is not.

Thus it is Derrida, not Kofman, who evinces that ambivalence, thereby threatening the positive inflection Derrida himself ascribes to her death. Is it that such a gesture (of substitution) implies that the name of Sarah Kofman ('for me too, of course, Sarah was unique') might, after death, be subject to the same opening up of the textualized body, the same examination, scrutiny, autopsy, the same dissemination of meanings to which the text is subject? In other words, are there potential, discomfiting ramifications for their relationship, whose singularity is now threatened? And what does it matter if Kofman authorizes this substitution?

It matters because this substitution is a dilemma for Derrida; it flies in the face of his own reckoning with Kofman's death. If, as he insists, she was unique – singular, exceptional, and bounded by space, time, and situation – then allowing the book 'to serve in place of its occupant' is neither desirable or feasible, for by definition the unique, once lost, cannot be replaced. It is here that I think we can return to Pavese, and to the spot where the pendulum of his posthumous reception has come to rest, in a critical position that privileges what above I called the mutually reinforcing hermeneutical codes of the life and the work. Derrida insists a fair amount on the inequity of the inevitable *substitution* of corpse and corpus; I think really, though, it is the *spectacle* of the exchange of corps and the corpse that is of greater concern to him. And Pavese is all about spectacle – reading the chronicles of his 'absurd vice' is like watching a man go down in flames, or 'perform an obscene act.'[45] Following Kofman, Derrida posits a unidirectional substitution of book for body, whereas in Pavese's case, that substitution takes place continuously and in both directions, so that there is neither an ur-body nor a point of origin. Pavese offers a way around the tension between singularity and multiplicity in his suggestion of a liminal space, in which the two can coexist.

Thresholds

Last blues, to be read some day
'Twas only a flirt
you sure did know
some one was hurt
long time ago.

All is the same
year has gone by –

someday you came
some day you'll die.

Some one has died
long time ago –
someone who tried
but didn't know.[46]

Derrida's discomfort with the implication that the book can substitute for the body seems to point to the challenges suicide poses to nihilist thought: if there is no foundational concept on which to build distinctions between truth and non-truth, then there is, in a sense, no reason why we should oppose the substitution between book and body, for they are equal and exchangeable values, and neither can make a greater claim to authenticity. For Derrida, it is not easy to get over the body in spite of Kofman's apparent espousal of a philosophy of difference that therefore privileges the non-hierarchical interpretive play implied in the substitution. And this is striking; typically, Derrida claims that the binaries of modernity are, paradoxically, self-identical (that is, interchangeable with one another) – this is one of the fundamental moves of deconstructionism. But here, Derrida does not fully allow for the exchange, preferring a hierarchical view of the terms without, however, stating as much. In other words, he stops short where he most resembles himself, when he does not fully espouse moving from a position that embraces the text as a de facto body with claims to certainty and truth (manifest as the body's materiality), to one marked by the ambivalent asseveration of the body-text as a site of de-centring, multiple meanings.

It is tempting to read in this partially, but not wholly, disavowed substitution an analogy to the end of modernity described by Gianni Vattimo as the point at which the de-centring and multiplication of meanings (whereby persuasion triumphs over truth and reason – recall the invocation of Nietzsche) prevails.[47] Pavese's suicide seems to endorse a non-hierarchical relation between the terms of his life and works, and thus functions analogously to this substitution. Diachronic readings of Pavese's various posthumous incarnations in the body of criticism that sprang up in the decades after his death – as well as the various 'Last blues to be read some day' that are written in the voice of the dead – can be seen to walk us through the same steps that lead to Vattimo's view of the imbricated relations between modernity and postmodernity. Pavese's suicide traces a path that leads to the threshold between modernity and postmodernity, on the one hand, and yet threatens the rejection of postmodernity (in the guise of nihilist thinking) on the other. It evolves from an act of thoroughly modern ideological (or psychological) discontent to a postmodern one in which bodily death is representative more simply (and infinitely, more openly) of a new kind of writing. In other words, we can refine our initial observation about the ways Pavese's suicide has been read recently (as someone who could/would not live when he could/would no longer write) in the following way: Pavese's suicide marks not the end of his writing but the beginning of a new kind of writing, an infinite autopsy, an examination without end. In the place of his body are a multitude of texts, a limitless corpus of writing.

We can think about this in another way. Philosopher Emanuele Severino's discussion of *becoming* is predicated on the possibility of the simultaneity of difference and identity, an apparent impossibility (or absurdity) that requires the annihilation of one set of relations among the (non-permanent) terms. Using the example of wood that becomes ashes (or rather that *is* ashes, if we understand the wood and the ashes to be defined in some relation to the amount of energy they contain), he notes,

> Anche nella prospettiva scientifica, dunque, qualcosa può diventare altro da sé solo se si *annulla*. Per potere pensare che una certa quantità di energia assume una nuova forma, il sapere scientifico deve pensare che, in questa trasformazione, va annientata la *relazione* tra tale quantità (che permane, cioè che non si annienta) e la forma da essa inizialmente assunta – e va annientata perché va annientata tale forma.[48]

> Even from a scientific perspective, therefore, something can become something other than itself only if it *annuls* itself. In order to be able to think that a certain quantity of energy assumes a new form, scientific knowledge must think that, in this transformation, the *relation* between such a quantity (which remains, that is, which does not annul itself) and the form it initially assumed is nullified – and gets destroyed because that form gets destroyed.

The decimation of one set of associations favours the emergence of another. Pavese's death institutes in the corpus a series of transformations among relations between author and text that enacts the impossible equation wood = ashes. Moreover, it is not simply that a new set of relations between two terms holds, but that the destruction of first of the two unleashes innumerable new manifestations of the second:

per pensare che l'ente diviene altro da sé (ossia un altro ente), il nichilismo pensa che l'ente diviene niente – e che dunque è niente – nell'atto stesso in cui incomincia ad essere altro da sé ... separando l'ente dal niente, astraendo dalla loro relazione, ponendo come niente la loro relazione.[49]

in order to believe that the entity becomes something other than itself (that is, another entity), nihilism believes that the entity becomes nothing – and therefore is nothing – in the same act in which it begins to be something other than itself ... separating the entity from nothing, abstracting from their relationship, positing as nothing their relationship.

As the wood is *also* ashes (and postmodernity is also, in this way, modernity), Pavese's body is *also* text, liberated of its burdensome aliquot of energy. Not binary but multiple, not vertical but reticular, Pavese's *becoming* takes place in limn between the models of readership delineated by Derrida and Kofman. Pavese inhabits the no man's land in which postmodernity can be understood at once as a form of modernity and its successor: the ashes and the wood.

Crossing Over

Rosetta, stupita, mi disse che non sapeva nemmeno lei perché era entrata nell'albergo quel mattino. C'era anzi entrata contenta. Dopo il veglione si sentiva sollevata. Da molto tempo la notte le faceva ribrezzo, l'idea di aver finito un altro giorno, di essere sola col suo disgusto, di attendere distesa nel letto il mattino, le riusciva insopportabile. Quella notte almeno era già passata. Ma poi proprio perché non aveva dormito e gironzava nella stanza pensando alla notte, pensando a tutte le cose sciocche che nella notte le erano successe e adesso era di nuovo sola e non poteva far nulla, a poco a poco s'era disperata e trovandosi nella borsetta il veronal ...[50]

Rosetta, astonished, told me that she had no idea herself why she had gone to the hotel that morning. In fact, when she entered, she was happy. She was feeling relieved after the dance. For a long time nights made her shudder; the idea of having got through another day, of being alone with all her disgusts, of waiting for morning stretched out in bed—all became unbearable. That particular night, anyhow, she had already got through. But then precisely because she hadn't slept but paced back and forth in the room thinking of night, thinking of all the stupid things that had happened to her in the night and now she was again alone and couldn't do anything, little by little she became desperate and finding the veronal in her bag ...[51]

Let us look to the texts for an illustration of Pavese's liminality. For that, I wish to call as evidence Pavese's *Tra donne sole* (*Among Women Only*, 1949) and its cinematic adaptation, Michelangelo Antonioni's film *Le amiche* (*The Girlfriends*, 1955), the latter of which illustrates the theoretical position on substitutions posited above in its considerations about the suicide of one of its protagonists.[52] I will argue that the structural positions of the suicide in *Le amiche* function primarily as shifts off-screen of the filmic action, to a vanishing point where previous relations nevertheless still obtain.[53] The film corroborates my reading of Pavese's suicide as his writing's replacement and its antecedent, as it were, in an apparently antithetical state whereby the corpse is at once exchanged for the corpus and constitutes it as well – to borrow from Severino, in which Pavese is *becoming*.

Tra donne sole has all the earmarks of what critics generally identify as *the* suicide text: written very late in his career, it deals specifically with a suicide method Pavese himself will employ, and offers a meditation on one possible motivation, at least notionally, of suicide. Although there are suicides in Pavese's previous works, here it is the event to which all others seem to lead.[54] It was Pavese's penultimate work, and was written quickly and uncharacteristically confidently, between March and May of 1949. But rather than focus exclusively on his own writing, I choose this time to look also at Antonioni's reworking of that text that reflects, from a short distance, on our author. The film is a comment on Pavese's text that takes Pavese's suicide into account, providing further support for what I have been describing as the fundamentally liminal quality of Pavese's posthumous writing. The discrepancies between Pavese's text and Antonioni's reworking of it are productive insofar as the inclusions and the omissions in Antonioni's adaptation serve to highlight elements in the written text that are useful for our argument. Antonioni offers the distillation of some of Pavese's key concerns – such as sex, work,[55] and myth[56] – and some of his enduring thematic preoccupations, such as voyages of return, knowledge as a function of re-vision, and the condition of rootlessness. He does this within a narrative structure that, based on Antonioni's intercalation of Pavese's suicide, models the kind of indeterminacy that we perceive in Pavese.

In this film (as well as Antonioni's 1957 *Il grido*) we may discern both the popular conception of suicide as the supreme gesture of despair, and the conception of it as something much more modest in its aspirations. Suicide for Antonioni becomes a simple act of crossing the border to an off-screen world that is not between life and death or life and afterlife, but between intra- and extra-text. It is a critical commonplace to observe that suicide lurks, in one form or another, in many of Antonioni's films. What I would like to suggest is that these suicides lend themselves to a mapping that is much less concerned with highlighting dramatic effects or existential crises than with identifying the sites at which the protagonist's suicide punctures the membrane between filmic and non-filmic. Suicide in my reading of Antonioni is a sprocket: located toward but not precisely at the ends of the filmic time limits, it marks the places where those borders are pierced by what lies in either direction much like perforations in the celluloid. Or, if you prefer, the suicides in *Le amiche* act as imperfect book-ends to the filmic action. The film's beginning coincides roughly but not precisely with the unsuccessful suicide attempt by one of the girlfriends, Rosetta, and the successful attempt marks, more or less, the film's ending. Thus Rosetta's suicidal aspirations do not lie at the centre of the film or constitute an exclusive or even primary focus. But taken into consideration alongside the film's greater concern with Clelia's thoughts and movements, Rosetta's death has ramifications for our reading. Antonioni's strategic placement of Rosetta's suicide attempts, and his repositioning of the relationship between Clelia and Rosetta, teach us about the reticular relations among life, death, and writing, with special emphasis on the spaces in between.

The film opens with shots of Clelia preparing for her bath in a Turin hotel room; these are soon interrupted by the arrival of a maid who seeks access to the room adjoining Clelia's; upon entering that room, she finds the unconscious Rosetta with an empty vial of pills at her bedside. Rosetta is dressed in an evening gown, suggesting that upon returning home from an evening out, she went about the business of killing herself without bothering to change.[57] The structural position of her suicide attempt in an evening gown links her suicide (and our understanding of it) to an event off-screen, the evening party. Besides serving as a shorthand indication of her social class, her evening gown carries pre-filmic events with her into her death (or what she assumes will be her death). We are consequently privy, in a limited way, to the knowledge of at least one aspect of her off-screen, pre-filmic life. Thus we must qualify our assertion that the suicide attempt more or less marks the opening and closing of the filmic text: the presence of the evening gown means that at least the initial suicide attempt also marks the *absence* of such a beginning, the *lack* of any sort of boundary between what happened prior to our viewing presence and after our arrival. Suicide is at once the film's founding act and a symptom of its temporal continuity with what came before – different from it, *and* identical to it. Nor does the film linger in any way on Rosetta's death attempts. Only the first three minutes of the film are devoted to her first attempt. The *successful* suicide, too, is shot with the utmost economy; the recovery of her body at the film's close is shown in only two shots, one from above and one from the river. And as was the case with the initial attempt, the final attempt occurs off-screen; we see only the result of her efforts. But the film continues after her death for another few minutes: first, long enough for Clelia to criticize roundly the cosmopolitan Momina for her irresponsible behaviour toward Rosetta, and second, long enough for Clelia (mortified at her outburst and aware that it may have cost her beloved job at the fashion-house) to arrange what she hopes will be a reconciliation with her on-again off-again companion, the young building foreman Carlo. Instead of reconciliation, however, Clelia's employer arrives and suggests that Clelia return to Rome, a suggestion that is met by Clelia with gratitude and relief.

In Pavese's text, Rosetta's drama is eclipsed by the figure of Clelia, the novella's first-person narrator. She is not as central a character in the film, which is rather more of an ensemble piece and divides its interest among the various members of the group.[58] Indeed, Clelia's importance in the film lies in the fact that she is *not* the principal in any sense; she is, precisely, a marginal figure throughout the film as a semi- (but not total) outsider who hovers on the fringes of the clique, whence she can offer a new perspective on the dynamics of the girl-friends. Bouncing between Turin and Rome, she worked among and socialized with people far above the social station into which she was born. She acts as mediator and translator between Rosetta and her friends, suggesting remedies for Rosetta's malaise (which, predictably, include work and marriage, though on a train ride home from the girlfriends' disastrous daytrip to the shore, she also suggests rather philosophically that the happiest people are the ones who can look

outside themselves). The final scenes of the film juxtapose her conflicting ambitions, envisioned respectively as independent 'career woman' (articulated movingly by her employer as a declaration of their
matrilineal genealogy) and as Carlo's wife: 'una moglie tranquilla
in una casa modesta' (a tranquil wife in a modest home). It is fitting
that these dialogues take place first in that liminal space that is the
hotel lobby and then, after she rejects what is effectively a proposal
from Carlo, at the train station: sites par excellence of the condition of
anomie that is her essential habitus.[59]

The question of norms and their absence (attributed generally to the
war) runs throughout both Pavese's and Antonioni's texts, in ways
that reflect their individual concerns as artists as much as the relations
between them. Though Antonioni significantly soft-pedals or discards
altogether dialogues and scenes in the novella that might be perceived
as unsympathetic toward the characters, such as indictments of the
sexual laxity of leisure-class women, evident in the remark made by
Momina ('I don't know what does matter. I am afraid nothing counts.
We are all whores')[60] or the quick threesome in the hotel room during
one of the group's less rewarding excursions, he does not expurgate
the sex from the film altogether. What remains is an attitude of general indifference toward sex that is typical of many of Pavese's male
characters (Corrado of *La casa in collina*, for example, or Anguilla in *La
luna e i falò*). In the case of the novella, the women are quite simply
unimpressed by sex, which, like love or maternity, is perceived as a
threat to freedom and a largely dull one at that. For example, one of
the wealthy women at the nightclub remarks with disdain, 'Adele vede
dappertutto il sesso ... Ma non è più di moda ... Solamente le serve e
le sartine vogliono uccidersi dopo una notte d'amore'[61] (Adele sees sex
everywhere ... But it is no longer in fashion ... Only housemaids and
seamstresses want to kill themselves after a night of love).[62] Momina
remarks in the novella that when you have a child, you have to accept
life;[63] and in the film, she tells Carlo that he must not be a father because
being a parent means being responsible. Ironically, their disinterest in
intimate relations of any stripe only erodes their precious freedom by
limiting their options (because anything that might lead to intimacy
must be ruled out). This is but a variation on Pavese's predilection for
characters who constantly reflect on the causes and sensations of their
own isolation – recall Corrado's relationship with Cate in *La casa in
collina*, or Anguilla's reflections on American women in *La luna e i falò*,
to limit our examples to the realm of genital love. Think, for example,

of the first pages of the first chapter in the novella when Clelia recalls her father's death – it prevented her from enjoying *carnevale* with her girlfriends.

> [P]ensavo che probabilmente proprio in quella sera lontana m'ero detto la prima volta che se volevo far qualcosa, ottenere qualcosa dalla vita, non dovevo legarmi a nessuno, dipendere da nessuno, com'ero legata a quell'importuno papà. E c'ero riuscita e adesso tutto il mio piacere era disciogliermi in quell'acqua e non rispondere al telefono.[64]

> I thought that it was probably in that distant evening that I really learned for the first time that if I wanted to do anything, to get something out of life, I should tie myself to no one, depend upon no one, as I had been tied to that tiresome father. And I had succeeded, and now my sole pleasure was to dissolve myself in warm water and not answer the telephone.[65]

Then again, we should not be surprised; the title of the book is after all *Tra donne sole*, which could mean, variously, *Among Women Only* (the standard published translation), *Among Women Alone* (i.e. without men), *Among Women Who Are Themselves Alone*, and so on – hardly a compelling title, in other words, for readers seeking a high percentage of pornographic content. (And, lest we forget, this is an Antonioni film and thus runs true to form when it depicts sex as a thrill comparable to an afternoon at the orthodontist's.)[66] It is also a variation on the theme of the vicious circle of writing and life (or its avoidance) evident in Pavese's letters: just as avoiding intimacy as a means of maintaining one's freedom actually forecloses the options afforded by intimacy, so is it impossible to live (that is, participate) while writing, or write while living. Writing excuses one from living and prevents it at the same time: 'If you had no faith in what you are doing, in your work, the material you are creating, the pages you write, what a horror, what a desert, what a void life would be! The dead escape this fate. They keep themselves intact … Fundamentally, you write to be as dead, to speak outside of time, to make yourself remembered by all.'[67]

These relationships between class identity and rootlessness, typical of several of Pavese's texts, are further manifestation of the author's concern with thresholds, margins, liminal spaces, and holding patterns. Here these are parsed, again typically, in terms of Clelia's voyage of return from Rome to Turin, where she had been a child in one of its distinctly working-class neighbourhoods. Not at all the way she imagined it (triumphant, full of admiration or recognition), this unsatisfactory return resembles those in other Pavese novels (*La luna e i falò*, for example) in the sense that the return – the re-vision or re-cognition so central to Pavese's epistemology – results in a kind of greater wisdom for Clelia than it had, say, for Anguilla. Similiarly, Corrado's return home at the end of *La casa in collina* from his *sfollamento* in the countryside produces self-knowledge – specifically about participation, resistance, writing, and life – that we must conclude will eventually be applied for the greater good. Instead, in *Le amiche*, Clelia can only hover on the margins of her neighbourhood and marvel at its squalor, and though she enacts the long-dreamt return in the novel, it is a moot victory, since Gisella fails to acknowledge Clelia's success in the same ways Nuto celebrates (in his non-demonstrative way) Anguilla's. Clelia's voyages of return, in other words, result in self-knowledge but not validation, whether of oneself or by others:

Chiamò le figlie. Avrei voluto andarmene. Quello era tutto il mio passato, insopportabile eppure così diverso, così morto. M'ero detta tante volte in quegli anni – e poi più avanti, ripensandoci – che lo scopo della mia vita era proprio di riuscire, di diventare qualcuna, per tornare un giorno in quelle viuzze dov'ero stata bambina e godermi il calore, lo stupore, l'ammirazione di quei visi familiari, di quella piccola gente. E c'ero riuscita, tornavo; e le facce, la piccola gente eran tutti scomparsi. Carlotta era andata, e il Lungo, Giulio, la Pia, le vecchie. Anche Guido era andato. Chi restava, come Gisella, non le importava più di noi né di allora. Maurizio dice sempre che le cose si ottengono, ma quando non servono più.[68]

She called her daughters. I would have preferred to leave. This was all my past, intolerable and yet so different, so dead. I had told myself many times in those years – and later, too, as I thought it over – that the aim of my life was really to be a success, to become somebody and one day return to those alleys where I had been a child and enjoy the warmth, the amazement, the admiration of those familiar faces, of those little people. And I had been a success and I had returned; and the faces, the little people, had all disappeared. Carlotta was gone, and Slim, Giulio, Pia, and the old ladies. Guido was also gone. Neither we nor those times mattered anymore to the people who were left, like Gisella. Maurizio always says that you get what you want, but only after you have no more need for it.[69]

Indeed, Clelia's arrival in Turin's exalted social circles (in possession of the long-fantasized furs that she has the good taste to leave in her hotel when she first goes to the old neighbourhood)[70] goes largely uncommented by her new moneyed (but not newly moneyed) friends, with the exception of Momina when she praises Clelia's fashion sense, noting that designers usually dress like tramps.[71] In a contrasting gesture of reverse snobbism, her social ascendance is trotted out by her working-class lover Carlo in a pathetic attempt at psychological and professional sabotage, when he implies that her problems result from moving above her station.

There are other journeys as well, and they are equally closely tied to the question of Clelia's social mobility. They also provide the opportunity for a little fantasy play for the rich girls, who display their easy virtue when they go slumming in dive bars, shady establishments, and finally to a restaurant in full view of a brothel on the night of Rosetta's successful suicide. It is not exactly *Belle de Jour* but it does bring new depth to Momina's remark – they are *not* all whores, they just want to be. But these trips outside their class milieu are ultimately unsatisfactory. They don't result in knowledge or even diversion so much as in failure – the women cannot escape their own psychological disenfranchisement no matter how hard they try to run away.

To what class does Clelia belong, anyway? To none and to all: she certainly does not wish to be able to return to her old (that is, working-class) life, as her rejection of Carlo makes patently clear. Nor is she fully a part of the world in which she spends all her time now – the moneyed circles accept her but she was not born to them, and she continually distinguishes herself from her friends with remarks apparently intended to raise class consciousness,[72] though wholly ineffective if her goal is to convert her friends to the joys of gainful employment: '"Se ti mancasse la pagnotta," dissi, "chiederesti di meno"'[73] (You would not scoff if you had to earn your bread); 'So che cosa vuol dire vedere un'altra con le calze di seta e non avercele'[74] (I know what it is like to see someone else wearing silk stockings and not to have them yourself).[75] The irony is that the most convincing desire she expresses in the novella is to live in a villa above the city, where she can decide when and where to see people.[76] Work is a means to an end that is begrudged by everyone till she reaches it. You work so that one day you don't have to, and resent those who don't have to.

Thus in the film, the affair with Carlo is nothing but an admission of the failure of her policy of *noli me tangere*. Their brief liaison represents a withdrawal to her origins insofar as she does not go to bed with any of the non-working-class men, as well as a regression to the comforting belief in the ('natural' – read 'animal') sanity of the proletariat,[77] who by these lights are not decadent and disillusioned like the milquetoasts, fops, and drunkards with unfortunate names like Carletto (little Carl), Loris (changed to Lorenzo in the film), and Fefé[78] who populate the over-classes. It is also, paradoxically, not a chink in her tower of solitude as it first appears, but the outward proof of its success – it gives her the opportunity to make pronouncements about her total autonomy, pronouncements that have larded her thoughts since the novel opened.

Thus it is not a huge surprise when the film ends as Clelia's train pulls out of the station, whisking her away to a new phase in the narrative of her life. In other words, like Rosetta's evening gown, which stitches us viewers into the thick of the fabric of her narrative, or the portrait painted by Lorenzo that she never has the chance to destroy, and that therefore remains as indelible proof of her existence (and as another posthumous text to be read) after she is gone, Clelia's train performs an analogous function: it transports us to the world beyond the film's boundaries. If we read Clelia as the other half of Pavese's alter ego (as Biasin does) then we see a new manifestation of the fraught question of identity. Was Rosetta's suicide an inevitable function of the story's economy of existential attrition, by which, as Gioanola suggests, all possible branches of the tree of life (love, work, friendship, sex, art, maternity) wither and die? If Pavese is indeed divided into Rosetta[79] and Clelia, then escape could mean suicide or getting on a train. There is life on either side of Rosetta's death.[80]

But what or whose is it? Insofar as suicide is *not quite* the alpha and omega of the film, insofar as it lies *almost* but not *exactly* at the termini, there is a way in which we can understand suicide as somehow impermanent or imperfect. The story neither truly begins nor ends with it, and life (or the life of the other characters and thus the body of the story) presumably continues off-screen. It is this spilling or crossing over of life from the edges of the filmic text, the non-terminal aspect of suicide, which seems relevant to the death by suicide of real authors. By placing the suicides at the margins of the film texts and particularly by linking the pre- and post-filmic events in the lives of both the dead and the surviving characters to the suicides, the film asks us to meditate on the relations between the bodies it depicts and the bodies of work that depict them. In other words, the corpses and the corpus are in a similarly ineluctable dialogue. The difference, perhaps, lies in the outcome of its outcome: where the death of the author, for some, demands somehow that we reread his or her opus with new eyes, so to speak, attuned to the possible harbingers of suicidal behaviour in its author (only ever visible in hindsight and of dubious anecdotal, not diagnostic, value), Rosetta's death in *Le amiche* engages us in a reading that takes suicide at least to some extent as a foregone conclusion. Instead, a different interpretative act is required: no longer a rereading, or a searching of the interstices of a text for signs of impending authorial demise, the protagonist's suicide transposes impending death to the margins of the filmic text in such a way that it is simultaneously ever present, and inconsequential. Rather than inextricably linking the corpse to the corps, the positioning of the suicide at the general outset of the text means that they are not co-extensive; our understanding of one does not begin and end with the other. In Roland Barthes's formulation, for the *author*, 'death has another importance: it denies the reality of the author's signature and makes the work a myth: anecdotal truth endeavors unsuccessfully to become symbolic truth… . By destroying the writer's signature, death establishes the truth of the work which is an enigma.'[81] In contrast, the films would seem to illustrate the opposite: the importance of death is that, far from making the work a myth, it situates it in the ongoing trajectory of *other* lives; it underscores precisely death's *anecdotal* (and not symbolic) nature.

We inevitably note, for example, that Pavese completed *Tra donne sole* in 1949, one year before his suicide. Consequently in the novel, Momina's obsessive musings about Rosetta's appearance during the initial suicide attempt (not just her eyes but her dress, the lighting in her hotel room, the presence of a mirror in which she could have viewed but chose not to view herself dying) take on the feeling of a kind of preliminary meditation on the visual aspects of death. There are two lengthy exchanges between Clelia, Rosetta, and Momina that focus precisely on one's appearance after death (or its close facsimile). It seems relevant that Momina (and not, say, Mariella, or Rosetta's mother, or one of the men) is present for both of these conversations, which take place in different places and on different occasions in the book. Momina directs the conversation in both instances, and her provocative questions force Clelia, who witnessed Rosetta's ordeal, to testify as to Rosetta's state.

Momina disse, 'Tu che hai visto Rosetta quella notte. Dicci almeno com'è stato. Non l'avranno spogliata i camerieri, spero?'
Rosetta fece una smorfia, come cercando di ridere. Arrossiva anche lei.

Se ne accorse e indurì gli occhi, fissandomi.

Dissi qualcosa, non so, che le stavano intorno la madre e un dottore. 'No no, com'era Rosetta' disse Momina con accanimento. 'L'effetto che faceva a un'estranea. Allora tu eri un'estranea. Se era brutta, stravolta, se era un'altra. Come siamo da morte. In fondo lei non voleva saper altro.' ...

Dissi ch'era stato soltanto un attimo, ma mi era parsa gonfia in faccia, vestita da sera di celeste, e non aveva le scarpe. Di questo ero certa. Tanto era in ordine e poco stravolta, dissi, che avevo guardato sotto la barella se gocciava sangue. Pareva una disgrazia, una comune disgrazia. In fondo, chi è svenuto è come uno che dorme.

Rosetta respirò forte ... 'Davvero ha creduto che mi fossi sparata?'

'Se proprio ci tenevi,' disse Momina 'era meglio spararsi. Ti è andata male.'

Rosetta mi guardava intimidita, dal fondo degli occhi—mi parve un'altra in quel momento—e bisbigliò: 'Dopo si sta peggio di prima. È questo che spaventa.'[82]

Momina said: 'You saw Rosetta that night. Tell us how it was. The waiters hadn't undressed her, I hope?'

Rosetta's mouth twitched, as if she were trying to laugh. She was red, too. She became aware of it and hardened her eyes, staring at me.

I said something. I don't know what--that her mother and a doctor were around. 'No, no. I mean how Rosetta was,' Momina said, not letting up. 'The effect it had on an outsider. . You were an outsider then. . Whether her face was ugly and distorted; whether she seemed like someone else. Like when we're dead. After all, that was what she wanted.'

They must have been very good friends to talk like that. Rosetta looked at me out of her deep eyes, attentive. I said I'd been there only an instant, but that her face was swollen, she had on a blue evening gown, and wore no shoes. Of that I was certain. Everything was so in order and so little disturbed that I had glanced under her stretcher to see if blood was dripping. It seemed like an accident, just a common accident. After all, a person who has passed out is like a person sleeping.

Rosetta breathed heavily, did not try to smile. Momina said: 'What time did you take the sleeping pills?'

But Rosetta didn't answer. She shrugged her shoulders, looked around and then asked hesitatingly in a low voice: 'You really believed I had shot myself?'

'If you really wanted to do it,' Momina said, 'shooting yourself would have been better. It didn't come off right with you.'

Rosetta looked at me out of her deep eyes, intimidated—at that moment she seemed to be somebody else—and she whispered: 'Afterwards you feel worse than you did at first. That's what's frightening.' [83]

In other words, it is through Clelia that Rosetta confronts her own corpse, when Clelia knowingly mounts the spectacle of death that Loris and the others will never manage to organize the way they intend. (Instead, Loris will mount a kind of performance piece meant to represent – complete with a catafalque – the death of art, though none of the painters invited to hear him read the eulogy bother to come!)[84] Note that this conversation takes place in the dark, exactly as the characters Loris, Mariella, and the others had discussed:

'Dicci almeno che cosa si prova. A chi si pensa in quel momento. Ti sei guardata nello specchio?'

Non parlava canzonando ma con voce bambina come se adesso recitasse. Anche prima, quando avevano spento, mi era parso una scena di teatro. Di nuovo mi venne il sospetto che quel giorno sulla barella non ci fosse addirittura stato nessuno.

Rosetta disse che non s'era guardato allo specchio. Non ricordava se nella stanza c'erano specchi. Anche allora aveva spento la luce. Non voleva veder niente, nessuno, soltanto dormire. Aveva un grosso un terribile mal di testa. Che a un tratto era passato, guarito, lasciandola distesa e felice. Com'era felice, le pareva un miracolo. Poi s'era svegliata, all'ospedale, sotto una lampada che le faceva male agli occhi.

'Seccata?' mormorò Momina.

'Uh,' disse Rosetta 'svegliarsi è orribile ... '

'Ho conosciuto una cassiera a Roma,' dissi 'che a forza di vedersi allo specchio, lo specchio dietro il banco, diventò pazza ... Credeva di essere un'altra.'

Momina disse: 'Bisognerebbe vedersi allo specchio ... Tu Rosetta non hai avuto il coraggio ... '

Chiacchierammo così, dello specchio e degli occhi di chi si uccide. Venne il momento che, tornando il cameriere con un nuovo vassoio, riaccendemmo la luce. La faccia di Rosetta era tranquilla, dura.[85]

'At least tell us what it feels like. Whom one thinks about at that moment. Did you look in the mirror?'

She didn't talk teasingly but with a child's voice as if she were acting. Before, when the lights were out, it had seemed to me a scene on the stage.

Again the notion came to me that there had been absolutely no one on the stretcher that evening.

Rosetta said she hadn't looked in the mirror. She didn't remember if there were any mirrors in the room. She had turned out the lights then, too. She didn't want to see anything or anybody, only to sleep. She had a tremendous, a terrible headache. Which suddenly went away, leaving her stretched out and happy. How happy she was. It seemed a miracle. Then she woke up, in the hospital, under a lamp which hurt her eyes.

'Disgusted?' Momina murmured.

'Uh,' Rosetta said. 'Waking up is horrible ... '

'I knew a cashier in Rome,' I said, ' who went crazy from seeing herself all the time in the mirror behind the bar. She got to thinking she was some-body else.'

Momina said: 'One should look at oneself in the mirror ... You've never had the courage, Rosetta ... '

We talked on like that, about mirrors and the eyes of a person kill-ing himself. When the waiter came in with another tray, we lit the lights, Rosetta's face was calm and hard.[86]

It is interesting that Rosetta takes up her initial observation about the dreadful morning after of the attempt ('After you feel worse than you did at first') in this second exchange ('Waking up is horrible'). One sort of reading might attribute this repetition to a personal concern on Pavese's part, whether as the narration of an experience (actual or imag-ined) or as the conjuring of an anticipated failure in order to neutral-ize the anxiety that girds Rosetta's remarks (what happens if it doesn't work? Am I not worse off than before?). I, however, prefer to read this as a form of play with the fantasy of discovery. To the extent that we are any of us apprehensive about appearances, novelists certainly are no different. Pavese's gaze lingers intently on Rosetta's body, he moves it around, surrounds it with other people, whether dressed, undressed, shod, or bare-footed ... Pavese narrates his manipulation of Rosetta's doll-like body until he finds a comfortable position: a little swollen in the face, but otherwise, you don't look bad! Then, when all is said and done, he removes the body altogether, until it can make its final appear-ance as rehearsed: 'Non pareva nemmeno morta. Soltanto un gonfiore alle labbra, come fosse imbronciata.'[87] (She didn't even seem dead. Only a swelling around the lips, as though she were being sulky.)[88] Thus in spite, perhaps, of textual evidence to the contrary, such as Loris and Mariella's conversation about the spectacle, initially about suicide, that they planned to mount, the threesome's conversations (and, for that matter, the betrayal of the suicide's whereabouts by the stray cat in the hotel room) are *not* proleptic gestures on his part:

> Io non so cos'abbia fatto Rosetta ... Mi piace anzi, questa fantasia della realtà, per cui le situazioni dell'arte perdono quota e diventano vita. Dove cominci il fatto personale non m'interessa ... Ma sarebbe troppo bello se davvero Rosetta avesse agito per suggestione ...[89]

> I don't know what Rosetta did, but this very real fantasy of hers strikes me as pretty good. By her mere act she concretized an abstract artistic situation into warm life. I don't care where the personal fact has its origin ... But it would be really too good if she did it from the suggestion in the play itself ...[90]

Though it feels almost like an invitation to view the body of the author, who, like his character, will die of an overdose alone in a hotel room, this is not the place, I would argue, to cry, 'Bingo' and claim the prize for deciphering the author's plan. It is, rather, a glimpse into the act of writing as it is inextricably linked to the question of life.[91] It is the book at the foot of the body, and our eyes alternating between them. To repeat our observation about Kofman, the substitution takes place continuously and in both directions, so that there is neither an ur-body nor a point of origin. Pavese is *becoming*.

By the same token, we may wonder at the notion that Rosetta, unlike her creator, can survive the ingestion of a massive dose of sleeping pills only to die by drowning in the film. Does this discrepancy not give us pause in the same way that the similarities do? Or, to return to our initial observation about the deaths in the Antonioni film, does not the body of the author exceed or cross over the margins of the text like Rosetta's, perhaps in the paradoxical evacuation of Pavese's bodily form? 'Di nuovo mi venne il sospetto che quel giorno sulla barella non ci fosse addirittura stato nessuno.'[92] Does Pavese inhabit a no man's land in that sense as well? The image of the empty stretcher is certainly suggestive of a landscape haunted by the disembodied dead – a metaphor, perhaps, for our readings too.

For it is in the move from anecdote to symbol (described by Barthes as unsuccessful) that we must view Rosetta's evening gown, and Pavese's sleeping pills as well.[93] Such a move permits the otherwise impermissible, namely the elision of the categories of fictional and 'real' suicides, by way of the analogous structural positions of the deaths. Just as the suicide in *Le amiche*, which is of a piece with the narrative world beyond the film's purview, punctures the margins of the film without marking its termination, so does Pavese's own death perforate the novel's narration, creating the space in which we pause before moving on. With the knowledge of the author's suicide, we read, and reread, at the same time, authorial intentions be damned. For the reader, suicide injects autobiography into the fiction, crossing generic and temporal boundaries: in short, retroactively shaping our interpretation of the text. Thus, like Rosetta's deaths ('Quella stupida si è uccisa un'altra volta'[94] [That dummy has gone and killed herself again]), the suicide of the protagonist is not so much the hallmark of a thematics of existential anguish common in Antonioni's films, but rather an invitation to contemplate the awful eternity of a subject whose attempt to flee is doomed to fail.

Pavese's death, too, is interminable and not terminal: inside and outside the story with no end. Or to return to the terms of the previous section, Pavese's death – at once ashes and wood – provides a hinge between modernity and postmodernity insofar as it at once makes assumptions about the relations between history, narrative, and time *and* overturns those assumptions. We are moving toward an understanding of my previous questions about how the author's life becomes a text to be read at the point of his death, and whether suicide is an act of writing and therefore subject to the same forms of critical interventions as writing per se. Reading these two texts, at least, it would seem that the answers are both yes: the author's life is in some sense inextricable from his text much like the portrait of Rosetta which, in the Antonioni film, she tries to have destroyed by the artist in order to erase all traces of her existence. That the portrait, proof of her past physical presence, remains, is inescapable much like the traces left in a text by an author once living.

The Post-Biological Author

A suicide of this kind is born, not made.[95]

The portrait remains. In doing so, it raises the same questions we have been asking throughout this study: what do you do with the knowledge of an author's suicide? How does suicide impact our reading strategies? On the face of it, these questions would seem not to have much to do with the issues of temporality that were under investigation in Severino, Derrida, and, indirectly, Vattimo, though it is my contention that Pavese's suicide illuminates them. The response Derrida seems to offer in *The Work of Mourning* is, we saw, an incomplete one, in that his essay on Kofman stops a step short of carrying out its promise of the substitution it seems to promote, on what appear to be the humanist grounds that that substitution of the corpse for the corpus compromises the integrity of the subject. Put in different terms, at issue is the axis: though Kofman proposes a horizontal exchange, Derrida's remains, ultimately, vertical. Borrowing Emanuele Severino's analysis resolves Derrida's exploration of substitution and antecedence as the paradox of ashes and wood: as we noted earlier, Severino's *becoming* is predicated on the possibility of the simultaneity of difference and identity, an apparent impossibility (or absurdity) that requires the annihilation of one set of relations among the (non-permanent) terms. For Vattimo, the terms might be simultaneity and sequentiality, that is, the way postmodernity is at once distinct from and predicated on the continued existence of modernity. Each of these sets of terms gets at the question of what we might call the paradox of the portrait as it is represented by Pavese's novella. In fact, besides Rosetta's attempts to destroy her portrait, each of our authors depicts protagonists in the act of erasing all traces of their bodies, if we consider that Morselli's eradication of all human life is tantamount to the eradication of all witnesses to his protagonist's bodily existence, since, if no one knows about him, he doesn't really exist. And Rosselli's poetic I, like Kofman, performs the exchange herself, when she directs the reader's gaze (do come see my poetry / sit for a portrait) to a text whose animation can stand in for her own bodily exertions.

The continued existence of the portrait – a bit like the portrait of Rebecca in the Daphne du Maurier novel by the same name[96] – stands as a marker of the dead body that, as Rosetta demonstrates, cannot be eradicated. On the contrary, having always already existed, it serves as an emblem of the temporal challenges particular to the suicidal author. Though it is articulated in different terms, the quote with which this section opens offers a pithy summation of this temporal logic: if a suicide really is born and not made, then Pavese's suicide was a foregone conclusion. What has not yet happened has already happened: Pavese was born dead. This is the specular opposite of Vattimo's positioning of postmodernity with respect to modernity: what is already over is not yet over. We note again support for the argument that in the case of an author's suicide, some of the positions held by critical theories that tend to exclude the author from the scene of reading come to resemble a popular, humanist, pro-subject position that embraces the singularity of the subject. More specifically, in this case, we might encapsulate the position articulated above, in which the author's death stands at once at the end of his or her life and as its inaugural gesture, as the quandary of what we might call the post-biological author: the suicidal author is an author whose status as living or dead is no longer relevant, having always already been dead.

With this term I mean to designate not only these temporal relations but also the way those relations are conditioned by the uses to which we as readers put the dead author. In other words it is not simply the author in a value-neutral, unmotivated state of corpse becoming corpus, but rather in a state of transformation whose starting and end-points are determined independent of the author. Unlike the ashes and the wood, whose meaning, if you will, is predetermined by their materials, the body of the suicidal author and his textual remains vary as a product so far as his readers vary. Thus the post-biological author stands in the same relation to his own death as to his work, at once prospectively and retrospectively. Another way we can think about this transformation of the author, upon his suicide, into a post-biological subject, is to view it as a gloss on the relationship Giorgio Agamben describes between sovereign and *homo sacer*, the sacred man.[97] If we understand suicide as a kind of threshold moment that redefines the relations between reader and author by way of textual mediation, we can borrow Agamben's terms to locate the suicidal author in a position akin to that of the *homo sacer*, and that author's readers in the position of the sovereign. This association elucidates the politicized nature of the stand-in for the authorial body (his textual remains), their new status as *bios*, where they had previously occupied the sphere of bare life. Through the intervention of the sovereign reader at the threshold moment of suicide, simultaneity ceases to pose as sequentiality, and the corpse joins the corpus much as bare life enters the polis, so that the pre-biological becomes post-biological, and that which was previously private is deployed in the public realm.

Hence our initial observation, with Morselli, that every scrap of writing became autobiographical for his readers, and at the same time every private thought, every piece of correspondence, once committed to paper, carries with it or refers back to the corps of writing, the writing corpse. Similarly, after her suicide, Rosselli's readers uncouple her writings from their historical moorings to reinscribe them in a kind of open sea. Is this not tantamount to an ideological reinscription of the bare life of the author? Pavese's case ('every shoddy line') is an illustration of that relationship, in the sense that his suicide marks a threshold not just between life and death (terminal and interminable) but also between the state of separation between those terms and a state in which they are coterminous. The post-biological author, made an accomplice to the reader, must engage in the act of dragging bare life into the polis or of offering for public consumption that which had previously been excluded, and in doing so confirms the possibility of the simultaneity of difference and identity that Agamben's dyad appears to refute. Suicide thus also elaborated on Barthes's assertions about the death of the author and the birth of the (sovereign) reader: the threshold event of authorial suicide positions the sovereign reader to locate the unqualified life of the suicide within the public domain, at the same time that it condemns and exalts the *homo sacer*, whose corpus of writing is inscribed on his corpse.

We started this chapter with the observation that from the moment of his death, discussions of Pavese's suicide have vacillated between two broad categories. The thinking goes that close readings of his texts demonstrate that his death was motivated either by personal reasons *or* by political ones; that his writing is interesting for stylistic and thematic qualities *or* for the ideological positions it questions; that he is either a navel-gazing decadent *or* a truly engaged intellectual courageous enough to look his own passivity in the face, and so on. We have seen an analogous tension in two very disparate theoretical stances, both of which have emerged at least in part from meditations about death: Derrida's apparent advocacy of the interchangeability of book and body, and Agamben's mutually defining sovereign and *homo sacer*. These dyads are constituted by morphologies of tension and opposition but never coexistence. In contrast, I have also argued for a reading, indebted to Severino and to Vattimo, of Pavese as occupying a more densely occupied space in which the relations of opposition that define these dyads are also relations of antecedence as well as of self–identicalness. In Pavese's *Tra donne sole* and Antonioni's *Le amiche* alike, the either/or question is diffused and subsumed by their greater occupations with questions of class, sex, myth, work, art, love that are too fully imbricated one with the others to countenance such reductionist thinking as the standard oppositional dyad implies. I have argued in this chapter, in other words, for a reading of Pavese that does not require a lifelong partisanship like to the Hatfields or the McCoys, but instead allows us to approach him from any number of positions. I have militated on behalf of an architectonics of the gaze that is a reticular or multiform realization whose borders, boundaries, points of origin, and destinations blur and overlap. 'For me, too, Pavese was unique,' I might conclude, but his is a singularity that depends only partly on Pavese's historical specificity and my relations to his status as post-biological. I have argued elsewhere for the importance of maintaining an open mind – of looking at books without slavish recourse to received knowledge. The tunnel vision that so often ensues after an author's suicide argues the point more strongly: death inspires a kind of hermeneutical conservatism that forecloses possibilities for less definitive readings. Perhaps what I advocate here, then, is that we resist the temptation of this conservatism and sacrifice certainties for curiosity, so that no matter how great the power of the reader, it always be tempered by a spirit of humility toward the dead.

4 Commemoration and Erasure: Primo Levi, Giorgio Agamben, Avishai Margalit

Silence

[E]ra sempre piú stanco di essere sano in un mondo che vedeva sempre piú insano. Così, un giorno, [p]ortò dentro la posta, lasciò nel suo studio il computer e l'archivio perfettamente ordinato, appena meno della sua mente, e se ne andò.[1]

[H]e was increasingly tired of being sane in a world he saw as ever more insane. So, one day, [h]e brought in the mail, left the computer and the filing cabinet perfectly tidy, barely less so than his mind, and he left.

More celebrated than any of the other three authors I have examined, the complex figure of writer, scientist, and Holocaust survivor Primo Levi (1919–1987) was venerated by a worldwide readership for forty-odd years, until his lethal plunge over the banister in his Turin apartment building in 1987, at the age of sixty-eight. Levi's suicide has been contested in some circles – not because there was no evidence of suicide (on the contrary) but because his writings deal, more often than not, with his experiences as a concentration camp survivor, and after all, we expect our survivors to survive. But for some readers, suicide threatens Levi's status as a survivor: it is as though survivorship were a club from which his membership could be revoked. Thus Levi's suicide has implications for his memory that exceed the relations between suicide and writing typical of other cases of authorial suicide, and the relations between writing and testimony common to Holocaust literature. His accounts of life in the camps have been unanimously praised for their elegant lucidity, their almost scientific clarity (often attributed to his primary professional career as a chemist), the lack of rancour of their expositions of the horrors of the camps and their aftermath, and for the life-long commitment to bearing witness to the events of the Holocaust, represented by his writings on behalf of those whose voices had been silenced. Much has been written about the possible effects of the camps on Levi, particularly about whether or not his death was in some way a belated response to the horrors experienced therein. Equally impassioned arguments have been made about the impossibility of suicide for Levi, according to which his courage and drive to survive precluded the possibility of such a renunciative act.[2] Of the four cases examined in this study, his is the only suicide under dispute.

Past chapters have juxtaposed our authors with figures who are not conventionally invoked in connection with them: in the case of Morselli, I have used Rensi and Monod; for Rosselli, it has been Kofman and Derrida; and Pavese has been read with Severino alongside Derrida and Agamben. In this chapter, I will not deviate from my methodology so much as redimension it. The readings that follow, of Levi through Giorgio Agamben and Avishai Margalit, do not represent provocative or unexpected choices. Nor is it surprising that I am using the suicidal author's works to provide the language for his commemoration. But where in chapters past I temporarily set aside the author's suicide, in this chapter the death stays front and centre, threatening the discourses about commemoration and witnessing that Levi himself embodies. The philosophical concepts of silence, testimony, and judgment, and the considerable tensions between them, form the pillars on which the majority of Levi scholarship is founded. And suicide compounds these tensions, confounds them individually as well as at the intersections between them.

The argument advanced here runs against readings that erase Levi's intermittent personal and intellectual preoccupations with suicide. After his death, Levi's concern with memory and with the vital task of bearing witness founds the discourses of commemoration/memory that emerge around him, at the risk of undermining the importance of, or indeed expurgating, his other concerns. What is more, having written about commemoration and bearing witness, Levi himself became a privileged object of commemorative acts that nonetheless do not commemorate him; instead, they instrumentalize his writings to support their own theoretical positions.

For many North American readers, Levi is a singular embodiment of Holocaust survivorship. In spite of convincing physical evidence that

Levi's death was a suicide, it has nonetheless been contested because people associate him so strongly with survivorship and with testimony. According to Risa Sodi,

> Over time, Primo Levi has come to represent the entirety of Italian Holocaust writing – and more. Much as Elie Wiesel is recognized today as both a superlative writer and an actor on the world stage, so Primo Levi has assumed a role that goes well beyond the realm of literature. He, like Wiesel, has come to assume the antonomastic mantle of 'survivor' and is increasingly invoked as a 'watchman' of Holocaust memory. Such is the international esteem for him that his works are excerpted in virtually every recent anthology of Holocaust writing, and his extraordinary success in America is ... 'one of the most interesting American cultural phenomena in recent memory.'[3]

If Levi is indeed a cultural phenomenon (American and Italian), then Levi's suicide has enormous significance. It is at once an individual act and also, effectively, a socially and historically symbolic act. The ramifications of his death for his readers – the thanatopolitics – are broader and deeper than those of, say, Amelia Rosselli, for reasons that stem from the kinds of expectations that have developed around the figure of Levi. Some of these take the form of highly personalized inflections; for example, at an academic conference roundtable panel on the legacy of Primo Levi, I heard eminent scholars discussing several recently published Levi biographies.[4] The central critique of one biography was that it did not conform to the speaker's personal image of Levi – 'my Levi.' To the best of my knowledge, no one really speaks of 'my Rosselli' in quite the same way that Levi's readers have appropriated him as their own. By the same token, it could equally be argued that part of the power of the particular biography under dispute lies in the ways the author eloquently channelled her own fascination with Levi into her scholarship. But beyond these two examples of individuals taking possession of Levi's persona – of the 'strong notional element' of these 'epistolary friendships'[5] – is the equally compelling mediatory use to which his books have been put. By mediatory I don't mean conciliatory; I don't understand his message to be one of forgiveness or of an exaltation of the human spirit. Instead, I mean something closer to exegesis and translation. Levi made legible his own camp experiences as well as the experiences of the dead; his books gave us the language and the tone with which to speak of the

Holocaust. In contrast, few people view Rosselli (or Pavese, or, for that matter, Hemingway or Plath) as the incarnation of an urgently ethical stance. Levi spoke – was made to speak[6] – for all; Rosselli, on the other hand, spoke only for herself.

There is a further distinction to be made between the responses to the suicides of the first three authors in this study and Levi's suicide. In the cases examined earlier, we noted how after a writer's suicide, his or her works were scrutinized for hidden clues that traced an ineluctable, if occult, path toward suicide. We further noticed the ways even the most intimate aspects of a writer's life were opened up to scrutiny – from sexual appetites to sartorial and culinary preferences; from political and religious beliefs to details about personal health and hygiene to which, in certain populations, only one's valet is privy. Does the volubility with which readers and critics rehash every detail of the writer-suicide's life mirror, in reverse, the pious silence that often surrounds other deaths? And what are the ramifications of this silence for examinations of the Holocaust? Recourse to the notion of the ineffability of the Holocaust has become a commonplace.[7] Putting aside the moral issues related to failure (or refusal) to communicate historical events and experiences (especially what scholars call 'limit events'), what can we learn from this juxtaposition of, on the one hand, the logorrhea inspired by suicide and, on the other hand, the deferential discretion that accompanies accounts of the Lager? Are our responses opposite as a function of the conflicting natures of the two phenomena, one intensely private, self-directed and self-willed, and the other public, forcibly imposed, and outwardly directed? In previous chapters, we noted the ways post-suicide criticism of an author seemed to revert precisely to the position condemned by Barthes as obsolete:

> The Author, when believed in, is always conceived of as the past of his own book: book and author stand automatically on a single line divided into a before and an after. The Author is thought to nourish the book, which is to say that he exists before it, thinks, suffers, lives for it, is in the same relation of antecedence to his work as a father to his child.[8]

The suicidal author's life, in other words, is usually inferred in every line of his work. With Levi, on the other hand, we can observe the opposite phenomenon: a critical averting of the eyes, so to speak, from the more private of the author's personal foibles[9] and, at the same time, a re-evaluation of his works not with an eye toward discerning foreshadowing of suicide, but rather the opposite. The critical tendency with Primo Levi, broadly generalized, is to reread his work in an effort to unearth yet further evidence of its life-affirming, not death-predicting, value; of its urgent and continued relevance; of its centrality to Levi's supposed life's mission to bear witness to his and others' experiences.

Thus many readers disregard the fact that Levi deals directly with the topic of suicide. The texts with which Levi is far and away most closely associated are *Se questo è un uomo* (1947) and *La tregua* (1963): both texts are staples on the reading lists of many universities' PhD qualifying exams, the latter to a lesser extent than the former, as well as being required reading in the Italian schools. His short stories (with the exception in the United States, perhaps, of *The Periodic Table*, 1975) and his poetry are much less well known and read mostly by specialists, though by no means consistently, if the rates at which these texts are cited in scholarly publications is any indication. Compared to the legions of readers of his masterpieces about survival, the readers of the fiction texts like 'Verso Occidente' (*Vizio di forma*, 1971) (to which I will return in a moment) are few and far between indeed. We might of course make the argument that this critical reticence is simply a discreet way to avoid passing judgment on these texts. Or, following Robert Gordon's thesis, we might question whether there is so much critical weight given to the notion of witnessing or bearing testimony in Levi's writings that critics (perhaps until Gordon himself) have simply not had the tools with which to investigate these texts in a productive way, for they are quite fruitless when read only in the key of testimony. (Or perhaps there is some truth in both of these positions.) But if the philosophical concepts of silence, testimony, and judgment form the pillars on which the majority of Levi scholarship is founded, I think in either case we can argue for the relevance of these texts, perhaps especially of those non-fiction essays that make explicit linkages between the concentration camps, writing, and suicide.

Thus there is reason, for example, to take into consideration passages like the following from the most synthetic of his meditations on writerly clarity, 'Dello scrivere oscuro' (in *L'altrui mestiere*), in which he sees a connection between the unclear, 'animal-like' writings of Georg Trakl and Paul Celan and their eventual suicides:

L'effabile è preferibile all'ineffabile, la parola umana al mugolio animale. Non è un caso che i due poeti tedeschi meno decifrabili, Trakl and Celan, siano entrambi morti suicidi, a distanza di due generazioni. Il loro comune destino fa pensare all'oscurità della loro poetica come ad un pre-uccidersi, a un non-vuol-essere, ad una fuga dal mondo, a cui la morte voluta è stata coronamento. Sono da rispettare, perché il loro 'mugolio animale' era terribilmente motivato: per Trakl, dal naufragio dell'Impero Asburgico, in cui egli credeva, nel vortice della Grande Guerra; per Celan, ebreo tedesco scampato per miracolo alla strage tedesca, dallo sradicamento, e dall'angoscia senza rimedio davanti alla morte trionfatrice.[10]

The effable is preferable to the ineffable, human speech to animal moaning. It is not by chance that the two least decipherable German poets, Trakl and Celan, both died suicides, two generations apart. Their shared destiny makes one think of the obscurity of their poetics as a kind of pre-suicide, as a not-wanting-to-be, as a flight from the world, to which wilful death was the climax. They are to be respected, because their 'animal moaning' was terribly motivated: for Trakl, by the shipwreck of the Hapsburg Empire, in which he had faith, by the vortex of the Great War for Celan, German Jew saved by miracle from the German slaughter, by the uprooting, and by the ceaseless anguish before death triumphant.

Levi makes careful distinctions between his own crystalline writing and the writings of these two. Note that his explicit justification for clarity was based on the desire for writerly longevity:

[N]on si dovrebbe scrivere in modo oscuro, perché uno scrittore ha tanto più valore, e tanta più speranza di diffusione e di perennità, quanto meglio viene compreso e quanto meno si presta ad interpretazioni equivoche.[11]

One should not write in an obscure way, because a writer has so much more worth, and so much greater hope of diffusion and of perpetuity, the better he is understood and the less he lends himself to equivocal interpretations.

The rest of the essay militates on behalf of clarity as the hallmark of the living, and specifically of the healthy. Thus the language of Celan is 'the language of him who is about to die' ('quello di colui che sta per morire').[12] He continues:

Il mugolio animale è accettabile da parte degli animali, dei moribondi, dei

folli, e dei disperati: l'uomo sano ed intero che lo adotta è un ipocrita o uno
sprovveduto, e si condanna a non avere lettori.[13]

The animal moaning is acceptable on the part of animals, the dying, the
mad, and the desperate: the sane and whole man who adopts it is a hypo-
crite or ill equipped, and condemns himself to not having readers.

These distinctions, however, do not survive Levi. In each of the cases
of authorial suicide we examined, we noted the impulse to jumble suicides together in a big promiscuous pile. As was the case with Amelia
Rosselli, whose name was inevitably linked with Sylvia Plath's after
her suicide, Levi, too, changed posthumous bedfellows, so that after his
death, he was frequently compared to Celan (and, in a not-too-distant
second place, suicide and Holocaust survivor Jean Améry) despite the
multiple and radical differences in their writings. What's more, Levi's
fixation with clarity in his own works does not preclude the possibility
that such clarity is ultimately impossible, as evidenced by this disavowal from the same essay:

È evidente che una scrittura perfettamente lucida presuppone uno scri-
vente totalmente consapevole, il che non corrisponde alla realtà. Siamo
fatti di Io e di Es, di spirito e di carne ed inoltre di acidi nucleici, di tradizioni, di ormoni, di esperienze e traumi remoti e prossimi; perciò siamo
condannati a trascinarci dietro, dalla culla alla tomba, un Doppelgänger,
un fratello muto e senza volto, che pure è corresponsabile delle nostre
azioni, quindi anche alle nostre pagine.[14]

It is obvious that a perfectly lucid piece of writing presupposes a totally
conscious writer, which does not correspond to reality. We are made of
Ego and Id, of spirit and of flesh as well as of nucleic acids, traditions,
hormones, experiences, and traumas both remote and recent; for that reason we are condemned to drag behind us, from the cradle to the grave, a
Doppelgänger, a mute and faceless brother, who is co-responsible for our
actions, and therefore also for our pages.

My point here is not to insist that there are indeed plentiful suicidal
prolepses in his work – such a position would run counter to the most
basic assertions of this study. More simply I want to note Levi's move
in these passages: where indecipherable writings are the wind-up, suicide is inevitably the pitch ('l'oscurità della loro poetica (è come) un

pre-uccidersi, a un non-vuol-essere, ad una fuga dal mondo, a cui la morte voluta è stata coronamento'). Hence his insistence on the goal of an admittedly impossible clarity of his own work, which he claims differentiates him from Trakl and Celan and thus trumps whatever other similarities might exist. Here the irony is that in the case of both of these figures, Levi gets it wrong: Trakl's highly purified, symbolist language and Celan's abstract distillations are anything but bestial moaning. So it would seem that Levi's invocation of these suicidal authors serves less as an authoritative assessment of good writing than as a kind of psychological necromancy, conjuring up the darkness ('l'oscurità') the more firmly to reject it ('L'effabile è preferibile all'ineffabile').[15]

Verso occidente

– Non ne hai mai avuti, di dubbi? Sii sincera!
– No, mai –. Anna meditò, poi aggiunse: – Quasi mai.
– Hai detto *quasi*.
– Sí, lo sai bene. Dopo che è nata Mary. È durato poco, pochi mesi, ma è stato molto brutto: mi sembrava che non ne sarei uscita mai, che sarei rimasta cosí per sempre.
– E cosa pensavi in quei mesi? Come vedevi il mondo?
– Non ricordo piú. Ho fatto tutto per dimenticarlo.
– Dimenticare che cosa?
– Quel buco. Quel vuoto. Quel sentirsi … inutili, con tutto inutile intorno, annegati in un mare di inutilità. Soli anche in mezzo a una folla: murati vivi in mezzo a tutti murati vivi.[16]

– Did you never have any doubts? Be honest!
– No, never – . Anna thought, then added: – Almost never.
– You said almost.
– Yes, you know very well. After Mary was born. It didn't last long, a few months, but it was very ugly: it seemed to me that I would never come out of it, that I would stay that way forever.
– And what did you think in those months? How did you see the world?
– I don't remember anymore. I did everything possible to forget it.
– Forget what?
– That hole. That void. That feeling of uselessness, with everything around me useless, drowned in a sea of uselessness. Alone even in the middle of a crowd: walled up alive in the midst of everyone walled up alive.

But, I repeat, it is not the case that Levi's writings are read for their suicidal intentions. On the contrary: if Levi followed the patterns of reading enacted in the cases of other suicides, we might expect readers who are convinced of the connections between Levi's concentration camp experiences and his suicide to get excited about texts like the one I mentioned above, 'Verso occidente,' in which a scientist named Walter (as in *alter*) champions suicide:

> ognuno di noi uomini … lotta per vivere e non sa perché. Il perché sta scritto in ogni cellula, ma in un linguaggio che non sappiamo leggere con la mente: lo leggiamo però con tutto il nostro essere, e obbediamo al messaggio con tutto il nostro comportamento. Ma il messaggio può essere più o meno imperativo: sopravvivono le specie in cui il messaggio è inciso profondo e chiaro, le altre si estinguono, si sono estinte. Ma anche quelle in cui il messaggio è chiaro possono avere delle lacune. Possono nascere individui senza amore per la vita; altri lo possono perdere, per poco o molto tempo, magari per tutta la vita che gli resta … [F]ra chi possiede l'amore di vita e chi lo ha smarrito non esiste un linguaggio comune. Lo stesso evento viene descritto dai due in due modi che non hanno niente in comune: l'uno ne ricava gioia e l'altro tormento, ognuno ne trae conferma per la propria visione del mondo … La vita *non* ha uno scopo; il dolore prevale sempre sulla gioia; siamo tutti dei condannati a morte, a cui il giorno dell'esecuzione non è stato rivelato; siamo condannati ad assistere alla fine dei nostri più cari … Sappiamo tutto questo, eppure qualcosa ci protegge e ci sorregge e ci allontana dal naufragio. Che cosa è questa protezione? Forse solo l'abitudine a vivere, che si contrae nascendo.[17]

Each of us men struggles to live and doesn't know why. The why is written in every cell, but in a language that we do not know how to read with our minds. But we read it with all of our being, and we obey its message with our every behaviour. But the message can be more or less imperative: the species in which the message is inscribed deeply and clearly, survive, others die out, they have died out. But even those in whom the message is clear can have gaps. Individuals without love of life can be born, others can lose it for a short time or a long time, perhaps even for the rest of the life that remains to them … [B]etween those who possess a love for life and those who have lost it, there exists no common language. The same event gets described by the two in two ways that have nothing in common: one derives joy from it and the other, torment, and each finds there confirmation of his own vision of the world … Life does *not* have a goal:

pain always prevails over joy; we are all [men] condemned to death to
whom the day of execution has not been revealed; we are condemned to
be present at the death of those we hold dearest ... We know all this, and
yet something protects us and sustains us and distances us from the shipwreck. What is this protection? Possibly only the habit of living, which one
acquires by being born.

This is a fairly forthright defence of suicide articulated with characteristic Levian equilibrium. Whether congenital or acquired, perma-
nent or transient, psychic dystopia is not just a natural (and therefore
value neutral) state of being but also, ultimately, the logical conclusion
that only an acquired ignorance keeps us from reaching. Interesting,
too, is the punitive outcome of Walter's search for the mysterious L
Factor, a natural biochemical substance that maintains the mandate to
live: the spokesman for suicide is killed off, in the end. And, in fact,
Levi inserts a double-edged parody in his description of Walter, who
functions as a *reductio ad absurdum* of Homer's epic hero Ulysses, also
punished for his hubristic thirst for knowledge. What's more, the recol-
lection of Ulysses is also a self-citation, when Levi recalls his own use of
Dante's description (*Inferno*, canto 26) of Ulysses drowning in *Se questo
è un uomo*: 'Tre volte il fé girar con tutte l'acque: / a la quarta levar la
poppa in suso / e la prora ire in giù, come l'altrui piacque.' Walter's
companion saw

una massiccia ondata di corpi inquieti sovrapporsi alla prima, e una terza
alla seconda, cosicché la massa ribollente giunse all'altezza della cintura
di Walter; vide Walter ... barcollare, strappato al riparo del masso, cadere
ed essere trascinato, sepolto e ancora trascinato, visibile a tratti come un
rigonfiamento sotto il fiume delle piccole innumerevoli creature disperate,
che correvano verso la morte.[18]

a massive wave of restless bodies superimpose itself on the first, and a
third on the second, so that the seething mass reached the height of Walter's waist; she saw Walter ... torn from the shelter of the boulder, sway,
fall and be dragged, buried and dragged again, visible at times as a swelling under the river of countless disparate little creatures, who ran toward
the sea.

Where Ulysses' ship rose and fell in the waves 'come l'altrui piacque'
(as pleased God), Walter's body submits somewhat more ignomini-

ously to death in a sea of rodents, as pleased Levi: the lemmings he was attempting to inoculate with the L Factor .

Moreover, Levi's story uses terms that complement the ones with which he described the bestial bellows of Trakl and Celan when he wrote, 'L'effabile è preferibile all'ineffabile.' Apparently, suicidality exists not just in the mind of the deficient writer but also in the reader: *l'ineffabile* here means both indescribable and *illegible:* 'Il perché sta scritto in ogni cellula, ma in un linguaggio che non sappiamo leggere con la mente.' I'll stop here with this line of inquiry; my point is simply that if we are mining his fiction for indices of a preoccupation with suicide, we need not dig very deep to strike gold. Not an anomaly within Levi's opus, 'Verso occidente' is, on the contrary, a very typically Levian story, and one that offers ample ammunition for a conventional reading of the suicidal author.

We might expect readers who are convinced of the connections between Levi's concentration camp experiences and his suicide to focus on *La zona grigia* ('The Gray Zone,' described in *The Drowned and the Saved*). By 'gray zone,' Levi means the idea that victims can also be guilty, in some limited way, of inflicting violence on others, and that perpetrators can also be capable of acts of kindness or virtue: that is, can also be innocent. Though it seems like unnecessary muddying of the waters of good and evil, it is, rather, typically Levian both in its nuance and in its preference for individual cases over wholesale generalities. But articulations of any form of survivor's guilt (of which this is a form) are like catnip to those readers who seek confirmation of the suicide in the opus, and who regard survivor guilt as a presage of suicide.[19] Thus (at the risk of further flattening the differences between writer-suicides), *La zona grigia* is *not* read in the same way as, say, Guido Morselli's *Capitolo breve sul suicidio* or *Dissipatio H.G.*—that is, though not necessarily his greatest work *in assoluto*, as the one most relevant to the question of his death insofar as it is a sustained meditation on the subject.[20] Let us return now to my observation at the beginning of the chapter about the uses and abuses of Levi's writings: specifically, let us examine the detachment of the gray zone from the historical circumstances in which Levi elucidated it, and its deployment in the service of contemporary theory.

The Moral Witness

La sua morte fa venire in mente il detto ebraico secondo il quale il mondo può essere distrutto fra il mattino e la sera. Ma la morte non distrugge il valore e quella di Levi non distrugge Levi; niente sarebbe piú insensato, dinanzi al mistero insindacabile della sua scelta, di chiedersi perché o di confrontare la vitalità dimostrata ad Auschwitz con la decisione di oggi. Smarriti e addolorati, piú per noi che per lui che ci lascia piú soli, noi possiamo solo abbracciare Primo Levi e ringraziarlo per averci mostrato, con la sua vita, di che cosa possa essere capace un uomo, per averci insegnato a ridere anche della mostruosità e a non avere paura.[21]

His death calls to mind the Hebrew saying according to which the world can be destroyed between the morning and the evening. But death does not destroy value and Levi's death does not destroy him; nothing would be more foolish, before the uncensurable mystery of his choice, to ask why or to compare the vitality he demonstrated in Auschwitz with today's decision. Lost and saddened, more for ourselves than for him, who leaves us more alone, we can only embrace Primo Levi and thank him for having shown us, with his life, of what a man is capable, for having taught us to laugh even at monstrosity and not to be afraid.

In his *The Ethics of Memory*, philosopher Avishai Margalit calls Levi a paradigmatic example of the 'moral witness,' that is, someone who both witnesses first-hand the suffering caused by evil deeds, and suffers from them him- or herself. For Margalit, the act of bearing witness, which may also carry the risk of further suffering or danger, is motivated by the desire to be heard by a moral community, who 'ascribes intrinsic value to his testimony, no matter what the instrumental consequences of it are going to be'[22] (in contrast, say, to a political witness whose testimony is meant to change the immediate political landscape): 'The hope with which I credit a moral witness is a rather sober hope: that in another place or another time there exists, or will exist, a moral community that will listen to their testimony.'[23] Such a motivation has been regularly ascribed to Levi's writings and is consonant with the mandate articulated most forcefully by the survivor community 'never to forget.' The question remains, however, about what happens to Levi's status as moral witness after his suicide. For Margalit, the 'minimum moral community ... is between oneself and one's future self, who the current self hopes will retain a moral outlook. The minimal hope of a moral witness is ... a belief about the future self.'[24] This would seem to imply that upon his death, indeed because of the method and manner of his death, Levi stops being a moral witness because he is no longer addressing himself to a future self.

Margalit does not draw this conclusion and neither do I; and yet, Levi's suicide does have ramifications for the category of moral witness: first, it prompts the question about the *value* of his testimony, casting a retroactive pall not on its truth-value, but rather on its therapeutic value. If remembering a humiliation means reliving it (Margalit notes Baudelaire's assertion: 'I am the wound and the dagger'), then are we not better off simply trying to forget? Must the wound be the dagger? According to this logic, Levi's suicide implies that the certain suffering caused by bearing witness (which is predicated on the ability to remember) outweighs any value it might have to a potential moral community. (And it thereby creates a kind of vicious circle. We want to survive to bear witness but bearing witness is too painful to survive.) Second, it mitigates the force of a potential moral community, which now seems an insufficiently ephemeral justification for the risks, psychological and physical, run by the witness. And third, it reinscribes the event being witnessed as the central or constitutive event in the witness's life, regardless of its actual relevance to the suicide. It becomes much more difficult, in Levi's case, to ascribe his suicide to anything but the 'bleeding scar'[25] of memory, whether or not that was its primary impetus. It has been my contention throughout this study that the motives for suicide are ultimately unknowable to any but the suicide. To attribute Levi's suicide to the memory of the camps is just a more exalted version of the commonly held belief that Morselli killed himself because of his failure to publish, or Pavese because of his failure to perform. I prefer instead to privilege elements of Levi's 'pretraumatic personality'[26] over the camps in a discussion of motives, mostly in an effort to balance my general discomfort with what sometimes feels like a wholesale pathologizing of survivors with a recognition of the enormity of their suffering. For these reasons, Levi's case, I believe, demarcates and illuminates the outermost limits of the category of the moral witness by virtue of the apparent contradiction between a lifetime of addressing a moral community and the seemingly sudden loss of interest therein. Levi's suicide does not disqualify him as a moral witness, but it does point out our anxiety about the inconsistencies that comprise anyone's life.

The Perfect Witness

During his lifetime, Levi's concern with memory and with the vital task of bearing witness founded discourses of commemoration and memory that threaten to undermine the importance of (or even expurgate) his other concerns after his death. Giorgio Agamben, for example, blurs the boundaries between discourses of meaning and of commemoration with his deployment of the category of the *perfect* witness, of which Levi is the apotheosis, proposed in *Remnants of Auschwitz*. Levi occasions Agamben's study of the (im)possibility of bearing witness, which he calls 'Levi's paradox.' Set on exploiting concepts in Levi's writing in order to conjure up aporias, particularly with respect to the category of the 'drowned,' Agamben's true witnesses are impossible witnesses:

> The 'true' witnesses, the 'complete witnesses,' are those who did not bear witness and could not bear witness. They are those who 'touched bottom': the Muslims, the drowned. The survivors speak in their stead, by proxy, as pseudo-witnesses; they bear witness to a missing testimony.[27]

Compared to Margalit, Agamben is much more instrumental in his use of Levi as the apotheosis of this category. Levi's status in this vision is already unclear – he is at once a survivor and a perfect witness, that is to say one of the drowned. But both of these positions require the excision of Levi's suicide as a Procrustean limb. The implication of Agamben's paradox – that the survivor speaks on behalf of the perfect witness – is that after his death, Levi no longer occupies either position. This is not because the determination with which he vaulted the railing in his apartment building is in direct opposition to the death-by-inches visited upon the barely sentient drowned. It is due, rather, to Agamben's insistence that the witness is always already dead. But there is, I would argue, a connection to be made between the critical reticence that surrounds his suicide and the collective avoidance of the drowned Agamben describes, which could also describe Agamben's own attitude toward the *suicide*: it is 'almost as if silence and not seeing were the only demeanor adequate for those who are beyond help.'[28]

My point is certainly not to mystify the commonplace observation that the dead no longer speak for themselves but are spoken for. Rather, I want simply to underscore the way that after Levi's death, the representative for Holocaust survivors no longer speaks on behalf of others. The problem of Levi's suicide for Margalit's moral witness and Agamben's impossible witnesses, taken together, forms a kind of Scylla and Charybdis on which, whichever way he goes, the figure of Levi must crash. Levi can't be dead and yet he must be dead. We are returning, from a different vantage point, to the idea of the post-biological author, whose suicide, we said, both terminates and inaugurates his life. Where

Pavese's post-biologicity involved the ideological interpellation of the body of the author, Levi is subject to a variation on this interpellation when the discourses of commemoration and memory he founded are co-opted. By constructing theoretical edifices around Levi's writerly memorials, Agamben and Margalit at once buttress the strength of those memorials and obscure their sources in Levi. They perform acts of ventriloquism so that Levi's own gestures of remembrance, such as when he claims 'We speak in their stead, by proxy'[29] or 'Nothing remains of [Hurbinek]: he bears witness through these words of mine,'[30] seem to emanate from them.

It is not surprising that Levian concepts such as *la zona grigia* form the very scaffolding in studies by both Margalit and Agamben. For Margalit, it is relevant for a subcategory of moral witness – one can occupy the gray zone if/when one behaves in a morally ambiguous manner, so long as that behaviour is motivated by the desire to survive and, eventually, bear moral witness. For Agamben, the gray zone occupies a central position in *Remnants of Auschwitz*, when he famously declares, 'This is the specific ethical aporia of Auschwitz: it is the site in which it is not decent to remain decent, in which those who believed themselves to preserve their dignity and self-respect experience shame with respect to those who do not.'[31] Note, however, that in neither of these cases is Agamben or Margalit speaking of a dead Levi; there is no discussion of suicide here. Instead, his term has been appropriated to apply, precisely, to a special category of living person. Margalit and Agamben, then, avert their eyes from the spectacle of suicide at the mere hint, in Levi's camp writings, that there might exist indices of potential motives for suicide. This blind spot tempts me to follow Agamben's neat formulation in *Remnants of Auschwitz* of a kind of biopolitics of reading: until the seventeenth century, he notes, 'Foucault characterizes sovereignty through the formula to make die and to let live.' Later, sovereign power increasingly becomes biopower, which is 'to make live and to let die.'[32] In the twentieth century, Agamben argues, we must even further amend the description: 'to make survive.'[33] Are we moving toward an interpretation of the suicidal author as the key to a new biopolitics of reading, whose goal is not (with Foucault) the creation of productive citizens, but rather of productive corpses, perhaps like Elvis Presley, who, as I said in my introduction, was never so busy during his lifetime as he is in death? In that sense, Levi, too, has been a productive corpse, made to survive in order to serve as an almost fetishistic object of commemorative acts that, like Elvis impersonators, seem designed less to commemorate him than they do to reflect glory on their own renditions of his greatest hits.

Communities of Memory

> Chi ha avuto l'occasione di confrontare l'immagine reale di uno scrittore con quella che si può desumere dai suoi scritti, sa quanto sia frequente il caso che esse non coincidano.[34]

> Whoever has had the occasion to compare the real picture of a writer with the one inferred from his writings knows how frequently it is the case that they do not coincide.

The question remains, however, about what happens to Levi's status as witness after his suicide. I am not interested in stripping him of his title but rather in understanding the modulations suicide imposes on this particular category, which seems so apposite during his lifetime.[35] As we said earlier, since his death, Levi has become a cultural phenomenon, a blank slate available for the inscription of agendas of all stripes. This has to do, I will argue, with the coexistence of widely diverse readers, all of whom believe Levi belongs to them – those who feel authorized to talk about 'their Levi'/'my Levi' (and these are, not coincidentally, often the same readers who contest his suicide). With Levi, in other words, conflicts have arisen between disparate factions whose only common denominator has to do not with reading Levi's writings, but precisely with reading *through* them to get to some more or less distant hermeneutical shore. Margalit's distinction between thin relations (concerned with our common humanity or some aspect thereof), and thick relations (concerned with our nearest and dearest), seems to me a useful way to get at the existence of readers for whom Levi is 'theirs.' For these, we might say that Levi occupies both of the usually discrete spaces, so that his thin relations are also thick.[36]

Alternatively we can borrow Margalit's concept of ethical communities of memory, which are, essentially, communities that care (and where caring can be used to mean mourning). If a community of memory is a community that, having evolved around a shared relation or set of relations to the dead, consists of members who care for the same reasons, then we must ask who cares, and why.[37] To begin with the first question, we can imagine any number of communities that might wish to claim him as their own. We might equally imagine potential conflicts between these groups, just as we saw exist between those for whom Levi constitutes a thick relation, a thin one, and both. Take, as an initial example, Levi's Judaism. The posthumous enlistment of Levi into the ranks of the practising religious rankled some critics: 'Non c'è niente di piú maliconico del tentativo di trasformarlo, dopo la sua morte, in una specie di santone ebreo'[38] (There is nothing sadder than trying to transform him, after his death, into some kind of Jewish dogmatist). Especially offensive is the declaration that Levi 'è morto di sabato come un rabbi' (died on a Saturday like a rabbi), given that 'il suicidio è l'atto irreligioso per eccellenza e si può tranquillamente escludere che nella vasta letteratura religiosa ebraica ci sia qualche testo che lo raccomanda per santificare il sabato'[39] (suicide is the profane act *par excellence* and one can tranquilly exclude the possibility that in the vast religious literature of Judaism, there exists any text that recommends it for sanctifying the Sabbath). Sergio Parussa cautions that we risk oversimplification when we draw too close a connection between Levi's writing and his ambivalent Jewish identity. Parussa observes that 'by describing Primo Levi's work and his interest in Jewish identity as consequences of Auschwitz, by tying the Jewish literary and artistic experience exclusively to the Shoah, Western culture risks reducing the renewal of Jewish culture in the twentieth century, and Jewish culture as a whole, to experiences *in negativo*, that is, shaped, kept alive, and made possible only by the external force of persecution.'[40] Thus Levi's status as a writer (one difficult to pin down to any one category, to boot) and the writings themselves (including the history of their publication, which is bound up at least initially with historical and political questions) are doubly inflected with his relationship to Judaism. These questions in turn effected the kinds of communities of memory that developed around Levi after his death, which privileged his identity as a witness to history, concentration camp survivor, Jew (an identity subtended by others – non-Yiddish-speaking, Sephardic, Italian, secular, and so on), and scientist, to name a few.[41] There is, of course, overlap between these groups, but there is a way in which we can argue that part of the difficulty of countenancing Levi's suicide lies precisely in his appurtenance, *volente o nolente*, to so many groups.

Thus, there is a community of memory comprising scholars interested in his literary legacy (it, too, fractured into various factions). Among these, the focus is almost exclusively on the content and tone of Levi's writings, and its content (in the case of the Holocaust writings) is important for autobiographical and historical reasons, never for literary ones. Compared to the body of writings that deal with Levi's position in history, relatively few critics talk about the literary or technical aspects of his writing. Readers might note his tone or discuss, sometimes in depth, the influence of Dante or Rabelais, but it is a small minority who discuss the nuts and bolts of his writings, even of his poetry.[42] What's more, Levi himself does a fair amount of the critical legwork for the reader, by providing a critical gloss on his works both within those same works and in other, related ones. In Elio Gioanola's words,

> Si può dire che la difficoltà di scrivere su Levi è direttamente proporzionale alla facilità dello stile, che mira alla chiarezza e alla trasparenza comunicativa, oltre che alla tendenza dello scrittore, ulteriormente frustrante per il critico, ad anticipare costantemente con le sue riflessioni metanarrative le velleità di interpretazione: cosa dire di testi tanto chiari che parlano da sé e tanto esplicitamente commentati da non lasciare margini, almeno in apparenza, per ulteriori commenti? Non è certo strano che molta critica si limiti ad un gioco di citazioni dell'autore, variamente combinate e accostate. È probabile che l'unica strada davvero percorribile per scrivere su Levi in modo non soltanto illustrativo sia quella di far problema dell'apparente mancanza di problemi ... Ma dire che è difficile scrivere su Primo Levi può anche suonare ambiguo, perché nasconde, o può nascondere, la diffidenza del letterato per un tipo di scrittura sentita come poco letteraria, troppo corriva rispetto alle intenzioni denotative per riuscire poeticamente creativa. Non c'è troppa deferenza verso i referenti realistici e mentali, troppo scoperta adesione alle idee chiare e distinte?[43]

One can say that the difficulty of writing about Levi is directly proportional to the facility of his style, which aims for clarity and communicative transparency, as well as to the writer's tendency, ultimately frustrating for the critic, of constantly anticipating with his metanarrative reflections the ambitions of interpretation: what can one say about texts so clear they speak for themselves, and so explicitly commented that they leave no margin, at least so it seems, for further comments? It is certainly not strange that much of the criticism is limited to a game of author citations, combined and juxtaposed in various ways. It's probable that the only road that really can be travelled to write about Levi in a way that is not just illustrative is to problematize the apparent lack of problems ... But to say

that it is hard to write about Levi can also sound ambiguous, because it
hides, or can hide, the critic's diffidence with respect to a type of writing
felt to be not very literary, too hasty with respect to its denotative intentions to succeed as poetically creative. Is there not too much deference
toward realistic and mental referents, too much naked adherence to clear
and distinct ideas?

The upshot of this 'naked adherence' to the value of clarity is that some
critics show a marked preference for certain of Levi's writings,[44] such
that the reverence we mentioned earlier toward Levi's texts of testimony (*Se questo è un uomo*, *La tregua*, and *I sommersi e i salvati* in particular) entails an attendant impatience with those works that don't deal
directly with the *univers concentrationnaire* and its aftermath.[45] Some of
Levi's texts enjoyed immediate and enduring public affirmation, but
there was also reluctance on the part of the critics to embrace Levi when
he deviates from the topic of the camps (think, for example, of critiques
of his imperfect Piedmontese dialect in *La chiave a stella*[46] or the accusation of triteness and predictability often levelled at his poetry unless it
deals with the camps, like the prefatory poem at the front of *Se questo
è un uomo*).

I contend that this is a function of the double-pronged approach
readers apply to Levi. First, I think we can observe the presence of an
implicit hierarchy of genres[47] with respect to Levi, by which I mean the
idea that the work of the witness is more valuable than that of the fiction writer, which in turn is more valuable than that of the autobiogra-
pher or memoirist.[48] Note that this view implies a fairly clear separation
between the various genres, seen as unalloyed and discrete entities.
This brings me to the second observation, namely that this separation or boundary explains the relative insistence with which readers
privilege Levi's camp writings. It is not grounded exclusively in their
superior craftsmanship but rather has also to do with a blind spot[49] in
our reading strategies, which prevents us from seeing the two sides
of the coin: the way fiction is autobiographical in some way, shape, or
form, and the way autobiography is (in some way or another) fictional. I repeat these are reading strategies, not writing strategies (recall
de Man's observation that autobiography is not a genre but a way of
reading),[50] hence their relevance to my question about communities of
memory. Thus we can identify sub-communities within what we might
call his professional readership, whose appreciation of Levi's works
varies depending on their theoretical convictions about the intersec-

tions of narrative, history, and autobiography. This is a function of the conflicting processes to which Levi's works constantly submit, visible in the play of citations to which Gioanola referred. Sara Vandewaetere calls this process *decontextualization* (that is, the citation of sound bytes that give a false sense of coherence to his work because they do not take into account the texts in which he contradicts or complicates the citation) and *hypercontextualization* (in which reader's digest versions of his writings are placed in dialogue with otherwise irrelevant sources).[51] I would add that these, in turn, are compounded by the fact of his suicide – what I called earlier the 'strange bedfellows' phenomenon of authorial suicide – which provides a whole new set of teammates with whom to play the game of citations.

Self-Fashioning and Trauma

> Che fare, adesso? Come staccarsene?
> Ad ogni opera nata muori un poco.[52]

> What to do now? How to detach oneself?
> With the birth of every work, you die a little.

But these communities, it should be said, did not simply spring up, full-grown and autonomous, after Levi's death; he himself must certainly have played a role in all this during his lifetime. Stanislao Pugliese's summary of Levi's psychological development gives us a clue as to how this role manifested itself: 'In a self-fashioning that overcame numerous physical, psychological, and external obstacles, Levi managed to move from trauma to transgression and finally testimony in an attempt to defeat the demons (real and imaginary) that plagued him most of his life.'[53] It is interesting to contemplate the possibility that his legacy derives at least in part from acts of self-fashioning, given the broad emphasis generally given to the truth-value of his writings, though this is perhaps belied by the vexed question of genre in the case of his early works. For example, Levi made claims – implicitly and explicitly – that *Se questo è un uomo* was simple, unvarnished testimony, when, as his biographer Ian Thomson puts it, 'it is in fact a teeming, intensely literary work of great complexity, and far more calculatedly bookish than Levi cared to admit.'[54] One need only read the chapter entitled 'The Canto of Ulysses' in *Se questo è un uomo* to understand that this is so.[55] This question of self-fashioning is important because it is at stake in the play between the dead and the communities of memory that surround and develop around them, communities who may be committed to preserving certain kinds of memories.

As a result, the question of what kind of writer Levi *considered himself* to be is particularly important when it clashes with public perceptions about his writings.[56] Levi himself attributes his career as a writer to Auschwitz: '[I]f I had not lived the Auschwitz experience, I probably would never have written anything. I would not have had the motivation, the incentive, to write.'[57] It is partly observations such as these that some commentators see as justification for the reduction of Levi's will to live to the will – or ability – to write.[58] As was the case with Pavese, it is tempting to see Levi's life and writings as coterminous – Levi died, goes the logic, because there was nothing more (or of sufficient importance) to write.[59] Note that in this instance we see an extension, in reverse, of the hunt for proleptic suicidal moments in his writings; once reassured of their absence, the critic is free to expound upon the inspirational moments in his work, then lay her pencil aside. Auschwitz, by this logic, means writing or communication, broadly writ: the wound become dagger:

> Così finalmente la moltiplicazione delle lingue diventa un tramite per superare le differenze e unire gli uomini in un lavoro concorde. Conclusione ottimistica, poi smentita però da Levi uomo, con la sua morte che è anche un messaggio. Egli è salito sulla Torre di Babele o Torre del Carburo, e se ne è gettato a capofitto.[60]

> Thus finally the multiplication of languages becomes a pathway by which to overcome differences and unite men in harmonious work. An optimistic conclusion, later disavowed by Levi the man, with his death that serves also as a message. He climbed the Tower of Babel or the Tower of Carbide, and threw himself off head-first.

Other, intermittently contradictory, interventions by Levi seem geared toward keeping the Holocaust before our eyes. This is certainly a worthy enterprise – never to forget – but coming from a writer who simultaneously asks not to be considered exclusively a witness/survivor, sometimes these acts of commemoration seem gratuitous, like his appearance on the radio program ('Little Theater of Memory,' which aired in Italy in 1982)[61] in which guest hosts chose fifteen or so of their favourite musical pieces.[62] In Levi's case, no fewer than seven of the pieces, as he described them, were directly associated either with the implementation of the Racial Laws or with his experiences in or on his way home from the Lager.[63] One might imagine that Levi might choose to see this as an opportunity to air another side of his work or interests, such as music that, say, comments in some way on scientific phenomena. Acts of self-fashioning – what Levi chooses publicly to remember or, as Gioanola would have it, the fundamental condition of difference on which Levi's identity depends – lay the foundations for future communities of memory.

But if, as Margalit asserts, the 'memory of humiliation is the bleeding scar of reliving it',[64] then the potentially therapeutic, political, and artistic value of remembering must be considered to come at a heavy price:

> Humiliation … is not just another experience in life, like, say, an embarrassment. It is a formative experience. It forms the way we view ourselves as humiliated persons … Humiliation, in the strong sense, in being a fundamental assault on us as human beings, becomes constitutive of one sense of who we are.[65]

Acts of self-fashioning such as the incessant reference to suffering – what Levi chooses publicly to remember – confound the tendency to promote bowdlerized visions of Levi. For this reason, we must resist the temptation to expurgate suicide from the record – to ignore the fact that this survivor did not survive the way we like them to – just as we must not dismiss the persistence of trauma as an explanation for Levi's suicide, but rather to acknowledge the after-effects of trauma without pathologizing the survivors. Both instrumental to his success as an artist – the wound and the dagger – and to his status as a 'moral witness,' Levi's enduring preoccupation with suffering is a way of maintaining a moral community of memory, that is, one galvanized by the memory of a crime against our common humanity.

Conclusions

Shemà
Voi che vivete sicuri
Nelle vostre tiepide case
Voi che trovate tornando a sera
Il cibo caldo e visi amici:

Considerate se questo è un uomo,
Che lavora nel fango
Che non conosce pace
Che lotta per un mezzo pane
Che muore per un sí o un no.
Considerate se questa è una donna,
Senza capelli e senza nome
Senza più forze da ricordare
Vuoti gli occhi e freddo il grembo
Come una rana d'inverno.
Meditate che questo è stato:
Vi commando queste parole.
Scolpitele nel vostro cuore
Stando in casa andando per via,
Coricandovi alzandovi:
Ripetetele ai vostri figli.
O vi si sfaccia la casa,
La malattia vi impedisca,
I vostri nati torcano il viso da voi.[66]

You who live safe
In your warm houses,
You who find, returning in the evening,
Hot food and friendly faces:
Consider if this is a man
Who works in the mud
Who does not know peace
Who fights for a scrap of bread
Who dies because of a yes or no.
Consider if this is a woman,
Without hair and without name
With no more strength to remember,
Her eyes empty and her womb cold
Like a frog in winter.
Meditate that this came about:
I commend these words to you.
Carve them in your hearts
At home, in the street,
Going to bed, rising;

Repeat them to your children,
> Or may your house fall apart,
> May illness impede you,
> May your children turn their faces from you.

Let us return to our discussion of the intersections between Agamben's and Margalit's terms. In the declaration about the gray zone cited earlier, Agamben notes the contradiction of indecent decency, or shameful dignity, that emerges in the backwards glance of the survivor. Margalit's gaze, in contrast, is trained forward to the future goals of this indecently decent or immoral moral witness. What has yet to be accounted for, in these visions, is a sense of the present, of a way for the protagonists to make meaning of their experiences as they take place, or, put differently, of the obfuscating nature of the paradox. My concern, in other words, is that the rhetorical structure of the paradox glosses over or mystifies the experience in a way that Agamben, at least, claims to bemoan. At the same time, Levi's suicide appears to ground the teleology of the reading Agamben makes in *Homo Sacer*, in which suicide is the threshold event that creates a new order, that brings *zoe* into *bios*, or bare life into the polis, in the one exemplary space or historical moment in which it was already there. That is, if the concentration camp is the site par excellence in which bare or unqualified life is transformed into a bio-political concept,[67] then my reading of suicide as that transformational event is redundant; the inscription of the corpus upon the corpse has already happened by the time Levi dies. Levi himself seems to say as much when he notes of the Muselmänner that '[o]ne hesitates to call their death death.'[68]

Levi's *Se questo è un uomo* (*If This Is a Man*) was written between December 1945 and January 1947, that is, almost immediately upon his return home from Auschwitz.[69] It was written, he says,

[per] fornire documenti per uno studio pacato di alcuni aspetti dell'animo umano. A molti, individui o popoli, può accadere di ritenere, piú o meno consapevolmente, che 'ogni straniero è nemico'. Per lo piú questa convinzione giace in fondo agli animali come una infezione latente; si manifesta solo in atti saltuari e incoordinati, e non sta all'origine di un sistema di pensiero. Ma quando questo avviene, quando il dogma inespresso diventa premessa maggiore di un sillogismo, allora, al termine della catena, sta il Lager. Esso è il prodotto di una concezione del mondo portata alle sue

conseguenze con rigorosa coerenza: finché la concezione sussiste, le conseguenze ci minacciano. La storia dei campi di distruzione dovrebbe venire intesa da tutti come un sinistro segnale di pericolo.[70]

to furnish documentation for a quiet study of certain aspects of the human mind. Many people – many nations – can find themselves holding, more or less wittingly, that 'every stranger is an enemy'. For the most part this conviction lies deep down like some latent infection; it betrays itself only in random, disconnected acts, and does not lie at the base of a system of reason. But when this does come about, when the unspoken dogma becomes the major premiss in a syllogism, then, at the end of the chain, there is the Lager. Here is the product of a conception of the world carried rigorously to its logical conclusion; so long as the conception subsists, the conclusion remains to threaten us. The story of the death camps should be understood by everyone as a sinister alarm-signal.[71]

If the xenophobia of which Levi writes ('every stranger is an enemy') is indeed endemic to all humanity, then so is the politicization of humanity as well: all bodies conceal enemy combatants. For Levi, the transformation of bare life into political life is an ever-present potentiality, in need only of incitement in the form of systematization or organization. Writing, then, is a double-edged sword – it is integral to the movement toward the transformation of bare life into political life, insofar as it can provide the scaffolding upon which to build the institutions of xenophobia, as well as protection against it in the form of warning. Indeed, the very title of the book Levi produced as 'documentation for a quiet study' encapsulates this progression from bare to political life, in the form of a question. The volume's prefatory poem, quoted above, supports such a reading when it questions the humanity of the Lager victims and by extension, the humanity of those who subjected the victims to the hardships, humiliation, and death of which the poem speaks.[72] The division of humanity into a series of implicit and explicit binaries – victim and tormentor, man and woman, man (understood as mankind) and non-man, speaker and interlocutor, bearer of experience and bearer of memory – leaves no neutral or third space (tertium non datur, as Morselli often remarked) from which to answer the question. 'Is this a man' implicates both elements in each dyad but in different ways: one's humanity is up for grabs for creating the Lager as it is for experiencing it. In either case, humanity means bodies (most forcefully embodied by the woman in lines 10–14, who is without hair, has empty eyes and a cold womb) and bodies are inherently of the polis, whether as its governors or its subjects.[73]

More broadly, Levi's suicide reframes the question articulated in his poem, to encompass the thanatopolitics always already constitutive of sovereign life itself. Levi's death does not reinscribe him as the double man of suicide, since, insofar as his life/works already inhabited a state of exception, he had already crossed the threshold – infinite corpus and finite corpse, individual and institution, mortal and immortal. Nor is he available for exaltation or condemnation, as we argued with Pavese. Instead, Levi's *homo sacer* disavows the ontological uncertainty evoked in the poem's rhetorical strategy of questioning ('is this a man?') and posits in its place the certainty of a pre-existing narrative to counter those of the Lager. Or, as one scholar puts it,

[I]n the last analysis, political power must absorb death, for death – the *right* to death ... (... the decision as to what *counts* as death and *when* and in *what way* death counts *as death* and not simply perishing, which is to say, if death, and thus the life it most intimately articulates, counts *at all*), is the ontological decision whereby the living being can remain possible *unto its own-most self.*[74]

Levi's articulation of a narrative thanatopolitics derives from the heart not just of the suicidal subject but of humanity itself ('ask yourselves if this is a man'): it partakes in this vision 'whereby the living being can remain possible *unto its own-most self.*' I began this book with the observation that all suicides seem in some way to speak to one another, that they form a society unto themselves. In my reading, far from being excluded from determining '*when* and in *what way* death counts *as death*,' that society is an all-inclusive one, in which we as readers must participate. To do otherwise is to create a new order built upon a double imperative – to refuse death to its members, and to consecrate those deaths to some kind of new hermeneutical rule. We have seen that Levi's posthumous fortune reveals the other side of the same coin I described in chapters past. Where other suicides' lives are scrutinized for clues identifying the death in the work, Levi's readers seek evidence of outside factors to explain the death, with ramifications for the discourses of survival and testimony interlaced throughout his opus. Levi makes for an even more dramatic argument for the dangers of this logic of exceptionalism, which renders the suicide's work ineligible for the rules of scholarly engagement. Readerly participation as I described it just now, therefore, means relinquishing our impossible desire to negotiate with these dead or to ask them to arise and explain themselves, where we would otherwise take up the challenge of tending to their work ourselves, and leave the dead in peace.

Postscript: Learning from the Dead

I started with the question of how the knowledge of an author's suicide changes our approach to a text. I have argued that authorial suicide repositions the author as central to our understanding of a text, and, more broadly, it reveals the continued critical challenges posed by authors and authorship. The suicide of an author complicates the possibility of negotiating between historicist and linguistic readings of literature by redimensioning or throwing into crisis the relationship between a work and the specific or situated subject who created it. Posthumous assessments of our authors' works inevitably attempt to reckon with or account for the suicide in some way. These accounts eventually gain the kind of critical mass that consolidates as doxy or received wisdom about the author. They adhere tenaciously in the popular imagination as interpretive keys (suicide for love, professional failure, mental illness, and so on) with which to unlock the meaning of the work. Rather like ultrasounds, these miniature explicatory narratives reveal the life noiselessly kicking within the work. But also like ultrasounds they require a certain degree of interpretation, and there is precious little consensus nonetheless about what the picture means: how best to understand the complex logic of interactions along the three axes of the triangle author – reader – work.

I proposed alternate readings of four authors that neither eschew the referential particulars of the writing subject, attending only to the formal qualities of his or her production, nor depend on limiting the text's possible meanings to the historical and cultural parameters embodied in the figure of the author. It is not simply a question of refusing to let the suicide over-determine the reading and, indeed, I have taken seriously criticism that approaches the author from the vantage point of his or her suicide, though it is not an approach I advocate, because engaging with how these authors have been read is a productive opening for discussing broader questions about literature and life. My consistent approach, instead, has been to bracket the suicide temporarily, in order to attend to the questions, themes, and issues of concern to the author, be they philosophical (Morselli), biological/psychological (Rosselli), historical (Pavese), or ontological (Levi). This bracketing has allowed other texts to emerge that a reading through the suicide might have precluded, texts whose relevance would not be readily apparent otherwise. Returning to the suicide in conjunction with these texts has also helped me to resist the urge to reduce the myriad messy episodes of a life into a neat, unified narrative. The historical particulars of a Kofman, for example, can incorporate and make meaning from the biographical specifics of a Rosselli without pretending that Rosselli's or Kofman's texts don't radically exceed the boundaries of that juxtaposition.

At the same time, it is somewhat disingenuous of me to imply that the conventions of reading lie at the two extremes of the spectrum with regard to the position of the author when, in practice, few readers these days are so militantly anti-authorial as to take at face value the notion that we are written by language and not the reverse, and, similarly, few critics expect literature to provide an unobstructed view of the bottom of the author's heart. But even so – even if the two positions are closer than my simplified view implies – one's belief in the author and especially his or her intentions, or lack thereof, is arguably one of the single most determinant factors in one's approach to the work: tell me what you think about authors and I will tell you who you are.

And yet it is not entirely hyperbolic to say that when an author dies by his own hand, he is resuscitated: sometimes by the very people who had signed his death certificate. That is, in the presence of certain corpses, we become somewhat more fluid in our theoretical positions, as is evinced in the parabolic relations between the popular, humanist, pro-subject responses to an author's death and critical ones apparent in, say, posthumous scholarly assessments of Rosselli. Crystallizing what had been a growing tendency (almost from the get-go in Barthes and Derrida) toward what in many ways resembles Foucault's author function, we infer coherence from the author's signature, seek signs of authorial intention both within individual texts and across the oeuvre, and bequeath authority upon the biography. The suicidal author assumes the contours of a Romantic author, becoming a transcendental signifier that anchors an otherwise free-floating chain of signifiers. S/he returns us to the realm of history and of representation although previously we professed to be interested only in language. The exception in this study has been Levi, who was always already a kind of transcendental signifier and whose death threatens that status.

Barthes, for example, was neither the singular source of the stance, nor was he totally against authors. Indeed, read as the culmination of Barthes's dissatisfaction with the kinds of uses and abuses to which authors and authorship had been put in the years before his 1968 essay, the vehement if purposely provocative stance of his 'Death of the Author' comes as no great surprise. Derrida, too, was much more nuanced in his approach to authorship than is commonly assumed. As we have seen, the suicide of Sarah Kofman occasioned, in *The Work of Mourning*, a return to a Romantic view of the subject that stresses her singularity. But that is not to say that his meditation on Kofman is a unique instance. On the contrary: Derrida's concern throughout *The Work of Mourning* is precisely to reconnect the subject in all his or her (Kofman is the only woman in the volume) historical and geographical specificity, giving names, dates, and titles as well as anecdotes about private conversations, disagreements, meals shared, travels undertaken together, all in the service of reconstructing the 'singularity' of his friendship with the dead, as well as the singularity of his or her death. Consider, in this regard, the essay on Gilles Deleuze, whose suicide meets with many of the same impulses that are typical of the popular press, such as the retrospective claim that it was always en route: 'More than anything else, Deleuze the thinker is the thinker of the event and always of this event in particular. From beginning to end, he remained a thinker of this event.'[1] Also common among survivors of a suicide is Derrida's urge to reread the suicide's works with the hope of finding insight: he will 'continue – or begin again – to read Gilles Deleuze in order to learn.'[2] His death offers 'the chance to think, thanks to him, by thinking about him':[3] in other words, to reinstate the subject within the author. And no fewer than three times in the course of this brief essay, Derrida remarks upon some exclusive quality of Deleuze: he was 'the philosopher of serial singularity';[4] 'the one among all those of my "generation" to whom I have always considered myself closest';[5] 'the one among all this "generation" who "was doing" philosophy the most gaily, the most innocently.'[6] Indeed, much of the collection contained in the *Work of Mourning* is devoted to recuperating the uniqueness of the departed, or trying to avoid the strange bedfellows move, that is, the inevitable association or pluralization of the dead, which Derrida calls 'infidelity.'

It might be argued that it takes time and retrospection to see where these reading practices (of which I have made Barthes and Derrida the champions, though Foucault would be relevant here as well) stop short of fully maintaining their premises, and that the equivocations of deconstruction with regard to death are clear to see once these practices, too, are dead. But I have relied upon and been inspired by the methods of deconstruction too regularly to make such claims, or, in any case, not to recognize that 'we speak with the words of the dead,'[7] who haunt us so that we can learn from them. And what they have taught is that authorial suicide is an instance that cannot be comfortably contained. To return to the image we used earlier, the critical quandaries it produces continue to loom, both hovering (as a passive presence) and weaving (as an active agent), actively shaping our engagement with a text: they give it colour and texture, enhancing the narrative fabric.

At the same time that suicide threatens critical practices (I called it critical kryptonite earlier), it equally bestows its powers on the author. But as at least one superhero will confirm, that power entails a certain responsibility, which here takes the form of discursive might. We expect an author (though not necessarily a cellist or a tennis pro) to make meaningful pronouncements about the state of things, including his or her inner life, and we assume these pronouncements are in some way accessible to us, given the proper tools. Though in three of the texts I examined, the speaking subject (the last man standing in *Dissipatio H.G.*, Clelia in *Tra donne sole*, the poetic I of *Sleep*) does not explicitly identify with the author (Levi, we have seen, is identified as his own protagonist in his texts on survival), each is narrated by a strong first-person narrator who, in an instance of heteropseudonymous identification, implicates the author nonetheless. Let me return to the observation I made at the beginning of the last chapter. Recalling the invocation of 'my Levi,' I described the deep engagements that bind us to the figure of the author. Here I want to suggest that far from being an anomalous characteristic of Levi readers, it is in fact also exactly the result of an author's death: we make him or her ours, by filling in the gaps of our knowledge, by *writing* the author in a paradoxical gesture of deconstructive reconstitution. It is not exactly that where there was once text in the Barthesian sense, there is now work, so that readers now consume a product instead of producing it themselves: on the contrary, readers have never been busier constructing the text, reducing the distance between reading and writing, creating a text to suit the need for Foucauldian author coherence. We resurrect the body of the author, now structured like a text.

We resurrect him, prodded by a new and urgent desire for him and particularly for as detailed and historically specific a knowledge of him as can possibly be imagined. The goal of this specificity is, precisely, to ascertain his difference from us. The very specificity of our knowledge of him guarantees that in some way he and I are different. It is a variation on what Helen Deutsch calls the 'autoptic desire to see the thing itself, a seeing by oneself and of oneself,'[8] except in this case, the viewer hopes precisely to see signs of difference from oneself. This resurrection stems not from a position of *faith* in some ultimate truth embodied by the author (the position against which Barthes was reacting) but, arguably, from some deep-seated *fear*. Our need for reassurance is greater than our need for knowledge. If it is true, as Robert Pogue Harrison asserts, that grieving is self-referential[9] – that is, that we mourn ourselves and our own mortality when we mourn others – then it also follows that we might nonetheless prefer to see as few connections (beyond our common humanity) as possible. Hence our posthumous obsession with the biographical particulars of the author; we accomplish his estrangement in his reconstitution as the totally exceptional writing subject of an organic and coherent narrative (he died for love, and so on). For English speakers, this need for signs of difference is even visible at the linguistic level. The identification, in the word *suicide*, of the act with the agent forecloses the possibility of representing the dead in any position other than her last: unlike, say, the turgid ankles of the victim of gout, the noose stays in the picture. That identification of suicide as both act and agent is another strategy by which the survivor differentiates herself from that particular dead, or rather, from that particular death.

This is not necessarily to argue that suicide is unique as a hermeneutical watershed. Surely political revelations, such as those regarding Günter Grass or Paul de Man, cause analogously radical re-evaluations of their works. Similarly, readers are quick to reconsider the works of writers whose claims of autobiographism have been disputed, as were the cases of Augusten Burroughs, for example, or James Frey. Then again, the line between watershed revelation and otherwise inconsequential ones can be tough to draw. For example, antisocial behaviours are apparently relevant to our readings when they are associated with authors whose works promote or protect human dignity. Though I would certainly also argue that it was first and foremost their suicides that provoked such careful scrutiny of their lives, Arthur Koestler's works are also in some way altered by the knowledge of his history of committing sexual violence; the accusations of plagiarism impinge, at least marginally, on Jerzy Kozinski's identity as a Holocaust writer. On the other hand, stories about (non-suicide) John Cheever's vexed intimate life seem *not* to call for a wholesale revision of his oeuvre. The point is not that suicide is the only instance in which the life of the author has significant ramifications for reading: but it is, I believe, undeniably significant.

This is for many reasons, the most banal of which perhaps is because it is easy to catalogue suicides, as the Wikipedia page entitled 'Writers Who Committed Suicide' (277 entries) implies: it is certainly a more reliable statistic than, say, writers whose ideological stances were conflicted or writers who lived with cats. But the fact remains that we care about suicide more than cats or political commitment. We can ignore these, in some way, and merrily read with only a vague notion of the author's catlessness; not so the possibility of disregarding the knowledge that the person whose words one is reading – a person who has, in a sense, achieved immortality by virtue of his or her discursive abilities – has, since writing them, decided that nothing in the world, including the reader, matters enough. Thus we care – evidenced by the changes in reading strategies I have been tracking for the last 170 pages – because suicide is perceived to be unique and irreducible in each case, so that our impulse as survivors (for that is what we are, whether in the manner of thin or thick relations) is to discover the *sui generis* quality of each life. That we care is also, I believe, a function of a crisis of listening, if the general feeling (evinced by the relative success of suicide hotlines, crisis prevention centres, groups like the Samaritans, and so on) is that the simple act of listening can sometimes prevent a self-inflicted death. It is also the case that listening serves as what suicidologists call a *postvention*, a therapy designed to help alleviate the pain of survival. We described above how we are attentive to a suicide's words for the self-serving reason of delimiting their difference from us; let us also note the altruism of that potentially therapeutic attention.

For what we said about responses to Levi's suicide is, in the end, true of suicide in general: we handle it badly. No one wants to be the last one to leave the party, and no amount of talk about agency or courage can fully mitigate the pain of abandonment. Thus in the debate about the value of criticism and the supremacy of various methodologies of critical readings, I would like to offer the thought that readerly engagements with suicide are also proof of the enduring civic value, if you will, of our work. This is but one instance of the social function of literary criticism, and of the way its practitioners continue to have some kind of apostatic faith in a universal value, even if in this case it is simply the value of sticking around to see how the story ends.

Mine is not a rescue mission. I am not out to prove that from my alternative readings of these authors emerges a better writer, a more appealing person, a nobler or better justified death. But writing this book has caused me to re-evaluate my own feelings about suicide. I no longer view it as from afar, as something fascinating but utterly alien, like, say, life in the Gobi Desert, but rather have a clear sense of how close, at least potentially, it might come, or under which circumstances it might even seem desirable. These are generally not of the back-against-the-wall varieties of self-inflicted deaths Guido Morselli disqualified as suicides in his *Capitolo breve sul suicidio*, but are rather more like the ground-has-fallen-out-from-under-me kind, which are sometimes called catastrophic losses. This realization that the temptation of suicide is not the provenance of 'others' is a discomfiting thought, which Morselli describes this way:

> Il suicida è giunto colà dove anche noi potremmo ridurci un giorno: egli ha scoperto che quella speranza per cui e di cui viveva, anche lui come noi, altro non è se non vana apparenza, e che sotto di essa si nasconde la catena con cui la natura, per un suo fine oscuro, ci vuol legati all'ingiustizia e al dolore, ossia alla vita.[10]

> The suicide has arrived at that point where we, too, might find ourselves one day: he has discovered that that hope for which and on which he lived, just as we do, is nothing if not vain appearance, and that underneath it hides the chain with which nature, for one of its obscure reasons, want us tied to injustice and to pain, that is to say, to life.

We care about suicide (and in many cases condemn it) because it gives us ideas that we prefer to repress, including the idea that far from being an unnatural act, it is very much a part of the natural human repertoire: 'è giunto colà dove anche noi potremmo ridurci un giorno' (The suicide has arrived at that point where we, too, might find ourselves one day). No wonder, then, that we commit the biographical fallacy when we read a suicide's works: we seek signs of the author's irreducible individuality. *Pace* Pirandello, life imitates life more often than it does art, hence the literature of a suicidal author is considered interesting for the life that precedes it, not what follows after. My habitual reading strategy involves suspending disbelief to the extent necessary to engage meaningfully with a text, but not so much as to conflate the characters or events of a book with their author, not even when I am instructed to do so, as Flaubert mandated with the equation, 'Madame Bovary, c'est moi.' But reading a suicide, we do the opposite: we seek out the author's voice within the story to find proof of its uniqueness. Like so many latter-day Russian Formalists, we attempt to *make strange* what we read: to make sure it remains squarely within the bailiwick of an Other, or an *alter*, as Levi's and Morselli's slightly uncanny shared predilection for the name Walter attests. Hence Derrida's emphasis on the uniqueness of the departed: underscoring their singularity means, also, underscoring their alterity. And hence our dismay when we don't find exceptionality, but commonality, as in the suicide of Franco Lucentini, reputedly a 'copy-cat suicide' modelled after Primo Levi's: there is certainly nothing strange about imitation.

But we also pay attention to the dead – we care, even if it is not sufficient to repay the debt we owe – for the simple reason that their experiences, by definition, exceed ours, and thus they have much to teach us.[11] In the end, our job as readers of the dead (by suicide *and* by gout) is to bear witness, through our readings, to others' lives and writings without feeling any urgency for an interpretation that forces disparate or chaotic accretions of signs into legible formations. For in the final analysis, authorial suicides teach more about us, the living, than about the dead. Most of all, they write us: they give us the language with which to live and, after words, to die.

Notes

Introduction

1 As the hero of the satirical novel *Jérôme Paturot à la recherche d'une position sociale* (1844) puts it, 'A suicide establishes a man. Alive, one is nothing; dead one becomes a hero ... All suicides are successful; the papers take them up; people feel for them. I must decidedly make my preparations.' Quoted in Alfred Alvarez, *The Savage God: A Study of Suicide* (New York: W.W. Norton and Co., 1990), 233.

2 For a fictional version of this tendency, see Eli Gottlieb's novel, *Now You See Him* (New York: William Morrow/Harper Collins Publishers, 2008), about a short story writer with writer's block who kills his girlfriend and then himself, becoming a famous literary personality and highly prolific posthumous writer in the process.

3 Robert Pogue Harrison, *The Dominion of the Dead* (Chicago and London: University of Chicago Press, 2003), 15.

4 See my *The Reinvention of Ignazio Silone* (Toronto: University of Toronto Press, 2003).

5 Roland Barthes, 'The Death of the Author' in *Image, Music, Text*, translated by Stephen Heath (New York: Hill and Wang, 1977) 142–8. This essay, written in 1968, can be said to mark the end of structuralism and the beginning of poststructuralism.

   It is interesting to compare the body of the author with that of the artist, whom we often assume to be represented in his/her self-portraits. The Author may be dead but the Artist, in many contexts, is alive and well.

6 In the *Pleasure of the Text*, Barthes refines his previous arguments about the death of the author. In the subsection entitled 'Fetish,' he remarks, 'The text chooses me, by a whole disposition of invisible screens, selec-

tive baffles: vocabulary, references, readability, etc.; and, lost in the midst of a text (not *behind* it, like a *deus ex machina*) there is always the other, the author. As institution, the author is dead: his civil status, his biographical person have disappeared; dispossessed, they no longer exercise over his work the formidable paternity whose account literary history, teaching and public opinion had the responsibility of establishing and renewing; but in the text, in a way, I *desire* the author: I need his figure (which is neither his representation nor his projection) as he needs mine (except to "prattle").' Roland Barthes, *The Pleasure of the Text*, translated by Richard Miller (New York: Hill and Wang, 1975), 27.

7   For a small sampling of recent work on trauma, see Cathy Caruth's *Unclaimed Experience: Trauma, Narrative and History* (Baltimore: Johns Hopkins University Press, 1996); Eric L. Santner's 'History beyond the Pleasure Principle: Some Thoughts on the Representation of Trauma' in *Probing the Limits of Representation: Nazism and the Final Solution*, edited by Saul Friedlander (Cambridge, MA and London: Harvard University Press, 1992), 143–54; Shoshana Felman, *The Juridical Unconscious: Trials and Traumas in the Twentieth Century* (Cambridge, MA: Harvard University Press, 2002), and Ruth Leys, *Trauma: A Genealogy* (Chicago: University of Chicago Press, 2000). Leys's *From Guilt to Shame: Auschwitz and After* (Princeton: Princeton University Press, 2007) is also of particular relevance for its concern with Primo Levi, but also more generally for its argument that guilt has been replaced by shame in philosophical and psychological discourses (whether scholarly or popular).

8   Jacques Derrida, *The Work of Mourning* (Chicago: University of Chicago Press, 2001), 14.

9   For Barthes in *The Pleasure of the Text*, reading is akin in some ways to watching a strip tease, though perhaps one you can speed up or skim through, so long as the garments are removed in the proper order (pp. 9–13); and reading criticism is like being a voyeur, watching someone else's (the critic's) pleasure. Reading the works of a successful suicide is like flipping to the end of the mystery to see who committed the crime before reading the clues.

10   The case of suicide notes offers an interesting gloss on the discussion, insofar as they privilege the written over the corporeal by giving the word (and not the suicide) 'the last word.' See Amelie Frost Benedikt, 'On Reading Valedictory Texts: Suicide Notes, Last Wills and Testaments' in ΠΑΙΔΕΙΑ, Contemporary Philosophy, http://www.bu.edu/wcp/Papers/Cont/ContBene.htm, accessed 18 August 2003.

11   For confirmation of this tendency among non-professional readers, one

need look no farther than Internet sites such as Amazon.com, which encourages readers to write their own reviews of the books they have purchased. A cursory glance at the reviews of books like Diane Middlebrook's biographies of Sylvia Plath and Ted Hughes (*Her Husband: Hughes and Plath – A Marriage* [New York: Viking, 2003]) and of Anne Sexton (*Anne Sexton: A Biography* [New York: Houghton Mifflin, 1991]), or reviews of personal memoirs such as the one written by Jillian Becker (*Giving Up: The Last Days of Sylvia Plath* [New York: St Martin's Press, 2002]), gives, I believe, a sense of the kinds of issues non-professional readers seek to see resolved in books that deal with authors who commit suicide.

12 In 'The Death of the Author,' Barthes laments, 'The image of literature to be found in ordinary culture is tyrannically centered on the author, his person, his life, his tastes, his passions, while criticism still consists for the most part in saying that Baudelaire's work is the failure of Baudelaire the man, Van Gogh's his madness, Tchaikovsky's his vice. The *explanation* of a work is always sought in the man or woman who produced it, as if it were always in the end, through the more or less transparent allegory of the fiction, the voice of a single person, the author "confiding" in us.' Barthes, 'The Death of the Author' in *Image, Music, Text*, 143. This study will argue that Barthes, here somewhat acerbically preparing to dispense with the author, articulates the position to which theoreticians of the author will return after a death, especially by suicide. Indeed Barthes himself, who was moving progressively farther from stances such as this one as his career wore on, returns to this kind of pro-humanist recentring of the individual subject in one of his last writings, *Camera Lucida*, written after the death of his beloved mother. Barthes, *Camera Lucida: Reflections on Photography*, translated by Richard Howard (New York: Hill and Wang, 1981).

13 I borrow this phrase from Georges Minois from among so many others (intentional self-killing, self-murder, felo de se, and so on); his *History of Suicide: Voluntary Death in Western Culture*, translated by Lydia Cochrane (Baltimore: Johns Hopkins University Press, 1999) offers an erudite and highly readable survey of instances of and attitudes toward suicide from the Middle Ages till the Enlightenment. See also Robert Campbell and Diané Collinson, *Ending Lives* (Oxford: Basil Blackwell, 1988); *Suicide: The Philosophical Issues*, edited by M. Pabst Battin and David J. Mayo (New York: St Martin's Press, 1980); and the introduction to Irina Paperno's *Suicide as a Cultural Institution in Dostoevsky's Russia* (Ithaca: Cornell University Press, 1997) for other histories of suicide. None of the authors I examine in this study are considered to have killed themselves for exclusively altruistic reasons. Such an assertion would be just as difficult to argue as it

is to assert that some suicides are exclusively narcissistic in motivation; it is my belief that the overwhelming majority have multiple causes, neither to be disdained nor celebrated.

14 For example, novelist Jack London's fatal overdose of sleeping pills was recorded as a uremic poisoning for years. Mark Seinfelt, *Final Drafts: Suicides of World-Famous Authors* (Amherst, NY: Prometheus Books, 1999), 376. T.E. Lawrence's motorcycle accident was considered just that, an accident, for over sixty years until a series of letters surfaced that indicated otherwise. Seinfelt, *Final Drafts*, 424–5.

15 'Suicide is not to be presumed,' said a 1967 coroner's case in Great Britain, synthetically summing up the general sentiment. See Campbell and Collinson, 51–2 for a discussion of cases in which coroners who delivered verdicts of suicide were scolded for absence of sufficient proof.

16 The recent debate over the attribution of a poem about suicide to Abraham Lincoln is educative on this score. Despite both the general agreement among historians that Lincoln had at least two suicidal breakdowns (one of which was dubbed the 'fatal first of January') and the argument put forth by Lincoln scholar Richard Lawrence Miller that 'The Suicide's Soliloquy' (published in the *Sangamo Journal*, 25 August 1838) shares stylistic traits with other poems written by Lincoln around the same time, historians are reluctant to credit Lincoln with the piece. Miller's findings and the ensuing scholarly debate are described by Joshua Wolf Shenk in his piece 'The Suicide Poem,' *New Yorker*, 14 and 21 June 2004:62–5.

17 This is not to say that there are no 'socially acceptable' suicides: those whose motives are considered predominantly altruistic. The most frequently cited examples of these are a mother who dies to save her child, or Captain Oates's famous walk in the snow to spare his comrades on Scott's last South Pole expedition the burden of his presence. Or they may have to do with the protection of some less personal, perhaps more abstract, good. Historically, these have included religious martyrdoms and acts of patriotism, though in the West, particularly under George W. Bush's presidency, these motives have changed valence in public discourse about religious and ideological beliefs (whether those of the suicide bomber or the fireman who re-enters a burning building to save others, knowing that it will kill him) as a result of the events of 11 September 2001. In the end, much revolves around the perception of motives: 'Suicide is an escape from an intolerable situation. If the situation be an external, visible one, the suicide is brave; if the struggle be an internal, invisible one, the suicide is crazy.' Karl Menninger, *Man against Himself*, 1966 reprint of original (New York: Harcourt, Brace and World, 1938), 17.

18 Note that for Kant, all suicides are 'ignoble'; suicide for altruistic reasons is, to his way of thinking, not suicide at all. For a discussion of the distinctions between permissible and impermissible suicides, as well as of Kant's approach to the subject, see Robert Martin's chapter, 'Suicide and Self-Sacrifice,' in Battin and Mayo, 49.

19 On the difficulty of a satisfactory definition of suicide such as open-textured versus closed, see Peter Windt's article, 'The Concept of Suicide,' in Battin and Mayo, 39–47. For a discussion of 'instrumental' versus 'expressive' suicides, see David Wood's 'Suicide as Instrument and Expression' in the same volume, 151–60. See also Emile Durkheim's *Suicide: A Study in Sociology*, edited by George Simpson, translated by John A. Spaulding and George Simpson (New York: Free Press, 1997), 152–276 for description of egoistic and altruistic suicides. I note these here, and not in the later discussion of motives for suicide, because of the impact of the definition on the moral judgment attached to each death.

20 Jacques Derrida, *Aporias: dying – awaiting (one another at) the limits of truth* (Stanford: Stanford University Press, 1993), 42. Italics in original. In fact, though this is not Derrida's point, any anthropologist will tell us there are many ways of *properly dying*, such as (to limit myself to a small sampling from the Catholic tradition) *il culto della bella morte*, Saint Camillus de Lellis's Congregation of the Fathers of a Good Death (Clerici regulares ministrantes infirmis), and the etymology of the word *euthanasia*.

21 I invoke Derrida here because he engaged so consistently in his later works with the relations between death and writing. His *Specters of Marx* seems particularly à propos in that his is a work that attempts to engage with Marx precisely now that he and Marxism (it seems) are dead. See *Specters of Marx: The State of the Debt, the Work of Mourning, and the New International*, translated by Peggy Kamuf (New York: Routledge, 1994). Indeed, it is here, speaking of spirits, that he summarizes the new, hypostatic nature of the suicidal author, who is both 'the *more than one/no more one* [*le* plus d'un].' *Specters*, xx.

22 Derrida, *Aporias*, 43. Italics in original.

23 Jacques Derrida, *The Gift of Death*, translated by David Wills (Chicago: University of Chicago Press, 1995), 10. Italics/brackets in original.

24 This seems particularly to be the case in his *The Work of Mourning*, though he touches on some of the issues in *Aporias*, and also in *The Gift of Death*.

25 Paperno, 43–4. The Western history of this notion is developed in Ernst H. Kantorowicz's magisterial *The King's Two Bodies: A Study in Medieval Political Theology* (Princeton: Princeton University Press, 1997).

26 Giorgio Manganelli, *La notte* (Milan: Adelphi, 1996). Quoted in Giorgio Agamben, *Remnants of Auschwitz* (New York: Zone Books, 2001), 130.

27 See also Foucault's 'What Is an Author' for an examination of the author's name. In Michel Foucault, *Essential Works of Michel Foucault: Aesthetics, Method, and Epistemology*, vol. 2, edited by James D. Faubion (New York: New Press, 1998), 209–10.

28 Emile Durkheim, *Suicide: A Study in Sociology*.

29 See also Paperno, 11.

30 We may also note that intentionality is made visible across a wide temporal range: at one end of the spectrum are the kinds of suicides that require but one gesture – pulling the trigger of a gun, for example – and those that occur over the span of years or even decades – what Menninger calls 'death by inches' or 'chronic suicide,' which he describes as 'prolonging existence for the purpose of enduring more deprivation' (Menninger, 77). Along the same lines as Paperno's binaries of attribution (victory or defeat, autonomy or surrender, and so on), Menninger notes the overlap between asceticism and martyrdom, pointing out that the same gestures and acts (self-starvation, for example) take on different names according to the moral-ethical spin they take on in the popular imagination. A martyr, by this logic, is engaged in heroic self-sacrifice, but an ascetic (who may perform identical acts of self-deprivation or self-violence) is considered weak, crazy, or narcissistic (Menninger, 77–8).

31 Alvarez, 106–7. For a discussion of the connections between the various phases of bipolar disease and suicide attempts, see Andrew Solomon, *The Noonday Demon: An Atlas of Depression* (New York: Touchstone, 2001), 71 and Kay Redfield Jamison, *Touched with Fire: Manic Depressive Illness and the Artistic Temperament* (New York: Free Press, 1994), 46.

32 Solomon, 275.

33 Alvarez, 107. In light of the activity required of a suicide, I therefore do not agree with Alvarez when he asserts that the suicide 'assists passively at the cancellation of his own history; his work, his memories, his whole inner life – in short of anything that defines him as an individual' (270). On the contrary, I would argue that suicide does precisely the opposite, throwing all aspects of the suicide's life into high relief.

34 Alvarez, 109.

35 Our fascination with the corpse of the suicide resembles that of the tabloid with the celebrity. In the case of the former, we want to know not just the method, time, and place of death, but also – indeed, especially – the appearance of the body, including clothes, hair, and makeup. For a literary version of this prurient interest, consider the amount of dialogue devoted

to Rosetta's blue evening gown in Pavese's *Tra donne sole*. The mandate made famous in Nicholas Ray's 1949 film *Knock on Any Door*, 'Live fast, die young and leave a good-looking corpse,' is the positive analogue, which forestalls this hunger for intimate details about the body.

36 Vincent Crapanzano, *Imaginative Horizons: An Essay in Literary-Philosophical Anthropology* (Chicago: University of Chicago Press, 2004), 72–3.

37 Paperno, 34–5.

38 Shoshana Felman makes a strong case for a definition of madness that is at once philosophical, psychoanalytical, and literary: the embodiment of this conjuncture, she rightly points out, is Nietzsche. On the question of the philosophical/literary hybridity of madness, see Shoshana Felman, *Writing and Madness (Literature/Philosophy/Psychoanalysis)*, translated by Martha Noel Evans (Palo Alto: Stanford University Press, 2003), 35–7.

39 The unholy alliance between literature, madness, and suicide is frequently gendered female; though for Hélène Cixous and Xaviere Gauthier, madness is the name used for 'female protest and revolution' in writing, others propound a less romantic view that suggests women writers are inevitably mad because, precisely, they are women writers. Quoted in Elaine Showalter, *The Female Malady: Women, Madness, and English Culture 1830–1980* (New York: Pantheon Books, 1985), 4–5. Sandra Gilbert and Susan Gubar, *The Madwoman in the Attic: The Woman Writer and the Nineteenth-Century Literary Imagination* (New Haven: Yale University Press, 1984) and Phyllis Chesler, *Women and Madness* (Garden City, NY: Doubleday, 1972), too, discuss madness.

40 A full 18 per cent of poets whose biographies appeared in the *New York Times Book Review* between 1960 and 1990 (an indication, she notes, of a certain degree of prominence) were found to have committed suicide (Jamison, 61). See Jamison on the relationship between artistic creativity and various forms of depression: major, manic, and cyclothymia, a milder form of manic depression. (Note Jamison's findings do not include schizophrenia, which operates differently from the forms of depression listed above.)

41 My thinking throughout this chapter is deeply indebted to James A. Knapp and Jeffrey Pence's brilliant 'Between Thing and Theory.' Their investigation of the tensions between historicist and 'high theoretical' modes of scholarly inquiry (as well as the terms of that discussion, including but not limited to the notion of 'pragmatic scholarly projects,' which they define as 'solvable research questions' [642]) has been instrumental in my conceptualization of the proper hermeneutical mean for authorial suicide, providing the frame with which to organize my observations. James A. Knapp

and Jeffrey Pence, 'Between Thing and Theory,' *Poetics Today* 24:4 (Winter 2003), 641–71.

42 She is talking primarily about madness in literature – narrators who are or seem to be mad, unreliable narrators, and the like. Madness per se is not immediately relevant to my study, unless you accept the standard psychiatric-juridical assumption that all suicides are manifestations of mental illness (analogous to those that equate mental illness with madness). Felman, *Writing and Madness*, 5.

43 Again, I find Derrida useful for the ways he implicates my own death in my encounter with the deaths of these authors. In *Aporias*, for example (and more broadly in the *Work of Mourning*), he talks about 'awaiting oneself' in death, and how one always waits for the other. He says that it is (maybe only) in death that 'the *awaiting oneself* may be no other than the *expecting the other, or that* the other may arrive' (*Aporias*, 65).

44 I would like to maintain a distinction between haunting and mourning. Though related, their structures are, to my mind, incommensurable. Mourning implies a one-sided reckoning with what/whoever is no longer present, whereas haunting is potentially a two-way street, implying interaction between the survivor and the departed and the possibility, at least, of communication. On mourning, see Judith Butler's *Precarious Life: The Power of Mourning and Violence* (New York: Verso, 2004), and Alessia Ricciardi's *The Ends of Mourning* (Stanford: Stanford University Press, 2003), as well as Derrida's *The Work of Mourning* and *Specters of Marx*.

45 Séan Burke, *The Death and Return of the Author: Criticism and Subjectivity in Barthes, Foucault, and Derrida* (Edinburgh: Edinburgh University Press, 1998), 27.

46 To limit myself to a very few examples from outside the United States, see Maurice Couturier, *La figure de l'auteur* (Paris: Seuil, 1995) and Carla Benedetti, *The Empty Cage: Inquiry into the Mysterious Death of the Author*, translated by William Hartley (Ithaca: Cornell University Press, 2005). See Séan Burke's piece entitled 'The Ethics of Signature' in the volume he edited, *Authorship: A Reader. From Plato to the Postmodern* (Edinburgh: Edinburgh University Press, 2004), 285–91, as well as the pages throughout his *Death and Return of the Author*.

47 See Burke, *Death and Return of the Author*, 33–41 for a discussion of this.

48 Burke, *Death and Return of the Author*, 124–6.

49 Burke, *Death and Return of the Author*, 127.

50 Burke, *Death and Return of the Author*, 127–8.

51 Derrida, *Specters of Marx*, 11: 'What seems almost impossible is to speak always *of the* specter, to speak *to the* specter, to speak with it, therefore

especially *to make or to let* a spirit *speak*. And the thing seems even more difficult for a reader, an expert, a professor, an interpreter ... Perhaps for a spectator in general ... The reasons for this are essential. As theoreticians or witnesses, spectators, observers, and intellectuals, scholars believe that looking is sufficient. Therefore, they are not always in the most competent position to do what is necessary: speak to the specter.'

1. The Posthumous Author

1 Morselli's testament, cited in Valentina Fortichiari, *Guido Morselli: Immagini di una vita* (Milan: Rizzoli, 2001), 124–5. Fortichiari is Guido Morselli's most prolific biographer and critic. All translations are mine unless otherwise indicated.

2 See Fortichiari, *Guido Morselli*, and Fortichiari, *Invito alla lettura di Morselli* (Milan: Mursia, 1984). See also Maria Fiorentino's *Guido Morselli tra critica e narrativa* (Naples: Eurocomp Edizioni, 2002), especially the section entitled 'Biografia Intellettuale,' and Marina Lessona Fasano's *Guido Morselli: Un inspiegabile caso letterario* (Naples: Liguori Editore, 1998). See also Simona Costa, *Morselli* (Città di Castello: La Nuova Italia, 1981).

3 In 1944, one of Morselli's two paternal uncles committed suicide by throwing himself out of a window in broad daylight, a gesture that 'colpì profondamente il nipote Guido, che gli era molto legato.' Fortichiari, *Guido Morselli*, 19.

4 Fortichiari, *Guido Morselli*, 26.

5 By 1934, Morselli had written several short articles and he was a published author, his story 'La dodicesima battaglia' having come out in *Libro e Moschetto*. (See Fortichiari, *Invito alla lettura di Morselli*, 18.) Morselli published his first essay, *Proust o del sentimento* (Milan: Garzanti, 1943), in 1943 during his military service in Calabria. In 1946, an article entitled 'Variazioni su un tema famoso' came out in *La Via*, and in 1947, Morselli's second study, *Realismo e fantasia: Dialoghi con Sereno* (Milan: Fratelli Bocca, 1947) was published: the last book published during Morselli's lifetime. Morselli also published articles in *Il Tempo* (Milan), *La Prealpina* (Varese), *Il Corriere del Ticino*, and *Il Corriere Lombardo*.

6 He published the short story 'Fantasia con moralità' in 1953 in *Il Contemporaneo*, a few articles, reviews, and the short essay 'Fulton J. Sheen' in 1963–4 in *La Cultura*, and 'I miti e Roland Barthes' and 'L'ideologia, un tramite,' both in *Questo e altro* in 1964–5 – certainly a dignified showing for this number of years, and yet his writerly production far outstripped its publication. This was true for essays as well as for fiction. As Fortichiari

points out in her meticulously edited edition of Morselli's diary, between 1957 and 1958 alone, Morselli had composed seven chapter-length essays on the subject of *Scienza e astrazione*, as well as numerous fragments of pieces and notes on the topic. For a list of chapter titles, see her footnote number 17 in Morselli, *Diario* (Milan: Adelphi Edizioni, 1988), 219.

7 *Incontro col comunista* (written 1947–8); *Un dramma borghese* (1961–2); *Il comunista* (1964–5); *Brave borghesi* (1966); *Roma senza papa* (1966–7); *Contropassato prossimo* (1969–70); *Divertimento 1889* (1970–1); and *Dissipatio H.G.* (1972–3), plus a piece of book-length philosophy, *Fede e critica*, written 1955–6. Adelphi published six of Morselli's novels within four years, starting in 1974 with *Roma senza papa*.

8 At least one of the novels was actually seriously considered by different presses before it was rejected; Rizzoli had, for example, accepted *Il comunista* for publication, and Morselli had made alterations and corrected proofs for months, until a change in the leadership at Rizzoli led to a withdrawal of their interest in the book. See Fiorentino, 41 for that novel's failed publication itinerary.

9 Italo Chiusano's enthusiastic prognostications about the novels that are sure to follow *Roma senza papa* (published 1974, one year after Morselli's death) are indicative of the tenor of the case. Italo A. Chiusano, 'Il libro postumo che fa inopportunamente gridare al caso letterario: *Roma senza papa* di Morselli, una acuta satira socio-politica,' *Il Globo*, 22 November 1974: 5.

10 Giulio Nascimbeni, 'Il romanzo di fantateologia che sta diventando un caso letterario: C'è forse un Gattopardo del Nord,' *Corriere della Sera*, 21 October 1974: 3.

11 See the chapter on 'Le reniement inaugural' in Maurice Couturier, *La figure de l'auteur* (Paris: Seuil, 1995).

12 See Marina Lessona Fasano's tellingly entitled *Guido Morselli: Un inspiegabile caso letterario*, 1.

13 One exception to this assertion about the reversal of critical conventions is psychobiography, a methodology grounded in part on assessments of authorial character and thus one not thrown into crisis by the suicide of an author.

14 P. Macchione, 'La solitudine di Guido Morselli,' *La Prealpina*, 16 April 1988. Quoted in Fiorentino, 31.

15 There is no significant discussion of suicide (explicit or implicit) in *Incontro col comunista* (written 1947–8). Some reviewers, however, perceive a kind of structuring absence in that omission; according to their logic, in the case of Morselli he has *not yet begun* to display the anxieties that will plague him in later years. Thus the fact that his literature does not evince that anxi-

ety (or address it directly, in any case) is supposedly an indication that it is brewing, latent, or inchoate. By the time he writes *Il comunista* (1964–5), on the other hand, he is said to be on the downward spiral, as indicated by the novel's ambiguous conclusion regarding its protagonist, Walter Ferranini, who has been overcome by a kind of exhausted despair at the novel's close. Fasano here as elsewhere insists that the novels follow or trace Morselli's emotional trajectory, thus recasting their foundations as autobiographically, not literarily motivated.

16 Barthes, 'From Work to Text' in Vincent B. Leitch et al., editors, *The Norton Anthology of Theory and Criticism* (New York: W.W. Norton and Company, 2001), 1473. Thus a work stands in stark contrast to a Text, wherein the author 'is inscribed in the novel like one of his characters, figured on the carpet; no longer privileged, paternal ... his life is no longer the origin of his fictions but a fiction contributing to his work' (1473–4).

17 J.C. Vegliante, 'Guido Morselli' in *Magazine Littéraire* no. 165 (October 1980): 44.

18 Vegliante, 44.

19 See, for one example, the assessment that he is disappointing and over-rated compared to what has been said about him, in Ferruccio Mazzariol, 'La narrativa del (caso) Morselli,' *L'osservatore romano*, 2 October 1976: 3.

20 Gilles Costaz, '*Rome sans pape* de Guido Morselli: Un romancier italien imagine l'Eglise à la veille de l'an 2000,' *Le Matin*, 24 March 1979: 24. One way or the other, suicide is the alpha and omega of reading the novels. In contrast, Carlo Bo's positive review of the essays contained in *Fede e critica* does not mention suicide, though this is as likely a place as any to seek it, insofar as the book's central theme is a meditation on the relationships between religious faith and suffering from the standpoint of someone profoundly critical of the idea of an all-capable healing power of faith. Instead, Bo focuses on the content of Morselli's text, which he finds sincere, controlled, and hopeful. Carlo Bo, 'La fede secondo Morselli' in *Corriere della Sera*, 16 October 1977: 10. And Carmine Di Biase is equally enthusiastic in his review of the book, and praises the depth and breadth of the author's preparation on issues of faith. Carmine Di Biase, 'Uno scrittore in cerca di Dio,' *L'Osservatore Romano*, 21 January 1978: 3. Both Bo and Di Biase focus on content, and engage with existential/religious crises as they are addressed in *Fede e critica* – not as they might have impacted its author. Is there something about the essay format that allows readers to detach from biography in ways that fiction does not brook?

21 Giulio Nascimbeni, 'Il terzo romanzo postumo conferma il caso Morselli: Re in incognito' (review of *Divertimento 1889*), *Corriere della Sera*, 29 June 1975: 12.

22 Fortichiari in *Guido Morselli*, 7–8. It should be noted, however, that Morselli's editorial fiasco (he drew an upside-down flask – the sign of failure – on the folder in which he saved rejection letters from publishers) was not total.

23 Fasano, 2.

24 Fasano, 1.

25 Fortichiari, *Invito alla lettura di Morselli*, 133.

26 Fortichiari, *Guido Morselli*, 105. Morselli owned and discussed in his diary several works by the philosopher Giuseppe Rensi. For all intents and purposes, Rensi's Latin citation and the variation used by Morselli mean the same thing.

27 See Fortichiari, *Guido Morselli*, 105–20 for more information from various sources, including Morselli's personal physician.

28 Fiorentino, 180–1.

29 Michael Caesar, 'The Seventies' in *The Cambridge History of Italian Literature*, second edition, edited by Peter Brand and Lino Pertile (Cambridge: Cambridge University Press, 2001), 595.

30 Ennio Flaiano (1910–1972) was a novelist, and a journalist, as well as one of Federico Fellini's collaborators through the period of the latter's *Giulietta degli spiriti* (1965).

31 Costa, 11–12.

32 Costa, 18–19.

33 Costa, 46.

34 Giuseppe Pontiggia, 'La Roma senza Papa di Morselli: l'altro ieri a Cortina il convegno sullo scrittore morto nel 1973,' *Corriere della Sera*, 26 August 1978: 3.

35 Pierre Ysmal's review of *Le Communiste* (translated by Claude Minot-Templier) is illustrative: 'Sa rigeur et sa probité expliquent mieux le communisme que tous les livres des "ex" qui trop souvent règlent des comptes. Morselli avec ce roman prend rang parmi les rares grands écrivains du monde communiste' (His rigour and probity better explain Communism than all the books written by 'exes' who too often attempt to even the score. With this book Morselli joins the ranks of the rare great writers of the Communist world). *Magazine Littéraire*, no. 141 (October 1978): 43–4. See also Alcide Paolini's 'Come sono vecchi i giovani narratori,' *Corriere della Sera*, 24 March 1975: 3.

36 Morselli received a special posthumous Premio Scanno for *Il comunista*. Alberto Frattini, 'Sulla poesia italiana degli anni Sessanta ad oggi,' *L'Osservatore Romano*, 12–13 July 1976: 5.

37 Giulio Nascimbeni, 'Il comunista che contesta Marx' in *Corriere della Sera*, 2

March 1976: 3. Laurand Kovacs, too, insists that this is not a *roman à thèse*. Laurand Kovacs, review of *Le Communiste* in *La Nouvelle Revue Française* no. 311 (December 1978): 133.

38 Costa describes the uses and abuses of the book's party politics on pp. 68–9.

39 Alfredo Giuliani, 'Comunista serio, deputato inutile,' *La Repubblica*, 3 March 1976: 10. This article is reprinted with new material (on *Dissipatio H.G.*) in Giuliani's *Le droghe di Marsiglia* (Milan: Adelphi, 1977). For Pierre Enckell, the novel is 'ample, humain, et terriblement précis' (ample, human, and terribly precise). Review in *Les Nouvelles Létteraires*, 31 August 1978: 21.

40 The first chapter of the novel was published with an introduction by Giulio Nascimbeni by the *Corriere della Sera*, 14 September 1980: 3.

41 Florestano Vancini (the filmmaker who transposed *Un dramma borghese* to the screen) posited that there were only two successful themes for writers in the 1950s and 1960s, sex and political engagement, neither of which, he maintains, Morselli took up. Giulio Nascimbeni, 'Morselli, quel lago, quel mistero ...' *Corriere della Sera*, 18 March 1979: 3.

42 Pontiggia, 3.

43 Pontiggia, 3.

44 I much prefer the observation of Michael Caesar, who distinguishes between writers who write '"for themselves" or "for literature", writers for whom the act of writing is part of a continuing process of linguistic or metaphysical research' and those who write '"for the reader", in general a pre-conceived reader who is already familiar with the conventions of narrative realism, is not keen to have his or her expectations disappointed, and is unlikely to welcome much formal experimentation' (596). Describing Morselli within the wider context of Italian writings of the 1970s, Caesar concludes that Morselli does not fit comfortably in either camp (though one might argue that they are not necessarily mutually exclusive).

45 Note the resemblance between the premise of *Contro-passato prossimo*, in which an alternative version of the outcome of the First World War is depicted, and André Maurois's *Mes songes che voici* (Paris: Grasset, 1933), whose point of departure ('Si Louis XVI avait eut un grain de fermeté ... '[If Louis XVI had had a grain of strength ...]) leads to quite a different history of France. See a brief discussion of Maurois in Rensi, *La filosofia dell'assurdo* (Milan: Adelphi, 1991), 195.

46 See Guido Lopez's appreciative review of *Divertimento 1889*'s delicious tone in *Uomini e libri* 55 (September-October 1975): 26–7.

47 Giulio Nascimbeni, 'La notte in cui sparì il genere umano,' *Corriere della Sera*, 26 February 1977: 3.

48 Derrida, *The Gift of Death*, 10. Italics in original.
49 The influence of Frédéric Amiel is not to be overlooked, either, though it is not nearly so great as that of Rensi or Monod. Indeed, in *Dissipatio H.G.*, Morselli's protagonist gently mocks Amiel as one of the 'pesi massimi (e eroi noiosi) dell'introversione.' *Dissipatio H.G.* (Milan: Adelphi Edizioni, 1977), 68.
50 There remains, however, the question of whether he read Rensi's *La filosofia dell'assurdo* (1937) or its original 1924 version, *Interiora rerum*, or if he simply extrapolated from *Le aporie della religione*, which he definitely read, and which deals in large part with the problem of chance.
51 Morselli mentions chance specifically on page 176 of his *Diario*, in an entry dated 15 February 1957. As Fortichiari notes, this is the first in a series of entries that will reflect upon the centrality of chance for daily life. Indeed the diary entries that follow this initial reflection on chance become increasingly pessimistic over the course of the next few days, till his thoughts return to things religious. More specifically, Morselli also wrote a review essay on Monod ('Il caso e la necessità,' 1971) now in *La felicità non è un lusso*.
52 Jacques Monod, *Chance and Necessity: An Essay on the Natural Philosophy of Modern Biology*, translated by Austryn Wainhouse (New York: Alfred A. Knopf, 1971), 45.
53 Monod, 4.
54 Monod, 15–16.
55 The name Walter appears in more than one of Morselli's novels. It can be parsed in various ways. W-alter suggests 'Long live' (W) and 'alter' as in alter ego, other, or the Other.
56 *Dissipatio H.G.*, 19. Both *Un dramma borghese* and *Dissipatio H.G.* have anonymous narrators whose profession involves writing, and who are surrounded, in some ways, by ambiguous deaths.
57 Giulio Nascimbeni, 'Quella febbre strana e sottile che arriva il pomeriggio,' *Corriere della Sera*, 21 May 1978: 11.
58 Alfredo Giuliani, 'A Crisopoli sono spariti gli abitanti,' *La Repubblica*, 12 March 1977: 11. Later republished, with material on *Il comunista*, in *Le droghe di Marsiglia*.
59 See Fortichiari for a typical example of the collapse of author into protagonist (*Guido Morselli*, 124). Apart from ubiquitous mentions of Morselli's suicide, most of the critical reception of the novel was chequered.
60 Morselli, *Dissipatio H.G.*, 22.
61 Morselli, *Dissipatio H.G.*, 22–3.
62 See Max Saunders's discussion of autobiography and autobiografiction.

Saunders, 'Autobiografiction,' *Times Literary Supplement* 3 October 2008:
13–15.

63 Morselli, *Dissipatio H.G.*, 39.
64 Morselli, *Dissipatio H.G.*, 87.
65 Morselli, *Dissipatio H.G.*, 31.
66 Morselli, *Dissipatio H.G.*, 90.
67 Morselli, *Dissipatio H.G.*, 24.
68 Morselli, *Dissipatio H.G.*, 25.
69 For a North American analogue, we might recall that treasure trove of
    fantastic themes, the television series *The Twilight Zone*. Aired in the United
    States between 1959 and 1964, Rod Serling's examinations of life, death,
    extraterrestrial life, and the general unreality of reality codified the genre
    with its curiously elegiac admixture of middle-class Americana and a pre-
    dilection for Borges-like plot twists. Indeed, *Dissipatio H.G.* bears a striking
    relationship to two episodes, including the well-cited episode entitled
    'Time Enough at Last,' which deals with bank clerk Henry Bemis, who
    locks himself in the bank vault on his lunch hour one day to read. Open-
    ing the newspaper, he is confronted with the headline 'H-Bomb Capable of
    Total Destruction' at the very moment that a huge blast shakes the vault.
    Stumbling out into a post-apocalyptic wasteland after coming to, Henry
    realizes that he is the last man on earth – just what he wanted, because
    now as the title indicates he has 'time enough at last' to do all the reading
    he wants. Unless, of course, the whole thing is a dream suggested by the
    newspaper headline and Henry is really asleep on his lunch break.
70 *Fantastic* is a term that Todorov ascribes to narratives that take place in 'our
    world, the world we know,' and in which 'there occurs an event which
    cannot be explained by the laws of this same familiar world. The person
    who experiences this event must opt for one of two possible solutions:
    either he is the victim of an illusion of the senses, of a product of the imagi-
    nation – and the laws of the world then remain what they are; or else the
    event has indeed taken place, it is an integral part of reality – but then this
    reality is controlled by laws unknown to us.' Tzvetan Todorov, *The Fantas-
    tic: A Structural Approach to a Literary Genre*, translated by Richard Howard
    (Cleveland: Press of Case Western Reserve University, 1973), 25.
71 See *Dissipatio H.G.*, 67–9 for an amusing excursus into self-analysis. The
    novel's first paragraph, too, deals precisely with the vicissitudes of mean-
    ing when its foundation is something as contingent as text.
72 'Once we choose one answer or the other, we leave the fantastic for a
    neighboring genre, the uncanny or the marvelous' (Todorov, 25).
73 Monod, 114.

74 Monod, 180.
75 Moselli, *Dissipatio H.G.*, 86.
76 Ilaria's affair with Gildo resembles the affair between the anonymous journalist and his daughter's friend in *Un dramma borghese* in that they share a whiff of incest in the transfer of the parent's desires for his/her child to the child's best friend, though Ilaria's feelings for her son are much deeper below the surface than the journalist's for Mimmina.
77 We might also mention Saverio's and Vito's military tours in *Uomini e amori*, or *Il comunista*'s Walter Ferranini, whose limbo journey is a return to the America of his early adulthood. What's more, his flight back to Italy is structured around the fantasy of flying forever, neither landing nor crashing but simply disappearing somewhere over the ocean.
78 Morselli, *Dissipatio H.G.*, 51.
79 Morselli, *Diario*, 332–3.
80 Morselli, *Dissipatio H.G.*, 19.
81 Rensi, *La filosofia dell'assurdo*, 27.
82 See also the following, which underscore the centrality of Rensi's position in Morselli's *Weltanschauung*: Rensi, *La filosofia dell'assurdo*, 119, 168–9, 187–8.
83 Morselli, *Dissipatio H.G.*, 54–5.
84 Valentina Fortichiari's assessment seems plausible: it entails 'il sospetto di una paradossale contro-ipotesi, lo scambio vita/morte a valenza capovolta, dove una vita apparente non è che l'altra faccia di una tragica assenza, una vera scomparsa ... Non è forse dei morti, dell'ombra degli scomparsi, l'aggirarsi inquieto fra gli oggetti degli umani senza poter avere con questi ultimi alcun contatto reale? Non è dei fantasmi l'incapacità di comunicare con i viventi, e la condanna a un perpetuo, vano vagare nel mondo perduto?' (the suspicion of a paradoxical counter-hypothesis, the exchange of life/death with valences reversed, whereby an apparent life is nothing but the other side of a tragic absence, a real disappearance ... Is not the worried wandering among the objects of humans, without the power to have any real contact with them, proper to the dead and to the shadow of the departed?). Fortichiari, *Invito alla lettura di Morselli*, 122–3.
85 Morselli, *Dissipatio H.G.*, 112.
86 Fortichiari provides the citation from Rensi in her capacity as editor of Morselli's diary. I borrow Rensi's citation from Fortichiari.
87 Cited in *Diario* by Fortichiari, note at bottom of pp. 57–8.
88 Note the resemblance here to the appearance of the philosopher in Pirandello's 'All'uscita.'
89 Morselli, *Dissipatio H.G.*, 77.
90 Here, too, Fortichiari provides the reference to Rensi (*Aporie*, 71): 'non è

vero, come si dice, che, a differenza degli animali, gli uomini sappiano che morranno. In realtà, il loro saperlo è saltuario e superficiale, non mai chiaramente e profondamente presente' (it's not true, as they say, that unlike animals, men know that they are going to die. In reality, their knowing it is intermittent and superficial; it is never clearly and profoundly present'). *Diario*, 67n12.

91 *Diario*, 67–8.

92 Morselli, *Dissipatio H.G.*, 33.

93 Morselli, *Dissipatio H.G.*, 32.

94 Claudio Toscani comes to a similar conclusion in his review of *Contropassato prossimo* in *Uomini e libri* no. 54 (June-July 1975): 64–5.

95 And here recall Henry Bemis's bank, whose solidity symbolizes the unshakeable foundation of American capitalism – both figuratively (his boss admonishes him 'I am an organization man who functions within an organization' – a reassuring identity that calms skittish investors) and literally (had he not been in the vault, analogous of course to Morselli's protagonist's underground cave, he would not have survived the blast).

96 In contrast, Henry Bemis's anonymous lunar landscape after the H-bomb could be France or China as easily as Main Street, USA.

97 The nearby village, for example, 'has the excessive perfection of a publicity brochure' (Morselli, *Dissipatio H.G.*, 40).

98 See Morselli, *Dissipatio H.G.*, 38.

99 See pp. 93–4 for a description of the *cronoformaggio*.

100 See p. 37, where he talks about the 'Rothschild-hour,' when the Bourse is closing: 'l'ora in cui si decide per l'indomani il destino finanziario dell'Europa e di mezzo Occidente. Ma il tempio non si è illuminato, non si è aperto. Finito anch'esso. Morto, come le colonne e gli atrii di Balbec' (the hour in which is decided the next day's financial destiny for Europe and half of the West. But the temple did not illuminate, it did not open. It, too, was finished. Dead, like the columns and the atria of Balbec).

101 Morselli, *Dissipatio H.G.*, 132.

102 Morselli, *Dissipatio H.G.*, 12.

103 Morselli, *Dissipatio H.G.*, 32.

104 See also p. 43 for a description of the hangar at the local airport, seen as a bulwark against infamy, disappearance, etc. – like the Christians of Turkey and their Santa Sofia mosque, whose columns and cupolas were strong enough to guarantee their safety: an ironic commentary on technology as spiritual armour, so to speak.

105 Morselli, *Dissipatio H.G.*, 12.

106 Morselli, *Dissipatio H.G.*, 57–8.

107 Morselli, *Dissipatio H.G.*, 60.
108 Morselli, *Dissipatio H.G.*, 53.
109 Morselli, *Dissipatio H.G.*, 40.
110 Morselli, *Dissipatio H.G.*, 69–70.
111 Morselli, *Dissipatio H.G.*, 122.
112 Morselli, *Dissipatio H.G.*, 84.
113 Morselli, *Dissipatio H.G.*, 140.
114 Morselli, *Dissipatio H.G.*, 35.
115 Rensi, *La filosofia dell'assurdo*, 195.
116 See the *Diary* entry for 29 June 1944. His conception of the absurd and its relationship to history and causality will appear throughout Morselli's opus until his death.
117 Morselli, *Diario*, 177–8.
118 See his *Diario* (8 October 1959) for both a clear anticipation of Monod, and for this application of his and Rensi's philosophies:

> Il caso governa, solo, l'esistenza. Un 'caso', voglio ammetterlo, 'qualificato', cioè non privo di certe accortezze e di certe regolarità, capace di dar luogo alla versatilità delle cellule cerebrali dell'uomo, alla soave bellezza dei boschi in un pomeriggio d'autunno; ma che rivela troppo bene, all'apice della evoluzione organica come nella ricchezza della natura vegetale e animale, la sua disordinata fortuità, la sua inconsapevolezza, la mancanza di un fine e di un piano, nella sua ignara crudeltà e ingiustizia.
>
> La sofferenza che io in questi giorni sto provando, di nuovo (dopo i due amarissimi mesi di luglio e di agosto), non ha un fine, non ha uno scopo, come non ha, nella mia condotta, una motivazione plausibile. Potrei in questi stessi giorni esser felice, come d'altronde potrei essere morto. La mia sofferenza nasce da circostanze esterne, che potevano, senza pregiudizio di nulla e di nessuno, essere occorse in modo del tutto diverso: nasce da esse, non ne è spiegata o giustificata. La nostra vicenda umana è troppo futilmente aleatoria, troppo legato al gratuito e all'accidentale, perché possa ispirarsi a un qualsiasi principio morale. L'interpretazione della nostra vita non si può fare 'a posteriori', e in termini statistici ... è stolto voler dare una legge morale alla vicenda degli individui. Perché, e come, dovremmo essere migliori del mondo in cui viviamo e da cui siamo trattati come le biglie della 'roulette'? (Morselli, *Diario*, 181–2)
>
> Chance alone governs existence. A qualified chance, I must admit, that is, one not lacking certain wisdoms or certain regularity, capable

of giving rise to the versatility of the brain cells of man, to the gentle beauty of the woods on an autumn afternoon; but one that reveals all too well, to the apex of organic evolution as to the richness of vegetal and animal nature, its disordered fortuity, its unconsciousness, its lack of a goal or of a plan, in its unknowing cruelty and injustice.

The suffering that I am feeling these days, again (after the two extremely bitter months of July and August) has no goal, has no purpose, just as it has, in my conduct, no plausible motivation. I could, in these same days, be happy, just as I could be dead. My suffering is born from external circumstances that could, without anything or anyone's prejudices, have occurred in a totally different way: it is born from them, it is not explained or justified by them. Our human adventure is too futilely aleatory, too tied to the gratuitous and the accidental to be able to aspire to any moral principle. The interpretation of our life cannot be made *a posteriori*, and in statistical terms ... it is daft to try to give a moral law to the events of individuals. Why, and how, should we be better than the world in which we live and by which we are treated like the balls in roulette?

119 He summarizes the question thus in his *Dissipatio H.G.*, 66: 'il solo male è la sofferenza. Un individuo che soffre, a cui manca quello che gli occorre per *essere*. Ma in questo senso ristretto e concreto, il male li assediava da ogni parte, a ogni istante, in ogni loro atto, e anche pensiero, visto che l'attesa della sofferenza, la paura, è perfetta sofferenza' (the only evil is suffering. An individual who suffers, who lacks what he needs in order *to be*. But in that resticted and concrete sense, evil besieges them from every side, at every instant, in each of their acts, and even thoughts, considering that awaiting suffering, fear, is perfect suffering). See also his book-length essay *Fede e critica* (written in 1955–6 and published in 1977), which deals precisely with this problem.
120 Rensi, *La filosofia dell'assurdo*, 196.

2. The Corpus and the Corpse

1 Amelia Rosselli, *Sleep: poesie in inglese*, translated by Emmanuela Tandello (Milan: Garzanti, 1992), 8.
2 Recall that *Il conformista*, Bernardo Bertolucci's film (based on Alberto Moravia's novel), loosely recounts the assassinations. Moravia and Rosselli were related: he was the son of Rosselli's grandmother's brother.

3   See for example Silvia De March's *Amelia Rosselli tra poesia e storia* (Naples:
    L'ancora del mediterraneo), which begins with a timeline with the follow-
    ing categories: *Carlo, Giustizia e Libertà e la Storia; Marion e figli;* and *nonna
    Amelia e famiglia di Nello.* Rosselli is subsumed, unnamed, under someone
    else's rubric, and the dates run from the famous *fuga da Lipari* (her father's
    escape from internal exile on the island of Lipari in 1929) to his and Nello's
    funeral in 1937.
4   Her entry in the *Enciclopedia Zanichelli 2003,* however, reads 'scrittrice,
    figlia di Carlo' (1613).
5   Stanislao Pugliese, *Carlo Rosselli: Socialist Heretic and Antifascist Exile* (Cam-
    bridge: Harvard University Press, 1999), 2.
6   See her *Epistolario familiare* (Milan: Sugar Co., 1979).
7   Parts of this chapter were delivered at the MLA convention in San Diego,
    California, December 2003, and at the AAIS conference in Colorado
    Springs, Colorado, May 2007. Portions also appeared in '"Nor do I want
    your interpretation": Suicide, Surrealism, and the Site of Illegibility in
    Amelia Rosselli's *Sleep,' Romantic Review* 97. 3–4 (2006): 445–59.
8   Rosselli, *Sleep,* 20.
9   By the same token we might note that Rosselli's *Elizabethan October* is often
    associated with the poetry of John Donne, author of *Biathanatos* (published
    in 1641), the first tract to defend suicide. For a discussion of the history
    and importance of Donne's argument to subsequent interventions in the
    debate, see Georges Minois's *History of Suicide: Voluntary Death in Western
    Culture,* translated by Lydia Cochrane (Baltimore: Johns Hopkins Univer-
    sity Press, 1999), 94–7, as well as Robert Campbell and Diané Collinson,
    Ending Lives (Oxford: Basil Blackwell, 1988).
10 This is from his preface to Silvia De March's *Amelia Rosselli tra poesia e storia,* 6.
11 Writing about an analogous situation, David Orr puts it perfectly: 'In the
    case made by Ted Hughes and Sylvia Plath, the myth made by gossip
    has long obscured the art made by a couple of poets. That's a pity. It's a
    pity not only because many people might enjoy the poetry if they were to
    read it on its *own* merits, rather than for the customary vicarious *frisson,*
    but also because many people might not enjoy it. They might instead find
    themselves wondering why so much time has been spent on two writers
    whose most notable shared feature is the ability to write a poem dripping
    with blood, moons, and psychic violence about anything from soccer to
    provincial beekeeping clubs.' David Orr, 'Love, Your Ted,' *New York Times
    Book Review,* 16 November 2008,: 15.
12 See Alessandro Baldacci, *Amelia Rosselli* (Rome-Bari: Gius. Laterza e Figli,
    2007), 141: 'E' indubbio che la poesis della Plath presenti, con la sua com-

binazione fra tensione grottesca, frantumazione schizofrenica del soggetto e visione tragica della vita, una delle esperienze poetiche più prossime alla scrittura rosselliana' (It is certain that the poeisis of Plath, with its combination of grotesque tension, schizophrenic shattering of the subject, and tragic vision of life, presents one of the poetic experiences closest to Rosselli's writing). He continues, 'E le traduzioni rosselliane sono l'esempio di un dialogo che tramite la forma della traduzione assume la caratteristica di un abbraccio quasi fisico, di uno scambio attivo, "poietico", fra l'originale e la versione in italiano' (And Rosselli's translations are an example of the dialogue that assumes the characteristic of an almost physical embrace, of an active exchange, 'poietic,' between the original and the Italian version, by way of the form of the translation). In this description, not only do Rosselli and Plath resemble each other, they hug, too! See also Emmanuela Tandello's discussion of Plath's 1959 poem 'Electra on Azalea Path,' in which Plath confronts her father's tomb for the first time, apposite for the way it imbricates the figures of Electra, Plath, Rosselli, and their fathers. Tandello, *Amelia Rosselli: La fanciulla e l'infinito* (Rome: Donzelli Editore, 2007), 39–42.

13 She also mentions John Berryman on a number of occasions in her list of 'all-time greats.' Another example of the loss of the subject alongside the text, John Berryman committed suicide in 1972.

14 See Baldacci, 140–3, for a discussion of her various engagements (starting in 1975, then again in 1985, and finally in 1991) with Plath. See also Andrea Cortellessa, 'Il bosco, il sonno, la sipida musica,' *Galleria* 48:1–2, edited by Daniele Attanasio and Emmanuela Tandello(1997): 96–112.

15 Sylvia Plath, 'Lady Lazarus' in *Ariel* (New York: HarperCollins Perennial Classics, 1999), 6–9.

16 And yet, such an emphatic denial is often the cover for its opposite, for the unqualified marginalization of her parents implicit in Rosselli's choice of date equally convincingly underscores their centrality to her life, in their very exclusion from that life's end. Rosselli's suicide implies at once a rejection of her illustrious forebears, and (by virtue of its insistent denial) a covert embracing of that ancestry. For our purposes, it is not important (even if it were possible) to ascertain the depth or authenticity of Rosselli's actual affective ties to her family; more relevant to my study is the way the symbolic ties between them are complicated by Plath's presence.

17 Rosselli herself contributed to this assessment when she refuted the epithet 'cosmopolitan' attributed to her by Pasolini in the 1963 *Menabò* essay with which he introduced her early poems, calling her 'questa specie di apolide dalle grandi tradizioni famigliari di Cosmopolis' (that species of displaced person of the grand familial tradition of Cosmopolis). Pier Paolo Pasolini,

'Notizia su Amelia Rosselli,' *Il Menabò di letteratura* 6 (1963): 68–9. Rosselli
responded: '[I]o rifiuto per noi quest'appellativo: siamo figli della seconda
Guerra mondiale. Quando sono tornata in Italia mi sono molto legata a
Roma. Cosmopolita è chi sceglie di esserlo. Noi non eravamo dei cosmo-
politi; eravamo dei rifugiati' (I refuse this appellation on our behalf: we are
children of the Second World War. When I returned to Italy I was tightly
tied to Rome. Cosmopolitans choose to be. We weren't cosmopolitan; we
were refugees'). In Francesca Caputo, *Amelia Rosselli: una scrittura plurale*
(Novara: Interlinea edizioni, 2004), 9. Again see Baldacci, especially the
section entitled 'Una vita sotto assedio' (pp. 10–16, 25, 26, 35). Though
Baldacci is single-minded in his reduction of Rosselli's life to a doomed
attempt to recover from the trauma of the war (exemplified by but not
limited to family trauma), his otherwise fine book does not shy away from
the formal complexities of her works, and his take on her suicide (not coincidentally the final paragraph in a section on Plath and Emily Dickinson) is
elegant and sensitive (Baldacci, 144). For a more complex view, see Mario
Moroni's chapter on Rosselli in *La presenza complessa: Identità e soggettività
nelle poetiche del Novecento* (Ravenna: Longo, 1998), 129–44. Emmanuela
Tandello (one of the most prolific and sophisticated Rosselli scholars, along
with Lucia Re) begins her *Amelia Rosselli: La fanciulla e l'infinito* with not
the usual two but four deaths: her father's and uncle's, her mother's, and
Rocco Scotellaro's. Nelson Moe argues that 'what distinguishes her work
from that of other Italian postwar poets is its particular engagement in
and negotiation of the power relations operant in contemporary capitalist society [which] have their origins in her unique personal history as
the daughter of the assassinated anti-fascist leader Carlo Rosselli.' Moe,
'At the Margins of Dominion: The Poetry of Amelia Rosselli,' *Italica* 69.2
(1992): 177. Attilio Manzi redimensions her work within the varying sites
of literal and figurative exile in his 'El espacio y la palabra: Reflexiones
acerca del exilio poético de Amelia Rosselli,' in *Exilios femeninos*, edited by
Pilar Cuder-Domínguez(Huelva, Spain: Universidad de Huelva, Instituto
Andaluz de la Mujer, 2000), 339–45. See also De March, 15–19. Manuela
Manera, in contrast, refutes the poet's reduction to her biographical data
when she says, à propos Rosselli's trilinguism, 'le commissioni linguistiche sono non inevitabile traccia di inalienabile condizione biografica,
ma ricercata scelta di adeguatezza espressiva' (the linguistic mixtures
are not the inevitable trace of an inalienable biographic condition, but
the highly sought choice of expressive adequacy). Manera, 'L'"ydioma
tripharium" di Amelia Rosselli: Ricognizioni linguistiche,' *Lingua e stile* 38
(2003): 267.

18 Her work is 'un perturbante classico, una declinazione per certi versi
unica, senza pari nel panorama della poesia italiana del secondo Novecento' (a perturbing classic, in some ways a unique declination, without
equals in the panorama of Italian poetry of the late twentieth century). It is
'una forma del finimondo' (a form of bedlam) (Baldacci, 3, 5,). Carbognin
calls it 'una lirica … del tutto inassimilabile a quella dei contemporanei' (a
lyric … that is totally unassimilable to that of its contemporaries). Francesco Carbognin, 'Amelia Rosselli: prove d'autore,' *Strumenti critici* 105.2
(May 2004): 245. Andrea Zanzotto remarks, 'Improbabili o nulla i suoi
effettivi rapporti con scuole o gruppi. Rare analogie con situazioni di altri
autori, e analogie possibili solo come premessa all'individuare meglio dif-
ferenze costituzionali' (Its effective relations with other schools or groups
are improbable or non-existent. Rare are the analogies with other authors'
situations, and these are possible only as a premise from which better to
individuate constitutional differences). Andrea Zanzotto, 'Care rischiose
parole sibilline' in *Corriere della Sera*, 18 July 1976: 11. For Pier Vincenzo
Mengaldo, Rosselli's poetry 'resta un fenomeno in sostanza unico nel
panorama letterario italiano' (remains a phenomenon that is substantially
unique in the Italian literary panorama). Pier Vincenzo Mengaldo, *Poeti
italiani del Novecento* (Milan: Mondadori, 1978), 994. For Ann Snodgrass,
Rosselli's supposed uniqueness is tied up in questions of gender: 'Amelia
Rosselli's position in contemporary Italian poetry is characterized by two
almost paradoxical triumphs. The first is the exceptional critical acclaim
her work has received, as exemplified by the publication of Mengaldo's
Poeti Italiani del Novecento, making her the first female poet ever to be
included in a major anthology of Italian poetry in this century. The second
triumph is her ability to baffle the very critics who have included her
work in an exclusively male canon. Forced to invent a new terminology
to accommodate the complexity and originality of her work, these critics
seem challenged by her project to express the inexpressible.' Snodgrass,
Knowing Noise: The English Poems of Amelia Rosselli (New York: Peter Lang,
2001), 9. On this particular count, however, we are not in total agreement.
Rosselli's inclusion in Mengaldo's anthology is a highly problematic one in
light of his generally dismissive readings of her poetry, which are coded as
a kind of linguistic Kristevan abject, veiled as an homage to *scrittura fem-
minile*: 'la poesia è qui vissuta anzitutto come abbandono al flusso buio e
labirintico della vita psichica e dell'immaginario, producendo una sorta di
simultaneità e ubiquità della rappresentazione, e l'abolizione di ogni confine fra interno ed esterno, privato e pubblico-sociale' (here poetry is lived
first and foremost as an abandonment to the dark and labyrinthine flux

of psychic life and of the imaginary, producing a kind of simultaneity and ubiquity of representation, and the abolition of every boundary between internal and external, private and social-public). Mengaldo, 995. For a discussion of Italian poetry anthologies, see Lucia Re, '(De)Constructing the Canon: The Agon of the Anthologies on the Scene of Modern Italian Poetry,' *Modern Language Review* 87.3 (1992): 585–602.

19 Rosselli, *Sleep*, 71–2.

20 It should be noted that Cave only spoke English in moments of great distress, according to her son John: he recalled, for example, that she spoke English when she told him about his father's assassination. See Giuseppe Fiori, *Casa Rosselli: vita di Carlo e Nello, Amelia, Marion e Maria* (Turin: Einaudi Editore, 1999).

21 Shoshana Felman, *Writing and Madness (Literature/Philosophy/Psychoanalysis)*, translated by Martha Noel Evans (Palo Alto: Stanford University Press, 2003), 19.

22 Caputo lists these as a review of Roberto Lupi, *Armonia di gravitazione*, in *Il Diapason* 1. 8–9 (August-September 1950): 24–9; 'La serie degli armonici,' *Civiltà delle macchine* 2.2 (YEAR?): 43–5; and 'Nuovi esperimenti musicali con un nuovo strumento,' *Il Diapason* 4.11–12 (1954): 12–114. See the bibliographical note in Caputo, 347. Rosselli signed 'Marion' in her private correspondence with Scotellaro, too. See F. Vitelli, 'Un lago della memoria: Rocco Scotellaro e Amelia Rosselli,' *La Nuova ricerca* (1998): 6–7, and 'Amelia Rosselli e Scotellaro,' *Trasparenze* 17–19, edited by G. Devoto and E. Tandello (Genova: Edizioni San Marco dei Giustiniani, 2003). Both are cited in Tandello, 22.

23 Though it was her first language (she was born in Paris), Rosselli wrote in French only from time to time: see, for example, her *Diario trilingue*.

24 Caputo, 319–20. Italics in original. 'Seven Sisters' was a term used to describe the seven most powerful oil concessions in the 1950s. The term was coined by Enrico Mattei, an industrialist and former partisan, most likely murdered by political opposition in 1962. We can imagine the possible interest his figure might hold for Rosselli, both as an active opponent of Fascism like her father and uncle, and as the (probable) victim of a political assassination plot. Moreover, his death was under investigation in 1970 by a journalist who then himself disappeared, as in turn did the investigators who went in search of the journalist. In short, the term would indeed have been familiar to Italians and certainly to Rosselli. The polyvalent term 'Seven Sisters' also has a distinctly American connotation (linked to the other American entity, Goodyear and Co.) when it is used to designate a group of colleges including Vassar College, in Poughkeepsie, NY, not

far from Larchmont, where Rosselli lived for several years; Sylvia Plath attended Smith College, another Seven Sisters school.

25 See Caputo, 322.

26 From Aldo Rosselli's *Prove techniche della follia*, 72–3, quoted in Caputo 346.

27 Caputo, 290.

28 Rosselli, *Sleep*, 52.

29 For this view of her English-language works as part of an apprenticeship stage, see Tandello's translation of Rosselli, *Sleep*, 215.

30 Tandello articulates the connection between poetry, the poet's gaze, and her death when she writes about Antigone, 'E mi sembra che sia questo il punto cruciale anche per Amelia Rosselli: ci troviamo di fronte cioè a un sé già postumo. La fanciulla che muore si osserva mentre muore, vittima, corpo tra corpi; e nel vedersi morire piange la propria sorte' (And it seems to me that this is the crucial point for Amelia Rosselli, as well: we find before us an already posthumous being. The maiden who dies observes herself while she dies, victim, body among bodies, and in the course of watching herself die, laments her own end). Tandello, 49.

31 Nelson Moe identifies the roots of her alterity in three facets of her identity: in her 'relationship to the *Italian* lyric (as English and French writer); the *masculine* lyric (as a woman); and to the *poetic* lyric (as musician and musicologist)' (Moe, 184). To this list, I would also add her illustrious political parentage, which we might phrase, to follow Moe, as her relationship to the patriotic lyric (as successful suicide): by this I mean the clash between the expectation of a poetics (and politics) of high-minded nobility aroused by her father's and uncle's political martyrdoms, and what is commonly held to be the ignoble defeat of suicide.

32 Pier Paolo Pasolini, 'Notizia su Amelia Rosselli' in *Menabò* 6 (Turin: Giulio Einaudi Editore, 1963), 66–9.

33 Pasolini, 66. Manuela Manera refines Pasolini's deployment of the lapsus, noting with Rosselli that the Freudian lapsus is largely unconscious, whereas Rosselli engages in conscious 'linguistic invention.' See Manera, 234. Cristina della Coletta, too, revises Pasolini's reading, emphasizing the way 'nothing is absolutely gratuitous, and what appears to be a chance occurrence has actually been carefully calculated.' Della Colletta, 'Amelia Rosselli (1930-),' *Italian Women Writers: A Bio-Bibliographical Sourcebook*, edited by Rinaldina Russell (Westport, CN: Greenwood Press, 1994), 363. Lucia Re, too, notes, 'Si tratta tuttavia di una strategia pienamente calcolata da parte della Rosselli, non importa quanto involuntariamente possa essere l'associazione quando si manifesta per la prima volta, perché deve essere rielaborata coscientemente per poter diventare produttiva di

significato all'interno del testo' (We are dealing in any case with a strategy fully calculated by Rosselli, no matter how involuntarily the association might have manifested itself the first time, because it has to be consciously re-elaborated in order to produce meaning within a text). Re, 'Variazioni su Amelia Rosselli,' *Verri: Rivista di Letteratura* 3.4 (1993): 142. For a discussion of the lapsus in another context, see Marìa Elena Gutierrez, 'La poetica del lapsus: inconscio e linguaggio nell'opera di Alberto Savinio,' *Forum Italicum* 312 (1997): 439–57.

34 Consequently the lapsus becomes a veritable poetic Frankenstein's monster, an unnatural hybrid of human and mechanical. A similar version of this pathologizing reading can be found in Pier Vincenzo Mengaldo: 'Il fatto è che la Rosselli sente e lascia agire la lingua, letteralmente, in quanto corpo, organismo biologico, le cui cellule proliferano incontrollatamente in una vitalità riproduttiva che, come nella crescita tumorale, diviene patogena e mortale: da cui anche uno dei primi paradossi di questa poesia, che il linguaggio vi è insieme forma immediata della soggettività e realtà autonoma che sta fuori e anche contro il soggetto' (The fact is that Rosselli feels language and allows it to act, literally, insofar as it is body, biological organism, whose cells proliferate uncontrollably in a reproductive vitality that, as in tumour growth, becomes pathogenic and mortal: from which arises one of the first paradoxes of this poetry, that its language is at once immediate form of subjectivity and autonomous reality that stands outside of as well as against the subject). Mengaldo, 1981 edition, 995. For Re, the consequences to this reading are significant and analogous to the ones I attribute to Pasolini's deployment of the language of tumours and atomic explosions: 'Quello che Mengaldo descrive è un linguaggio malato, impazzito o meglio – senza dirlo in termini espliciti – un linguaggio della pazzia. Ancora una volta troviamo la Rosselli privata della propria voce: non è lei che parla in questi testi, ma piuttosto la sua malattia, cioè una forma di pazzia. La ragione della reticenza, del silenzio che circondano la Rosselli o nel caso di Mengaldo, la strana resistenza alla possibilità di concederle legittimità come cittadino della poesia, è ora chiara' (What Mengaldo describes is a sick language, language gone crazy or rather – without saying it in explicit terms – a language of madness. Yet again we find Rosselli deprived of her own voice; it is not she who speaks in these texts, but rather her illness, that is, a form of madness. The reason for the reticence and for the silence that surround Rosselli or, in the case of Mengaldo, the strange resistance to the possibility of conceding her legitimacy as a citizen of poetry, is now clear). Re, 'Variazioni su Amelia Rosselli,' 132.

35 Pasolini, 66.

36 Pasolini, 67. In contrast, Thomas Peterson notes with Rosselli herself that there is a decidedly Surrealist component to her work. Thomas E. Peterson, 'Il soggiorno in inferno and Related Works by Amelia Rosselli,' Rivista di Studi Italiani 17.1 (1999): 275–6. Peterson is also one of the few Rosselli critics to grasp 'the pleasure, even the erotics, of the text' (278).

37 Nelson Moe comes to similar conclusions about Rosselli's perceived uniqueness when he says, 'Discussions of her work repeatedly mention the singular nature of her poetry, along with such variant adjectives as solitary, unique, anomalous' (177). In a note he provides both a list of critics who have difficulty locating Rosselli's poetry within any tradition or school, and a list of those poets to whom we can reasonably make comparisons.

38 Stefano Agosti, Poesia contemporanea: saggi e interventi (Milan: Bompiani, 1995), 133–51.

39 Agosti, 136. This is not unlike the procedure visible in Surrealist Michel Leiris's 1925 Glossaire j'y serre mes gloses.

40 Rosselli, Sleep, 10.

41 Pasolini himself has created a neologism much in the style of Rosselli's lapsus: 'imposseduta' is an invented word, related both to 'possedere,' to possess, and impossessar(si), to master, grasp, or appropriate.

42 Franco Fortini, I poeti del Novecento (Bari: Laterza, 1978), 205.

43 Rosselli, Sleep, 124.

44 See, for example, her references to André Breton, Tristan Tzara, Louis Aragon, and Paul Eluard in the critical writings contained in Caputo. These references make explicit the connection between figures such as Gyula Illyés and Giordano Falzoni; speaking in connection to her own Spazi metrici, she mentions Breton as an example of one of the few poets who know how to use free verse (Caputo, 59).

45 Caputo, 'Cercare la parola che esprime gli altri' in Amelia Rosselli, 12.

46 Both Rosselli and Breton, however, were involved at various points with the PCI, and their respective works are ideologically engaged.

47 It is tempting after such a statement to evoke the unforgettable eye scene in Surrealist filmmaker Luis Buñuel's Un chien andalou, though such an evocation does not propel my argument beyond the obvious: an instance in which Rosselli's surrealism is, besides methodological or technical, thematic as well. Instead I will note that Rosselli's insistence on the (female-gendered) I further tips the scale, in some ways, toward her connection to the Surrealists over the masculinist Gruppo '63. See also Walter Benjamin's 1929 essay entitled 'Surrealism: The Last Snapshot of the European Intelligentsia,' which emphasizes the importance of experience as much as language for Surrealist poetics (against, say, the focus on language's materiality more typical of the

Gruppo '63). Benjamin, *Reflections: Essays, Aphorisms, Autobiographical Writings*, edited by Peter Demetz, translated by Edmund Jephcott (New York and London: Harcourt Brace Jovanovich, 1978).

48 Anna Balakian, *André Breton: Magus of Surrealism* (New York: Oxford University Press, 1971), 36. For Balakian, these 'disparate entities' derive from what for Abbé Constant is the principal of '*coincidentia oppositorium*, the coexistence of opposites, and the reversal of one into the other.'

49 This network or 'lacework of interrelations,' as Balakian calls it (33), can be linked in genealogy to Janet, and is made visible in the relative paucity, in Breton, of images linked through the adverb *comme*. For a discussion of metaphor in Breton, see Lino Gabellone, *L'oggetto surrealista: il testo, la città, l'oggetto in Breton* (Turin: Giulio Einaudi Editore, 1977), 23–34.

50 Gabellone describes the Surrealist 'object' similarly: 'L'oggetto è allora un significante privilegiato che sussume tutta una serie di significati instabili, ineffabili o aleatori, entrando in una catena diacronica di significanti (correlativi oggettivi) aperta nei due sensi (passato-futuro) e virtualmente infinita' (The object is thus a privileged signifier that subsumes a whole series of unstable, indescribable, or aleatory signifieds, entering into a diachronic chain of signifiers (objective correlatives) open in both directions (past – future) and virtually infinite). Besides the emphasis Gabellone places on multiple meanings in Breton, the notion of the aleatory, key to Breton's poetics, is similarly mobilized in Rosselli as the 'chance' outcome of word combinations(Gabellone, 19).

51 Gabellone describes automatic writing thus: 'il testo automatico (e per estensione la poesia surrealista) funziona solo attraverso la denegazione della scrittura in quanto materialità, e deve poter dare di sé un'immagine senza storia e senza paternità, rimandarci a un linguaggio orfano, tagliato fuori dal mondo, perfettamente autoriproduttivo' (the automatic text (and by extension surrealist poetry) functions only by way of the negation of writing as materiality, and needs to be able to give an image of itself as being without history and without paternity, to return us to an orphan language, cut off from the world, perfectly self-reproductive). Gabellone, 16.

52 Alongside the tumours and atomic explosions that compose her language, Rosselli's texts are 'epilettici' (epileptic), and the lapsus reveals the word 'sotto un aspetto orrendo … putrefatta o ridicola' (in a horrible light … putrefied or ridiculous). Pasolini, 67.

53 See Balakian, 28–9, for a discussion of the impact of Janet of Breton (and Jung).

54 For a thorough description of the influence on Breton of Janet's automatism, see Balakian, 28–35.

55 Balakian, 29. She quotes Janet: 'Let the pen wander automatically, on the page even as the medium interrogates his mind.' Pierre Janet. *L'Automatisme psychologique*, ninth edition (Paris: Felix Alcan, 1921), 464.

56 Fortini, 208.

57 Rosselli, *Sleep*, 66.

58 Rosselli, *Sleep*, 134.

59 Rosselli, *Sleep*, 144.

60 Compare this to Lucia Re's observation in 'Mythic Revisionism: Women Poets and Philosophers in Italy Today': 'By placing Antigone in the role of silent guardian to her poems, Rosselli implicitly wishes that they might be un-written, be allowed, like Polyneice's remains, to decay and disintegrate without being *seen* and preyed upon.' In Maria Ornella Marotti, editor, *Italian Women Writers from the Renaissance to the Present: Revising the Canon* (University Park: Pennsylvania State University Press, 1996), 227.

61 From Sylvia Plath, *Ariel* (1962), 8–9.

62 Jacques Derrida, *The Work of Mourning* (Chicago: University of Chicago Press, 2001), editor's note p. 14. See endnote iv.

63 Kaja Silverman, *Male Subjectivity at the Margins* (London: Routledge, 1992), 130.

64 Jacques Lacan, *Four Fundamental Concepts of Psychoanalysis*, quoted in Silverman, 130.

65 Silverman, 142–3.

66 Lacan, quoted in Silverman, 151.

67 Here again we may recognize the presence of a clear and identifiable poetic tradition into which Rosselli's works fit.

68 Giacomo Leopardi, 'L'infinito' in *The Poems of Leopardi*, translated by Geoffrey Bickersteth (Cambridge: Cambridge University Press, 1923), 208–9.

69 *Sleep*, 120. See also her 'Tu non ricordi le mie dorate spiagge, se come penso' (*Serie ospedaliera*, 77), which more explicitly posits 'L'infinito' as intertext:

> … O il naufragare. Ed è dolce il naufragar in questo
> Sonno così spiritato, ed è dolce il non pensare
> Altro che la mania di vedere, toccare, sentire
> Odorare il tuo riposo pieno.

> … Or the shipwreck. And it is sweet to wreck in this
> Sleep so spirited, and it is sweet not to think
> Anything else but the mania of seeing, touching, feeling
> Smelling your full repose.

70 For the account of the psychological surveillance to which Rosselli was
    subjected, see her *Storia di una malattia* in Caputo, 317–26.
71 See Octave Mannoni, 'Je sais bien mais quand même' in *Clefs pour
    l'Imaginaire ou l'Autre Scène* (Paris: Seuil, 1969).
72 Rosselli, *Sleep*, 96.
73 This is an illustration of what Kofman's translator Ann Smock calls
    Mémé's 'treacherous rescue' or 'generous swindle.' Kofman, *Rue Ordener,
    Rue Labat* (Lincoln: University of Nebraska Press, 1996), xi.
74 Kofman committed suicide, as did Gilles Deleuze, a fact that goes only
    obliquely mentioned in Derrida's commemorative piece on her life and
    works in *The Work of Mourning* (as her interest in 'conjuring death,' 171,
    and in his remark, 'and what a death,' 172).
75 Derrida, *The Work of Mourning*, 169.
76 Derrida, *The Work of Mourning*, 172.
77 Derrida elaborates on what he calls 'slippage from one death to another,'
    cautioning against the dangers of applying observations or feelings about
    one death to another, thereby reducing the individuality of each 'act of
    mourning'; at the same time, one might argue that that slippage enriches
    our understanding of the ties that anchor the dead to the world, to each of
    us as mourners(*The Work of Mourning*, 8).
78 Kofman, *Rue Ordener, Rue Labat*, 3.
79 Kofman, *Rue Ordener, Rue Labat*, 3.
80 Ann Smock in Kofman, *Rue Ordener, Rue Labat*, xii.
81 This is the expression Ann Smock uses in her translator's introduction to
    Rue Ordener, Rue Labat, xii.
82 Kofman quoted in Derrida, *The Work of Mourning*, 177.
83 Derrida, *The Work of Mourning*, 176
84 See also Foucault, 'What Is an Author,' when he describes the relationship
    between writing and death: 'This link subverts an old tradition exemplified
    by the Greek epic, which was intended to perpetuate the immortality of
    the hero: if he was willing to die young, it was so that his life, consecrated
    and magnified by death, might pass into immortality; the narrative then
    redeemed this accepted death. In another way, the motivation, as well as the
    theme and the pretext of Arabian narratives – such as *The Thousand and One
    Nights* – was also the eluding of death: one spoke, telling stories into the ear-
    ly morning, in order to forestall death, to postpone the day of reckoning that
    would silence the narrator. Scheherezade's narrative is an effort, renewed
    each night, to keep death outside the circle of life.' Michel Foucault, *Essential
    Works of Michel Foucault: Aesthetics, Method, and Epistemology*, vol. 2, edited
    by James D. Faubion (New York: New Press, 1998), 206.

85 Rosselli, *Sleep*, 40.
86 Of course, Durkheim was much less interested in individual suicides than his inclusion in this list implies.

3. The Post-Biological Author

1 Obituary signed G.Z. and published in *Il giornale dell'Emilia* (Bologna), 29 August 1950. Excerpted in Vincenzo Arnone, *Pavese: tra l'assurdo e l'assoluto* (Padua: Edizioni Messaggero, 1998), 86.
2 Lorenzo Mondo published Pavese's *Taccuino segreto* in *La Stampa*, 8 August 1990. See Vincenzo Binetti for an examination of the polemic surrounding the *Taccuino*. 'Marginalità e appartenenza: La funzione dell'intellettuale tra sfera pubblica e privato nell'Italia del dopoguerra,' *Italica* 74.3 (1997): 360–74.
3 Indeed, Lajolo (among others) claims to have written his book precisely in order to make reparations for not loving him more: 'Having arrived at the conclusion, and realizing how difficult it has been to reconstruct the life of Cesare Pavese, I'm at least certain that I have tried to show him that warmth that none of us, his friends, were able to show him during his life … My book is also an act of reparation. Could we have done more when he lived among us?' So as we saw with Morselli, in Pavese's case, too, there is a certain amount of self-flagellation, though it is for personal, not professional reasons. Davide Lajolo, *An Absurd Vice: A Biography of Cesare Pavese*, translated by Mario and Mark Pietralunga (New York: New Directions, 1983).
4 Rimanelli's characterization of Pavese's double-edged reputation recalls Moravia's assessment of the author. By January 1950, Rimanelli says, Pavese 'was already a kind of myth … On the one hand there was the man of culture who under fascism kept open the dialogue – prohibited by fascism – against every form of chauvinist autarchy in the realm of culture; on the other hand there was the Pavese of legend, woven of petty nature, which defined him as an acute but harsh man, all of one piece, distant, ungenerous, and even envious like a discontented God, extremely severe (especially) in regard to young writers.' Giose Rimanelli, 'Myth and De-Mythification of Pavese's Art,' *Italian Quarterly* 49 (1969): 3.
5 'Quella di liquidare Pavese con poche battute e una facile etichetta era una tendenza abbastanza diffusa nei primi anni '50' (Liquidating Pavese with a few remarks and a facile label was a fairly diffuse tendency in the early 1950s). Mauro Ponzi, *La critica e Pavese* (Bologna: Cappelli, 1977), 185.
6 R.W. Flint, 'Translating Cesare Pavese,' *Delos: A Journal on and of Translation* 1 (1968): 153.

7 Giuditta Isotti Rosowsky, 'La luna e i falò, una rilettura,' *Narrativa* 22 (2002): 106.

8 Implicit in these remarks is the idea that Pavese's suicide was a foregone conclusion. See, for example, 'A Man and His Novels,' *Times Literary Supplement* 15 September 1961: 612; Linda Hutcheon, 'Pavese's Intellectual Rhythm,' *Italian Quarterly* 60–1 (1972): 12; and Davide De Camilli, 'Pavese e altri diaristi,' *Italianistica* 5.1 (1976): 93–109. Of all of the pieces on Pavese's suicide I have read, Giose Rimanelli's is striking for its lack of rhetoric, and its elegant and utterly simple acceptance of the act. Rimanelli, 'Pavese's Diario: Why Suicide? Why Not?' in *Italian Literature: Roots and Branches. Essays in Honor of Thomas Goddard Bergin*, edited by Giose Rimanelli and Kenneth John Atchity (New Haven: Yale University Press, 1976), 383–405. Another interesting move is the subsuming of Pavese's supposed psychological foibles under the rubric of a discourse of love for humanity, by eliding the intellectual interest with the character who exhibits it: see Ada Ruschioni, 'Appunti su Pavese,' *Vita e Pensiero: Mensile di cultura dell'Università cattolica* 49 (1966): 602. We have seen this in the case of Amelia Rosselli as well, when Andrea Zanzotto interprets her poetry as a sign of her tremendous 'generosity.' Zadie Smith's article on the recent suicide of novelist David Foster Wallace, too, makes similar claims on his behalf. See Zadie Smith, 'Always Another Word,' *Harper's Magazine*, January 2009: 26–30 as well as Duncan Murrell's follow-up suggestion of the word *agape* as more appropriate than her 'prayer.' Duncan Murrell, 'Letters: Love Match,' *Harper's Magazine*, March 2009: 4. Of course, not all suicidal authors are considered generous or loving: just, apparently, most of them.

9 There are a number of excellent anthologies of Pavese criticism, including *La critica e Pavese* by Mauro Ponzi, Sergio Pautasso's *Cesare Pavese oltre il mito: Il mestiere di scrivere come mestiere di vivere* (Genoa: Marietti, 2000), and Marziano Guglielminetti and Giuseppe Zaccaria, *Cesare Pavese: introduzione e guida allo studio dell'opera pavesiana: storia e antologia della critica* (Florence: Le Monnier, 1976). There are also essay collections devoted to Pavese by authors who have written about him over the decades, such as the retrospective *Trent'anni con Cesare Pavese: Diario contro diario* by Geno Pampaloni (Milan: Rusconi, 1981).

10 A quick and unscientific survey of the review articles published during the decades before and after his death bears this out. Between 1941 and 1949, I counted 142 reviews of Pavese's works; in 1950, the year of his death, I am aware of 96, of which 36 were published posthumously. There were 60 articles published in 1951; 74 in 1952; 50 in 1953. Then the numbers decrease,

so that the total between 1954 and 1960 is 95, unevenly distributed. Also interesting is the fact that none of the reviews before his death contained in their title anything but the title of the work being reviewed, whereas in the year 1950, in the period between January and 21 August, 14 have descriptive or polemical titles; after 27 August, 20 have them. We can attribute this modest shift to a change in the fashion, certainly, but after 1950 the titles are roughly evenly divided between those that simply refer to a Pavese text and those that say something about the reviewer's own arguments: in other words Pavese scholarship consists more and more of review articles, as critics stake their claims from the outset and foreground their own positions.

11 See for example *Rinascita* (Rome) no.3, March 1950, no.6, June 1950, and no.7, July 1950.

12 And perhaps they were partly right: it was revealed in 1990 that pages initially expurgated from Pavese's diary, written 25 October 1942, expressed ironic admiration toward the Fascists (in particular for their discipline, in contrast with the antifascists, 'che sanno tutto, superano tutto, ma quando discutono litigano soltanto' (who know everything, overcome everything, but when they discuss, only argue), as well as disbelief about Nazi atrocities: 'Tutte queste storie di atrocità naz. Che spaventano i borghesi, che cosa sono di diverso dalle storie sulla rivoluzione franc., che pure ebbe la ragione dalla sua? Se anche fossero vere, la storia non va coi guanti. Forse il difetto di noi italiani è che non sappiamo essere atroci' (All these stories of naz. atrocities. [Is it] that they frighten the bourgeois, how are they different from the stories of the Fr. revolution, that had right on its side? Even if they were true, history does not happen with gloves on. Perhaps the flaw of us Italians is that we don't know how to be atrocious). The tone of these and other similar entries, however, precludes reading much into his critique of anti-Fascism other than a reactionary objection on stylistic grounds, nor do his remarks on Fascism or Nazism constitute a genuine endorsement of their policies, disturbing – and naïve – as these remarks are. See *La Stampa*, 8 August 1990: 15–17 for the full text of the expurgated pages. Monica Lanzilotta provides an interesting analysis of this new *caso Pavese* in her *La parabola del disimpegno: Cesare Pavese e un mondo editoriale* (Rende: Centro Editoriale e Librario Università degli Studi della Calabria, 2001), 113–30. Similarly, Sergio Pautasso's lucid discussion of the discoveries can be found in his *Cesare Pavese oltre il mito*, 26–32. Also on the limits of Pavese's political engagement, see Carlo Annoni, 'Appunti di antifascismo e resistenza nella narrativa di Pavese,' *Vita e Pensiero: Rassegna Italiana di Cultura* 51 (1968): 205–13.

13 Moravia's *Pavese decadente*, in *Corriere della Sera*, 22 December 1954, reprinted in *L'uomo come fine e altri saggi* (Milan: Bompiani, 1964), 187–91, and in Ponzi, 186–90. Here quoted in Guglielminetti and Zaccaria, 168. Contrast this with attempts to assert Pavese's neorealism, exemplified by Carlo Salinari's 'La poetica di Pavese,' cited in Ponzi, 190–200.

14 Davide Lajolo, *Il vizio assurdo: Vita di Cesare Pavese* (Milan: Il Saggiatore, 1960). Translated by Mario and Mark Pietralunga as *An Absurd Vice: A Biography of Cesare Pavese* . Other personal recollections followed, such as Natalia Ginzburg, 'Portrait of a Friend,' *London Magazine* 8.5 (1968): 21–7.

15 Dominique Fernandez, *L'échec de Pavese* (Paris: Grasset, 1967). See also Gian Paolo Biasin, 'L'inconscio di Pavese,' *Italica* 46.3 (1969): 310–21.

16 This is *Sigma* no. 3–4, December 1964.

17 Annoni, however, makes a decent case for the argument that Pavese's interest in the Resistance is secondary to his interest in the solitary nature of man, an interest well served by the questions raised by the Resistance about communal action, solidarity versus individualism, and the role of the intellectual.

18 Piero De Tommaso, 'Ritratto di Cesare Pavese,' *Rassegna della letteratura italiana* 69.3 (1965): 546. See also Christian Dedet, 'Cesare Pavese,' *La Revue de Paris* 71 (1964): 122.

19 On myths in Pavese as well as Pavese as myth, see Armanda Guiducci, *Il mito Pavese* (Florence: Enrico Vallecchi, 1967); Francesco Mattesini, 'L'echec di Pavese,' *Vita e Pensiero: Rassegna Italiana di Cultura* 51.3 (1968): 201–4; Giovanni Cillo, *La distruzione dei miti: Saggio sulla poetica di Cesare Pavese* (Florence: Enrico Vallecchi, 1972); Giovanni Caserta,*Realtà e miti nella lirica di Pavese* (Matera: BMG, 1970); Alain Clerval, 'Cesare Pavese: De la naissance du mythe au suicide comme art de vivre,' *Nouvelle Revue Francaise* 239 (1972): 83–8. See also Furio Jesi, 'Cesare Pavese, il mito e la scienza del mito,' *Sigma* no. 3–4, (December 1964):, 95–120. A much rougher assessment is to be found, once again, in Moravia, who writes, 'Probabilmente il mito di Pavese va spiegato con l'incapacità di creare il mito nei suoi libri. Non vogliamo dire con questo che Pavese si è ucciso perché era consapevole di non essere riuscito a dire certe cose. Pavese aveva della propria opera e di se stesso un'opinione altissima, come si può vedere nel diario. Ma, strano a dirsi, è proprio questo idea esagerata di se stesso che in parte ne ha provocato la morte ... Pavese non è riuscito a creare il mito nella pagina; e il suo suicidio va interpretato come un tentativo di crearlo nella vita ... l'operazione tristissima e orgogliosissima è riuscita. Il mito di Pavese, il mito dello scrittore che si è ucciso per motivi esistenziali, sopravviverà alla sua opera. Ma i motivi erano soltanto apparentemente

esistenziali. In realtà erano letterari' (The myth of Pavese can probably be explained by the incapacity of creating myths in his books. With this we don't mean to say that Pavese killed himself because he was aware of failing to say certain things. Pavese had an extremely high opinion of his work and of himself, as one can see from the diary. But, strange to say, it is precisely this exaggerated idea of himself that partly provoked his death ... Pavese did not succeed in creating a myth on the page; and his suicide can be interpreted as an attempt to create it in life ... The terribly sad and extremely proud operation succeeded. The myth of Pavese, the myth of the writer who killed himself for existential reasons, will survive his work. But the motives were only apparently existential. In reality they were literary). Alberto Moravia, 'Fu solo un decadente' and 'Il mito di Pavese' in *L'Espresso*, 12 July 1970 and 26 July 1970. Cited in Gian Carlo Ferretti, 'Pavese e la scelta del silenzio,' *Studi in memoria di Luigi Russo* (Pisa: Nistri-Lischi, 1974), 478.

20 À propos of anthropology, Pavese's supposed obsession with masturbation is not to be confused with his other 'preoccupazione ossessiva,' according to Italo Calvino: human sacrifices! See Italo Calvino, 'Pavese e i sacrifici umani,' *Revue des Etudes Italiennes* 12.1 (1966): 107–10.

21 See 'Pavese, niega toda posibilidad de evolución histórica,' in Manuel Carrera,'Cesare Pavese,' *Revista de Occidente* 12 (1976): 13–22.

22 Gioanola, among others, compellingly argues for this coterminousness. The strong exceptions to this rule include Pavese's good friend and first biographer Davide Lajolo, who forcefully objected to the publication of Pavese's diary *Mestiere di vivere*, considering it degrading to Pavese: '*Il mestiere di vivere* non è da leggere. Non aggiunge nulla a Pavese scrittore, deprime la figura di Pavese uomo. Non è un libro da leggere' (*The Business of Living* is not for reading. It doesn't add anything to Pavese the writer; it degrades the figure of Pavese the man. It is not a book to be read). *L'Unità*, 11 October 1952, quoted in Pautasso, *Cesare Pavese oltre il mito*, 15. In this edition (but not in *Cesare Pavese, L'uomo libro: il mestiere di scrivere come mestiere di vivere* [Milan: Arcipelago, 1991]), Pautasso provides a careful overview of the debate sparked by the diary's publication.

23 Elio Gioanola, *Cesare Pavese: La realtà, l'altrove, il silenzio* (Milan: Editoriale Jaca Book, 2003), 62. In his study, Gioanola argues for a return to Pavese's life – or to examination of it, in any case, for evidence of the relationship between it and Pavese's writing.

24 Gioanola, *Cesare Pavese: La realtà, l'altrove, il silenzio*, 63–4. For a similar argument about the prevalence of the *mal du siècle* among cultural figures in the early part of the century, see Thomas Harrison, *1910: The Emanci-*

pation of Dissonance (Berkeley and Los Angeles: University of California Press, 1996).

25 I personally prefer Clelia's justification for living in *Tra donne sole*: 'finché la vita aveva un bagno, valeva la pena di vivere' (as long as you can have a bath, living is worth the effort). Cesare Pavese, *Tra donne sole* in *La bella estate* (Turin: Oscar Mondadori, 1999), 230; Pavese, *Among Women Only*, translated by D.D. Paige (London and Chester Springs: Peter Owen, 2004), 6. Translations of *Among Women Only* are from this edition where noted.

26 Gioanola in *Cesare Paves: La realtà, l'altrove, il silenzio*, 65. Citations to this effect from Pavese's letters are to be found on pp. 64–5. Also relevant are studies like Lorenzo Mondo's 'Le dernier roman di Pavese,' which understands the list of towns with which *La luna e i falò* opens to function as a literary farewell: 'Le sens en est manifeste dès la première page, où l'auteur rassemble autour de soi, pour les embrasser d'un seul regard, les villages e les pays de son enfance, en répétant avec tendresse leurs noms qui chantent: Canelli, Barbaresco, Alba, Ponticello, Neive, Cravanzana ... ' (The meaning is manifest from the first page, where the author gathers around him, in order to take them in with one single glance, the villages and the towns of his childhood, tenderly repeating their names which sing: Canelli, Barbaresco, Alba, Ponticello, Neive, Cravanzana ...). Mondo, 'Le dernier roman de Pavese,' *Lettres Nouvelles* 13 (1965): 116.

27 Vincenzo Guerazzi, 'Alle foci del Po con Pavese, Morselli ed Hemingway,' *Forum Italicum* 33.1 (1999): 280.

28 Pavese in a letter to Constance Dowling. See Davide Lajolo, *Pavese* (Milan: Rizzoli, 1984), 12 and again on 279, as well as Gioanola, *Cesare Pavese: La realtà, l'altrove, il silenzio*, 70.

29 Alfred Alvarez, *The Savage God: A Study of Suicide* (New York: W.W. Norton and Company, 1990), 123.

30 Ferretti, 481.

31 A notable exception can be found in Gioanola in *Cesare Pavese: La realtà, l'altrove, il silenzio*. For Ignacio Fontes, on the other hand, the motives behind Pavese's suicide are worthy of comment, of censure. Fontes locates the source of Pavese's long-standing suicidal tendencies in his difficult relations with women, whom he considers adversaries if not outright enemies. In this way Fontes locates Pavese's suicide among the suicides for love, a category whose connotations of immaturity are apparent from the anecdotal examples of otherwise unknown Spanish teenagers who killed themselves over broken relationships. Ignacio Fontes,'Una interrogación sobre el suicidio de Pavese,' *Revista de Occidente* 142 (1993): 121–35.

32 Alvarez, 123: 'Suicide often seems to the outsider a supremely motiveless

perversity, performed ... for reasons which seem trivial or even impercep-
tible. Thus Pavese killed himself at the height of both his creative power
and his public success, using as his excuse an unhappy affair with a dim
little American actress whom he had known only briefly.' Note the attribution of a single motive.

33 Cesare Pavese, *Lettere 1924–1944* (Turin: Einaudi, 1966) and *Lettere 1945–*
1950 (Turin: Einaudi, 1966).

34 Marziano Guglielminetti and Silvia Savioli, 'Un carteggio inedito tra
Cesare Pavese e Mario Bonfantini,' *Esperienze Letterarie: Rivista Trimestrale*
di Critica e Cultura 25.3–4 (2000): 62: 'ogni infimo rigo di Pavese recuperato
è un rigo guadagnato.'

35 Rimanelli suggests that Pavese's diary, though perhaps begun for private
reasons, evolved into a document intended for eventual publication.
Rimanelli, 'Pavese's Diario,' 385. The unnamed author of the *Times Literary*
Supplement's review of Pavese's diary says, 'it was only at the eleventh
hour that he gave permission for its posthumous appearance' ('A Man and
His Novels,' 612). Writing in 1954, however, Angela Bianchini Fales noted
that according to the preface to the published diary, 'molti dei suoi amici
ne conoscevano l'esistenza da tempo e ad alcuni di loro Pavese aveva
espresso il desiderio che fosse pubblicato' (many of his friends had for
some time known of the existence of the diary and Pavese had expressed
to some of them the wish that it be published). Angela Bianchini Fales,
'Cesare Pavese e le sue opere postume,' *Italica* 31.3 (1954): 160. Ester Dolce
offers a summary of critical interpretations in her 'Appunti dopo la lettura
dell'epistolario pavesiano,' *Vita e Pensiero: Rassegna Italiana di Cultura* 51
(1968): 230–46. Carmine Di Biase looks for insights about Pavese not as
writer but as critic and theoretician of his own works in the diary, in 'Dal
verso alla prosa: Autocritica e chiarificazione nel *Diario* di Pavese,' *Vita e*
Pensiero: Rassegna Italiana di Cultura 51 (1968): 214–29. Gilbert Bosetti traces
the evolution of the diary in his 'L'Intimite du journal pavesien: Ecrire
pour vivre' in *Le Journal intime et ses formes litteraires*, edited by V. Del Litto
(Geneva: Droz, 1978), 119–28. Finally, Ferretti reads Pavese's diary as an
intensely literary entity, conceived to be read. Ferretti, 479.

36 For Biasin, suicide is a consistently important thematic element, apparent
even in Pavese's very early works. He cites poems such as 'Agony,' 'Paradise on the Rooftops,' and 'The Cats Will Know,' his short novel *Among*
Women Only, and the short story 'Suicides.' Gian Paolo Biasin, *The Smile*
of the Gods: A Thematic Study of Cesare Pavese's Works, translated by Yvonne
Freccero (Ithaca: Cornell University Press, 1968).

37 It would be inaccurate to consider it alongside, say, Vittorini's *Diario in*

pubblico, a text that was conceived and executed with a plural reader-ship in mind. For a sensitive (and sensible) comparison of Pavese's and Vittorini's diaries, see Glauco Cambon's 'Truth as Fiction: Pavese's Diary,' *Michigan Quarterly Review* 16.1 (1977): 5. Davide De Camilli compares it to Leopardi's *Zibaldone* and Baudelaire's *Journaux intimes* in his 'Pavese e altri diaristi.' At the other end of the spectrum we might locate Morselli's diary, which resembles Pavese's for its interests (indeed, it is in many ways much more impassioned and verbal about literature, philosophy, science, politics, and, of course, sex – which Morselli did in fact have) but was writ-ten, to the best of my knowledge, without a posthumous publication plan, as we might expect from a largely unpublished author.

38 And in fact it contains plenty. For starters, see Davide De Camilli's list of references in 'Pavese e altri diaristi,' 98–9. Biasin notes the diary entries of 23 March and 25 March 1950. See *The Smile of the Gods,* 272–3n6 for a lengthy list of diary entries that deal directly with the author's suicidal thoughts.

39 Pautasso, *Cesare Pavese oltre il mito,* 46.

40 See Michel Foucault's 'What Is an Author?' in his *Essential Works of Foucault: Aesthetics, Method and Epistemology,* vol. 2, edited by James D. Faubion (New York: New Press), 205–22.

41 Pavese's last journal entry, dated 18 August 1950. Pavese, *Il mestiere di vivere – Diario 1935–1950* (Turin: Einaudi, 1952).

42 Jacques Derrida, *The Work of Mourning* (Chicago: University of Chicago Press, 2001), 169.

43 Derrida, *The Work of Mourning,* 175–6

44 Derrida, *The Work of Mourning,* 176.

45 This is Rimanelli's description of the sensation of reading Pavese's diary ('Pavese's Diario,' 384).

46 Cesare Pavese, 'Last blues, to be read some day' from the collection *Verrà la morte e avrà i tuoi occhi,* published in *Le poesie* (Turin: Einaudi Tascabili, 1998), 143. The poem was composed in English and is dated 11 April 1950.

47 I am thinking in general terms about Vattimo's *The End of Modernity: Nihil-ism and Hermeneutics in Postmodern Culture,* translated by Jon R. Snyder (Baltimore: Johns Hopkins University Press, 1991).

48 Emanuele Severino, *Tautótēs* (Milan: Adelphi, 1995), 19.

49 Severino, 24.

50 Pavese, *Tra donne sole* in *La bella estate,* 298–9.

51 Pavese, *Among Women Only,* 118–19.

52 Note the structural similarity between Morselli's suicide after *Dissipatio H.G.* (the suicide novel), and Pavese's after *La bella estate,* whose third com-

ponent is *Tra donne sole*. It was the book for which he won the 1950 Premio Strega. Not his last work but the one in which suicide is most visible, it is the book generally privileged by his readership as having the most to say about the author. Morselli writes of shooting himself (though not in his last novel, *Dissipatio H.G.*) and Rosetta poisons herself in a rented room like her creator in his hotel room.

53 Portions of the section that follows were presented at the AAIS 2004 Convention in Ottawa.

54 Biasin's discussion of *Among Women Only* highlights the immanence of Rosetta's suicide throughout the story, and rightly points out that we might be tempted to read much into the multiple similarities between the figures of Rosetta and Pavese. But Biasin de-emphasizes suicide when he observes that it is Clelia around whom much of the interest of the narrative revolves, and it is she alongside Rosetta who forms a dyad that much more fully speaks to their creator than can Rosetta alone: 'In reality, Clelia and Rosetta are dialectic poles in Pavese's personality: there is the author who, like Clelia, forges tenaciously his destiny on the faith of his profession; and there is the man who, like Rosetta, cannot find any value in life (despite the many books he wrote, as opposed to his character's sterility). There are two Paveses: one the responsible adult who knows how to accept life, like Clelia; the other the young Pavese, eager for the absolute who refuses any compromise whatsoever, like Rosetta' (*The Smile of the Gods*, 161). See also Donald Heiney, 'Pavese: The Geography of the Moon,' *Contemporary Literature* 9.4 (1968): 522–37; and Linda Hutcheon's article.

55 What is work, here? For the protagonist Clelia, it is many things: financial necessity, class-jump facilitator, source of independence, and, after her impolitic outburst at work in front of clients and her superior, an exit strategy. For other characters such as Rosetta, it is potentially a way to pass the time until she falls in love or marries (the former and the latter not necessarily causally linked in the text); it is, equally problematically, a source of castration anxiety for Lorenzo because his wife Nene is so much more successful. The only one who works well is Febo (in the novella), and Clelia recognizes this before their quick erotic adventure – she admires the way his hands move across the page.

56 Gioanola gestures toward the text's mythical nature when he envisions the three women standing on the edge of the abyss, in the throes of a ritual whose high priestess is Momina, whose victim is Rosetta, and whose horrified initiate is Clelia. The invocation of myth and ritual here does not convince me completely because it carries with it a sense of the inevitable, and Rosetta's death is not inevitable at any single point. Nor does Gioanola's

sense of Momina's superiority (described, for example, in his *Cesare Pavese: La poetica dell'essere* [Milan: Marzorati, 1971], 350–1) – although she is the most outspoken of the women and perhaps the most consistent in her rejection of any transcendent purpose to life, she is more like the mouthpiece for her class, not the instigator of its foibles. I think one could equally argue that Rosetta occupies the position of authority, as the only one to put her money where her mouth is.

57 At least, I assume it is a question of not even bothering; neither the novel nor the film attributes other motives to Rosetta (such as wanting to be dressed in a particular way when her body was found), and indeed the dialogue between Rosetta and Momina about looking in the mirror (discussed below) would seem to indicate that Rosetta was precisely not concerned with her appearance but rather with expediently acquitting herself of the immediate task – the diminution of pain.

58 *The Group*, the novel by American Mary McCarthy written in 1963, is not entirely off the mark as a point of comparison with *Tra donne sole*. As in Pavese, McCarthy's clique of young co-eds muddles through some of the various adventures of young womanhood, including but not limited to, in no particular order, marriage, sexual initiation, childbearing, lesbianism, unfaithful husbands, and class struggle. What's more, one of the group in McCarthy's novel commits suicide as well. See *The Group* (New York: Harcourt, 1963).

59 For a discussion of Clelia's (and Pavese's) relationship to Turin, see Vincenzo Binetti, 'Contextualizing Marginality: Urban Landscape and Female Communities in Cesare Pavese's *Among Women Only*' in *Italian Women and the City: Essays*, edited by Janet Levarie Smarr and Daria Valentini (Madison/Teaneck: Fairleigh Dickinson University Press, 2003).

60 'Tutte siamo puttane' (Pavese, *Tra donne sole* in *La bella estate*, 333). See also the scene in which Becuccio takes Clelia's hand as they work together to unpack a crate: 'Un bel momento mi sentii prendere la mano nella paglia. Gli dissi di fare attenzione. "È una merce che costa." Mi rispose: "'Lo so"' (Pavese, *Tra donne sole* in *La bella estate*, 287) (Suddenly I felt him take my hand in the straw. I told him to be careful. 'That stuff's expensive.' 'I know,' he replied. 'All right then,' I said (Pavese, *Among Women Only*, 99). Later, when she seduces him (it could hardly be said to be the reverse, since the only time Becuccio showed any initiative was when he chose the restaurants), she continues the equation between sex and commerce: '"Ci vengo" gli dissi. "Ma è un regalo di stanotte. Ricòrdati"' (Pavese, *Tra donne sole* in *La bella estate*, 327) ('Of course [I'll come with you],' I said. 'But it's a present. For tonight only. Remember' (Pavese, *Among Women Only*, 161).

61 Pavese, *Tra donne sole* in *La bella estate*, 242. Note here, as well, that the question of suicide is inextricable from questions of sex and class. That Clelia is, effectively, a *sartina* (seamstress) and yet moves in the same circles as the women whom she dresses (see too the scene where a wealthy husband angers his wife by mistaking Clelia for one of their set, not recognizing her as a mere seamstress) makes this attribution interesting (Pavese, *Tra donne sole*, 240). Clelia, after all, is not the aspiring suicide but rather Rosetta, who comes from the most distinguished family of all of the girlfriends. In any case, sex is clearly outmoded, and in spite of her humble upbringing and her *parvenue* status, Clelia, too, does not feel particularly bad the morning after a roll in the hay. What's more, the continuous references to suicidal seamstresses – 'Tu invece mi hai l'aria di una sartina abbandonata,' Momina spits at Rosetta on p. 295 (You, on the other hand, look like an abandoned seamstress) – serve to accentuate the kinship, or twinship, of Rosetta and Clelia. Comments such as these at once identify Clelia as a stand-in for Rosetta and hint at the nature and degree of the three girlfriends' self-loathing, as the epithet *sartina abbandonata* implies. Finally, there is Rosetta's rejection as a potential prostitute at the end of the novella ('Crocerossina,' *Tra donne sole* in *La bella estate*, 346), followed by her successful suicide that same night.

62 Pavese, *Among Women Only*, 24.

63 Pavese, *Tra donne sole* in *La bella estate*, 266

64 Pavese, *Tra donne sole* in *La bella estate*, 231.

65 Pavese, *Among Women Only*, 8.

66 It is perhaps worth noting, though, that the film deviates from the book in its treatment of the potentially redeeming power of love. Rosetta's affair with Lorenzo, though unsavoury (for the petty jealousy it inspires) and slightly tawdry (for reasons of class, not of morality – they must meet in a hotel room just like the plebes), is otherwise a source of unexpected, and hitherto unknown, happiness. The end of the relationship and its attendant, very public, rejection, is thus all the greater a loss for Rosetta.

67 This passage from Pavese's diary, written 10 April 1949, is quoted in Biasin's *The Smile of the Gods*, 162. Recall that the novel was composed between March and May of 1949.

68 Pavese, *Tra donne sole* in *La bella estate*, 270.

69 Pavese *Among Women Only*, 71–2.

70 She does wear a fur coat (one of several she owns) on her second visit, and takes note twice of the sort of looks Gisella gives her coat and stockings.

71 The novella deals in greater detail with this question than the film; Clelia's wealthy gentleman-friend Morelli, for example, obliquely remarks on her

ascent to social glory on a few occasions early on in the text. Perhaps this is the reason they do not consummate their relationship in spite of his assiduous courtship.

72 Gioanola sees her remarks in a slightly different light: 'Ma sono battute dettate piú che da un'indignata coscienza di classe, dalla rabbia di sentirsi aggrappata a un mito che si dissolve di fronte alle gelide proposte nichil-iste di Momina e compagne' (But these are remarks dictated less by an indignant class consciousness than by the anger of feeling oneself clinging to a myth that dissolves before the frosty nihilist proposals of Momina and her companions). Gioanola, *Cesare Pavese: La poetica dell'essere*, 344. I, however, am not as convinced as Gioanola that Momina as an individual holds Clelia completely in her thrall, preferring to understand her philo-proletarianism as an attempt at self-individuation vis-à-vis the group in general. Clelia is not clinging to a crumbling myth so much as building a myth of her own.

73 Pavese, *Tra donne sole* in *La bella estate*, 338. The translation that follows is mine.

74 Pavese, *Tra donne sole* in *La bella estate*, 302.

75 Pavese, *Among Women Only*, 123.

76 Pavese, *Tra donne sole* in *La bella estate*, 338

77 Gioanola reaches similar conclusions when he describes Clelia's choice of Becuccio as 'un tentativo di salvataggio nel mito della sanità del popolo di cui Becuccio, con la sua serena capacità di lavoro, senso dei limiti e della concretezza vorrebbe essere un esempio tipico' (an attempt at salvation in the myth of the health of the people of whom Becuccio, with his serene ability to work, sense of limits, and concreteness, is a typical example). Gioanola, *Cesare Pavese: La poetica dell'essere*, 342–3.

78 There is also the indeterminate Pupé, who would better support my claim that Pavese's upper class is populated exclusively by people whose names can be made into affected diminutives and term of endearment if only I knew his/her gender. My thanks to Alessandro Vettori and Alberto Bianchi for information on this name.

79 Vincenzo Binetti asserts that Pavese offers a 'reclaiming of the Flaubertian confession, a provocative "Rosetta, c'est moi"'('Contextualizing Marginal-ity, 209).

80 We might also consider the death of Aldo at the end of *Il grido* (1957), which Antonioni released one year after *Le amiche*. Though there is no explicit suicide attempt at the beginning of the film, Aldo's suicide is antic-ipated early on. His introduction occurs when he is seen to peer precari-ously over the edge of the enormous tower of the sugar-refining factory in

which he works. Spying his companion Irma, he rushes down to meet her and collect his lunch, only to discover that she has gone. His suicide at the film's end will replicate that position: as Irma stands below, Aldo teeters over the edge again rushing down to meet her, unsuccessfully again this time because it is he who has gone. The film ends soon after Aldo's fall: closing shots reveal Irma crouching over the body of her former mate, which has fallen to a modified figure of the cross.

Thus Aldo's death ends *Il grido* much as Rosetta's initial suicide attempt begins *Le amiche*. Its location *toward but not exactly at the end* has the same effect: its prolepsis at the beginning of the film and its enactment at the end forms a kind of false bracket, a kind of enjambment where we carry over our participation beyond what appears to be its logical conclusion. Aldo's unsuccessful journey to Irma, which leads first to his metaphorical descent (which much of the film was dedicated to documenting) then to the (deadly) physical one, like Rosetta's evening gown (which reappears, in the novella, almost but not exactly at the end of the book) and the coda revolving around Clelia, is located such that Irma herself organizes the pre-and post-filmic events. Their presumptive happy relationship at the film's beginning, and their failed reunion at the film's end, create the space for the structuring absence that will be Aldo's fall: from Irma's good graces, from the comfort of social and erotic stability, from the top of a high tower.

81 Roland Barthes, *Critique et verité* (Paris: Editions du Seuil, 1966),. 59–60.
82 Pavese, *Tra donne sole* in *La bella estate*, 278–9.
83 Pavese, *Among Women Only*, 85–6.
84 As soon as the lights go out at Loris's party, Clelia makes explicit the link between Rosetta's attempt and Loris's mise-en-scène of this death of art: 'Cercai subito Rosetta nell'ombra. Mi parve di tornare a quella notte nella mia stanza, quando lei aveva spento' (Pavese, *Tra donne sole* in *La bella estate*, 342) (I sought Rosetta immediately in the dark. I was reminded of that night in my room when she had turned out the lights) (Pavese, *Among Women Only*, 183–4).
85 Pavese, *Tra donne sole* in *La bella estate*, 296–7.
86 Pavese, *Among Women Only*, 114–15.
87 Pavese, *Tra donne sole* in *La bella estate*, 351.
88 Pavese, *Among Women Only*, 198.
89 Pavese, *Tra donne sole* in *La bella estate*, 257.
90 Pavese, *Among Women Only*, 50.
91 I read Clelia's only half-ironic question 'C'è gente che per morire si circonda di fiori?' (Are there people who surround themselves with flowers

in order to die?) in the same way, as meta-narrative – how shall I narrate this? – and not meta-autobiographical – how shall I die? Pavese, *Tra donne sole* in *La bella estate*, 233.

92 Pavese, *Tra donne sole* in *La bella estate*, 296.

93 Aldo's call to Irma from the top of the refinery tower in Antonioni's *Il grido* functions analogously.

94 Pavese, *Tra donne sole* in *La bella estate*, 350.

95 Alvarez, *The Savage God*, 149.

96 I refer to English novelist Daphne du Maurier's *Rebecca* (New York: Harper Collins, 1938), about a beautiful woman whose death (by suicide, indirectly) does not diminish her presence in the lives of her husband or his second wife. Rebecca's posthumous prominence in the house, maintained by the devoted and sinister Mrs Danvers, finds its visual correlative in the portrait of her – in a costume the nameless second wife is tricked into copying, badly – that stands in the centre hall.

97 See Giorgio Agamben's *Homo Sacer: Sovereign Power and Bare Life*, translated by Daniel Heller-Roazen (Stanford: Stanford University Press, 1998).

4. Commemoration and Erasure

1 Cesare Cases, 'L'ordine delle cose e l'ordine delle parole' in *Primo Levi: Un'antologia della critica*, edited by Ernesto Ferrero (Turin: Piccola Biblioteca Einaudi, 1997), 33.

2 I accept the conclusion that Levi's death was suicide; but it is more important to me here (as in previous chapters) to investigate the ramifications of that conclusion than it is to attempt to prove or challenge it. My reluctance to prove or disprove his suicide, however, is not in order to discredit or to legitimate a 'reassessment of his literary production that takes into account the irrevocable silence he has willed,' as Jonathan Druker argues in his 'On the Dangers of Reading Suicide into the Works of Primo Levi' in *The Legacy of Primo Levi*, edited by Stanislao Pugliese (New York: Palgrave Macmillan 2005), 221–31. On the contrary, as I hope is by now clear, my point of departure is precisely this compulsion that Druker articulates so clearly. I am not interested, in other words, in the results of the reassessment but, rather, in the very fact of it. I also agree with Druker (221–2) and others who note that the trick with Levi has to do with the fact that survivorship, which might seem to preclude the possibility of suicide, was always already part and parcel of his identity as a writer. In interviews, Levi owns up to and disavows (in the same interview) suicide as an

option in the camp: 'There was no time to think about killing yourself.' 'I thought about it a number of times, but never seriously.' *The Voice of Memory: Interviews 1961–1987 Primo Levi*, edited by Marco Belpoliti and Robert Gordon, translated by Robert Gordon (New York: New Press, 2001), 246.

Among those who are disinclined to accept a verdict of suicide is Massimo Giuliani in *A Centaur in Auschwitz: Reflections on Primo Levi's Thinking* (Lanham, MD: Lexington Books, 2003), 3, who notes that in the event that his death was suicide, it was (against Wiesel) committed for distinctly 'banal,' that is, not mythical, historical, transcendental, reasons – a private act by a private individual, that is, and not further proof of the iron grip of the concentration camp. See also the highly controversial article by Cynthia Ozick, 'The Suicide Note,' *New Republic* 198.12 (21 March 1988): 32–6. German newspaper obituaries point unambiguously to Auschwitz as the cause. See 'Spätes Opfer,' *Deutches Allgemeines Sonntagsblatt* no. 16, 19 April 1987: 21; 'Primo Levi, 67,' *Der Spiegel* no. 17, 20 April 1987: 272. See also the Austrian newspaper obituary 'Schriftsteller Primo Levi in Turin gestorben' (in *Die Presse*, 13 April 1987), which indirectly attributes multiple causes to his death. The *New York Times* obituary, in contrast, begins with a mention of serious, recent depression. See John Tagliabue's 'Primo Levi, Holocaust Writer, Is Dead at 67,' *New York Times*, 12 April 1987.

3 Risa Sodi, 'The Rhetoric of the Univers Concentrationnaire' in *Memory and Mastery: Primo Levi as Writer and Witness*, edited by Roberta S. Kremer (Albany: State University of New York Press, 2001), 35. Or, as two of the students in my first-year seminar ('Surviving the Holocaust: Personal and Social Reflections in Italy') who are 'totally into the Holocaust' put it, Levi is believed to be all one needs to read to become conversant in Holocaust studies.

4 These were Myriam Anissimov's *Primo Levi: Tragedy of an Optimist*, translated by Steve Cox (New York: Overlook Press, 1999); Ian Thomson's *Primo Levi: A Life* (New York: Henry Holt and Company, 2002); and Carol Angier's *The Double Bond: Primo Levi, A Biography* (New York: Farrar, Straus and Giroux, 2002). Of these, it was Angier's biography – in some ways the least conventional of the three, though by no means the least scholarly – that did not mesh with the speaker's ideas about Levi.

5 These expressions are borrowed from Avishai Margalit's discussion of 'thick relations' in his *The Ethics of Memory* (Cambridge, MA: Harvard University Press, 2004). My thinking in this chapter is heavily indebted to his work.

6 This holds true both for Holocaust victims and survivors in general (for

whom his experience was considered broadly representative) and for Levi's friends – see the chapter 'Levi Uomo' in Carole Angier's *The Double Bond* for examples of survivors who left the remembering, so to speak, to Levi: for Jean and Charles, Levi 'remembered for all of them' (434) and Luciana 'did not speak about her experiences until Primo, "who spoke for all of us" had gone' (445).

7 For an elegant example, see especially the beginning (pp. 73–4) of the chapter 'Discretion, or Language and Silence' in Robert S.C. Gordon's *Primo Levi's Ordinary Virtues: From Testimony to Ethics* (New York: Oxford University Press, 2001). For a much fuller look at the issue of representations of limit events, see Saul Friedlander's edited volume, *Probing the Limits of Representation: Nazism and the 'Final Solution'* (Cambridge, MA: Harvard University Press, 1992). Contrast Agamben, who investigates this as a paradox (and will develop from it what he calls 'Levi's paradox' regarding the Muselmann or perfect witness): 'the survivors bore witness to something it is impossible to bear witness to,' but does not accept silence as a tolerable or reasonable response: 'Why confer on extermination the prestige of the mystical?' *Remnants of Auschwitz* (New York: Zone Books, 2001), 13 and 32.

8 Roland Barthes, 'The Death of the Author' in *Image, Music, Text*, translated by Stephen Heath (New York: Hill and Wang, 1977), 145.

9 Carole Angier's fascinating and controversial biography is the most notable exception to this rule.

10 Levi, 'Dello scrivere oscuro' in *Opere* vol. 2 (Turin: Einaudi, 1997), 676–81.

11 Levi, *Opere* vol. 2, 677.

12 Levi, *Opere* vol. 2, 680. See also Elio Gioanola's take in his *Psicanalisi e interpretazione letteraria* (Milan: Editoriale Jaca Book, 2005), 382–3.

13 Levi, *Opere* vol. 2, 681

14 Levi, *Opere* vol. 2, 677.

15 Gioanola reaches similar conclusions: '[T]anta lucidità ha anche funzione di difesa: ma difesa contro cosa? Potremmo dire … difesa contro la "diversità", e l'esclusione che questa comporta. Sentirsi "diversi" è lo stesso che sentirsi in colpa, cioè meritevoli di condanna per qualcosa di oscuro che è avvenuto alle origini, di cui si ha certezza ma non coscienza' (Such lucidity also functions as a defence: but defence against what? We might say … defence against 'difference' and its attendant exclusion. To feel oneself to be 'different' is to feel oneself to be culpable, that is, deserving of condemnation for something obscure that occurred at the origins, of which one feels certain but not conscious). Gioanola, *Psicanalisi e interpretazione letteraria*, 384.

16 Levi, 'Verso occidente' in *Vizio di forma* (Turin: Einaudi, 1987), 24.

17 Levi, 'Verso occidente' in *Vizio di forma*, 24–5.

18 Levi, 'Verso occidente' in *Vizio di forma*, 32–3.

19 The usual equation holds that experience of the gray zone compounds survivor's guilt and thus must figure prominently in the suicide's motives. See pp. 17–24 in Ruth Leys, *From Guilt to Shame: Auschwitz and After* (Princeton: Princeton University Press, 2007) for a theoretical discussion of this manner of thinking. For a reading of Levi's suicide as a self-declared function of survivor guilt, see Gioanola, *Psicanalisi e interpretazione letteraria*, 387–8, as well, of course, as Levi's poem 'Il superstite': 'Indietro, via di qui, gente sommersa, / Andate. Non ho soppiantato nessuno, / Non ho usurpato il pane di nessuno, / Nessuno è morto in vece mia.' In *Ad ora incerta* (Milan: Garzanti, 2004), 76. Gioanola sees a link between survivor guilt and the feeling of being different to which he referred above: 'L'ultimo Levi è letteralmente in preda, non più solo nel profondo, ai sensi di colpa per essere sopravvissuto, un superstire appunto, e non basta più a lenire la "vergogna" l'essersi preso l'incarico del testimone dell'orrore, ma la colpa del non essere morto è la stessa cosa della colpa dell'essere nato, quella che da sempre abita in lui e lo ha fatto "diverso" *ab origine*' (The later Levi is literally prey, no longer only deep down, to feelings of guilt for having survived, for being, precisely, a survivor, and having taken on the burden of bearing witness to the horror no longer suffices to alleviate the 'shame,' but the sin of not having died is the same thing as the sin of being born, one that has always resided in him and made him 'different' from the start). Gioanola, *Psicanalisi e interpretazione letteraria*, 388.

20 Robert S.C. Gordon pays attention to it as part of his discussion of virtue(s) in Levi. See especially pp. 87, 91–3, and 165–6 of his *Primo Levi's Ordinary Virtues*. So does Agamben in *Remnants of Auschwitz* – not surprising, perhaps, considering how closely their interests overlap.

21 Claudio Magris in Ferrero, 52.

22 Margalit, 167.

23 Margalit, 155.

24 Margalit, 158–9.

25 This is Margalit's description of the memory of humiliation (130).

26 The expression is borrowed from Jack Terry, who writes about the risk of demonizing survivors: 'The pretraumatic personality had a great influence on the individual's reaction to the trauma: the degree of libidinal and ego and superego development played a great role. An external experience cannot be independent of one's personal history if it is to have an effect.' Jack Terry, 'The Damaging Effects of the "Survivor Syndrome"' in *Psychoanalytic Reflections on the Holocaust: Selected Essays*, edited by Steven A. Luel

and Paul Marcus (New York: Holocaust Awareness Institute, Center for Judaic Studies, University of Denver; Ktav Publishing House, [Denver], 1984), 139–40. Cited in Leys, *From Guilt to Shame*, 85. I agree with Terry on this point but do not support an understanding of survivor's guilt that wholly expurgates the external stressor from the scene.

27 Agamben, *Remnants*, 34. I am not comfortable with the uncontested translation of the word *Muselmann* as *Muslim* because of the way it subsumes an identification (presumably unintentional) of Muslims at prayer with bestiality, non-sentience, and soullessness under the guise of an unconvincing profession of ignorance. Although Agamben investigates the etymology, I know of no study that objects to the term. Instead, I prefer the terms drowned and submerged, which, though not exact equivalents to Muselmann, are justified by Levi's frequent use of them.

28 Agamben, *Remnants*, 63.

29 Levi, *The Drowned and the Saved*, quoted in Agamben, *Remnants*, 34.

30 Levi, *Survival in Auschwitz and The Reawakening: Two Memoirs*, translated by Stuart Woolf (New York: Summit Books, 1986),192. Quoted in Agamben, *Remnants*, 38.

31 Agamben, *Remnants*, 60.

32 Agamben, *Remnants*, 82.

33 Agamben, *Remnants*, 155.

34 Levi, 'Stanco di finzioni' in *Lilít e altri racconti, Opere* vol. 2, 48.

35 Margalit, for example, would seem to think it does; he mentions Adam Czerniakow (1880–1942) as someone who would have qualified as a paradigmatic moral witness, had he not committed suicide. His diary, written from 1939 to 1942, was published by Ivan R. Dee in 1999: Raul Hilberg, *The Warsaw Diary of Adam Czerniakow: Prelude to Doom*.

36 Note that I am borrowing Margalit's thick versus thin but not B. Williams's 'thick ethical concepts,' as in *Ethics and the Limits of Philosophy* (London: Fontana, 1993) or Clifford Geertz's 'thick description' as offered in *The Interpretation of Cultures* (London: Fontana, 1993), both of which are mentioned by Robert S.C. Gordon in his *Primo Levi's Ordinary Virtues*, 24nn49 and 51.

37 Margalit, 31.

38 Cases, 20n5.

39 Cases, 20n5. Cases continues in the note by giving credit to the Jewish community of Turin for taking on 'il compito di occuparsi della morte di Levi' (the task of occupying itself with Levi's death), but that does not, he opines, authorize them to appropriate him, 'dichiarando che "è uno dei nostri", quando ha appena dimostrato con la sua morte che non è' (declaring that he is 'one of our own' when he has just demonstrated, with his

death, that he is not). Cases, too, privileges Levi's suicide as a defining moment, as much as the community he criticizes ('ha appena dimostrato con la sua morte che non è'); I would argue, however, that it was not his death that demonstrates this but his life. After all, plenty of self-identified practising Catholics have committed suicide; the suicide (or adulterous behaviour, or infraction of any other sort) of a believer does not signify the end of his religious faith but rather a deviation from its practices, as Dostoevsky exhaustingly depicts in *The Brothers Karamazov*.

40 Sergio Parussa, 'A Hybridism of Sounds: Primo Levi between Judaism and Literature' in Pugliese, *The Legacy of Primo Levi*, 90. Indeed, Parussa further argues that 'it is the hybrid character of Levi's writing, its imperfection, its tension between testimony and narrative that reveals deep consonances between his writing and his Jewish background. For Levi, Judaism and writing are both experiences of hybridism: they both speak of a subject divided between belonging to the religion of his ancestors and to the identity of the place in which he lives, between Hebrew and Piedmontese dialect, between testifying to a historical truth in a certain language and the narrative modes, the literary codes, offered by that same language. It is precisely through this hybrid character that Primo Levi's works reawaken the ethical dimension of writing and challenge consolidated notions about literature' (91). Parussa's observations seem important to me because, besides underscoring the fundamentally split nature of Levi's writings, they put that split in the service of a critique of literature, rather than attribute that split to some underlying flaw in his writing.

41 Indeed, Levi himself was interested in the notion of the hybrid. See Levi's 'Quaestio de centauris' in *Storie Naturali* in *Opere* vol. 3 (Turin: Einaudi, 1990), 119–30.

42 This has not escaped the notice of some North American readers; Roberta S. Kremer attributes this to Levi's subject matter in the introduction to her edited volume, *Memory and Mastery*: 'Some writers, by nature of their subject, are not often given, or escape the luxury of a careful examination of their literary devices. This is especially the case when the writer is a Holocaust survivor: it is as though the "sacredness" of the subject matter imposes a respectful silence when it comes to a critical analysis, as though the Holocaust content defies or takes priority over a serious examination of the writer's means of expression' (ix). This is another version of what Friedlander and others so compellingly parse in discussions of the Holocaust as a limit experience. See Saul Friedlander's edited volume, *Probing the Limits of Representation*:

43 Gioanola, *Psicanalisi e interpretazione letteraria*, 371–2.

44 The new English translation of his short-story collection, *A Tranquil Star*, for example, has come and gone largely unremarked in the United States.

45 Cesare Cases is not afraid to criticize both Levi's theoretical assertions (like the ones that posit the supremacy of sanity over insanity, and of clearly communicative texts over those in which clarity does not feature prominently) and his writing, which is compelling when it is 'animato dall'intensità delle esperienze e dall'urgenza delle idée, [ma] freddo e un po' monotono quando ad esse si sostituiscono invenzioni alquanto cerebrali o riflessioni di buon senso, che non meriterebbero tanta precisione da orafo' (animated by the intensity of the experiences and by the urgency of the ideas, [but] cold and a bit monotonous when these are substituted by somewhat cerebral inventions or common sense reflections, which do not merit a goldsmith's precision) (7).

46 Cases, 9.

47 Sergio Parussa draws broader theoretical conclusions on the question of possible hierarchies of genre. He notes, 'If writing is born out of a need to testify, if creativity is a response to ethical urgency, then a tension between witnessing the truth and telling stories, between the work of the witness and that of the fiction writer, between a notion of writing as a purely aesthetic use of language and writing as the site where ethics and aesthetics meet, becomes unavoidable. The inclusion of ethics within the literary discourse, in fact, opens up the literary text to the rhetorical needs of the witness and sets it free from all the strict rules that tend to confine writing to a purely aesthetic and self-referential work on language' (90).

48 Cases, 32.

49 I refer to the Demanian idea of blindness, linked to autobiography. See also Max Saunders's discussion of autobiography and autobiografiction in 'Autobiografiction,' *Times Literary Supplement*, 3 October 2008, 13–15.

50 See Paul de Man, 'Autobiography as De-Facement,' *MLN* 94 (Baltimore: Johns Hopkins University Press, 1979): 919–30.

51 Sara Vandewaetere, 'Use and Abuse of the Work of Primo Levi,' paper delivered at AAIS-AATI conference, Taormina, May 2008.

52 Primo Levi, 'L'opera' in *Ad ora incerta* in *Opere* vol. 2, 568.

53 Pugliese in *The Legacy of Primo Levi*, 3. We need not be wedded to such a reading, however compelling it may seem; one might be tempted to propose an alternate reading whereby the proper trajectory is not trauma-transgression-testimony but rather trauma-testimony-transgression. This reading of Levi's suicide is one that places it squarely in the realm of the concentration camp. According to this reading, Levi's suicide mimics death in Auschwitz, but in civilian life decades later. Historian Yaffa Eliach asserts, 'Primo Levi

chose a brutal death as if in Auschwitz, where and when the only control the inmates could have was the time of their death, the end to their miserable lives. Primo Levi made sure that he completed his cycle of life in the Auschwitz tradition. As a prominent chemist, who even knew how to use chicken manure to enhance lipstick, he could probably have chosen a peaceful, more respectable death. But he probably felt that this would not fit the Auschwitz time and style of death.' Levi's method of suicide, in other words, was the civilian equivalent of touching the electric fence. Such an iconoclastic interpretation runs counter to the convention by which, in the battle for Levi's psychic space, Auschwitz did not ultimately win. Eliach, 'Primo Levi and His Concept of Time' in Kremer, 32.

54 Ian Thomson, 'The Genesis of *If This Is a Man*' in Pugliese, *The Legacy of Primo Levi*, 47.

55 My graduate seminar students, for example, are more or less evenly divided about whether or not *If This Is a Man* should be considered a novel.

56 Pugliese observes that Levi 'aspired to the simple title of "writer" without any adjective ("Holocaust," "Italian," or "Jewish")'(*The Legacy of Primo Levi*, 10). Thomson notes, 'Most galling [to Levi] were those critics who pigeonholed Levi as a "witness." This word – in Italian, testimone – would settle on Levi like an albatross, and he came to resent it thoroughly, It seems the most backhanded praise: Levi thought of himself as a writer first, and a witness second' ('The Genesis of *If This Is a Man*') in Pugliese, *The Legacy of Primo Levi*, 56.

57 In Belpoliti and Gordon, 206.

58 Nicholas Patruno, for example, remarks that by 1984, Levi 'admits, with obvious disappointment, to having exhausted his creative reservoirs and that he is writing poems to which he does not give much value.' Nicholas Patruno, 'At an Uncertain Hour' in Kremer,100.

59 Levi himself confounds that interpretation of his suicide, as Marco Belpoliti points out: 'There is an almost standard reply that he uses after a certain date – around 1978 – when he is asked, "What are you writing now?" "Nothing," he says, "I think I've exhausted all avenues"; or "I've run out of supplies, I don't have much more to say"' (Belpoliti and Gordon, xxi). See Marco Belpoliti's chapter, 'I Am a Centaur,' in *The Voice of Memory*, xxi-xxii, for a fuller discussion of the Holocaust as an ambiguously acknowledged well-spring for Levi's writings.

60 Cesare Segre, 'Primo Levi nella Torre di Babele' in *Primo Levi as Witness: Proceedings from a Symposium Held at Princeton University April 30-May 2, 1989*, edited by Pietro Frassica (Fiesole: Casalini Libri, 1990), 97.

61 The broadcast dates were 10, 17, 24 November and 1 December 1982.

62 'Little Theater of Memory' in Belpoliti and Gordon, 47–55.

63 Note, however, that Levi disavows the importance of the concentration camps on his reading habits: 'Non avrei previsto, accingendomi al lavoro, che fra gli autori preferiti non si trovasse né un furfante, né una donna, né un appartenente alle culture non-europee; che la mia esperienza concentrazionaria dovesse pesare cosí poco; che i magici dovessero prevalere sui moralisti, e questi sui logici' (I would not have predicted, setting about my work, that among my favourite authors there were not to be found one rogue, woman, or member of a non-European culture; that my concentration camp experience would count for so little; that the magical thinkers would prevail over the moralists, and these last over the logicians). Levi, *La ricerca delle radici* in *Opere* vol. 2, 1362–3.

64 Margalit, 130.

65 Margalit, 130

66 Levi, 'Shemà' in *Ad ora incerta* in *Opere* vol. 2, 525.

67 For a discussion of Levi's 'drowned' and *Remnants*, Pugliese's volume is useful. See (among many others) Antoine Philippe's 'The Drowned as Saviors of Humanity: The Anthropological Value of *Se questo è un uomo*' (Pugliese, *The Legacy of Primo Levi*, 125–31); William McClellan's 'Levi, Agamben, and the New Ethics of Reading' (Pugliese, *The Legacy of Primo Levi*, 146–52); and Dan Leshem's 'The Question of Ethical Discorse: Emmanuel Levinas, Primo Levi, and Giorgio Agamben'(Pugliese, *The Legacy of Primo Levi*, 153).

68 Levi quoted in Agamben, *Remnants of Auschwitz*, 70. Note that Agamben will take issue with this debate about deathless death in the camps; for now it is enough to note the liminal position inhabited by the submerged – not so much walking corpses, as Levi and others call them, but as paradigms of the coexistence of zoe/bios.

69 Cesare Segre parses Levi's motivations in his 'Lettura di *Se questo è un uomo*' in Ferrero, 57.

70 Levi, *Se questo è un uomo*. Prefazione in *Opere* vol. 1 (Turin: Einaudi, 1997), 5.

71 Levi, *If This Is a Man*, Author's Preface, translated by Stuart Woolf (Suffolk: Chaucer Press/Penguin Books, 1979) 9.

72 Robert S.C. Gordon interweaves subtle and convincing analysis of the relevance of this poem to an ethical understanding of Levi's works, especially *If This Is a Man*, in his *Primo Levi's Ordinary Virtues*.

73 With respect to the distinction between man and animal, Franco Ferrucci rightly notes the paradoxical nature of Levi's remarks about suicide in *I sommersi e i salvati*, in which Levi associates suicide with the human, and not animal realm; thus, there were very few suicides in the camps pre-

cisely because of the animal nature to which the prisoners were reduced. Here, unlike in Levi's discussion of Trakl and Celan's 'animal-like' poetry (which presages their suicide), suicide is not connected with reduction to the animal-like but rather is proof of humanity. Franco Ferrucci, 'La casa di Primo Levi' in Frassica, 52–3.

74 Thomas Carl Wall, 'Au Hasard,' in *Politics, Metaphysics and Death: Essays on Giorgio Agamben's Homo Sacer*, edited by Andrew Norris(Durham, NC, and London: Duke University Press, 2005), 38.

Postscript

1 Jacques Derrida, *The Work of Mourning* (Chicago: University of Chicago Press, 2001), 192.

2 Derrida, *The Work of Mourning*, 195.

3 Derrida, *The Work of Mourning*, 192.

4 Derrida, *The Work of Mourning*, 193.

5 Derrida, *The Work of Mourning*, 193.

6 Derrida, *The Work of Mourning*, 193.

7 Robert Pogue Harrison, *Dominion of the Dead* (Chicago and London: University of Chicago Press, 2003), 72. My thinking in this chapter is indebted to this work.

8 Helen Deutsch, *Loving Dr. Johnson* (Chicago and London: University of Chicago Press, 2005), 7.

9 Robert Pogue Harrison, 70.

10 Guido Morselli, *Il suicidio e Capitolo breve sul suicidio* (Pistoia: I quaderni di Via del Vento, 2004), 23–4.

11 Robert Pogue Harrison calls this debt 'insoluble' (154).

Works Consulted

Agamben, Giorgio. *Homo Sacer: Sovereign Power and Bare Life*. Translated by Daniel Heller-Roazen. Stanford: Stanford University Press, 1998.
– *Remnants of Auschwitz*. New York: Zone Books, 2001.
Agosti, Stefano. *Poesia contemporanea: saggi e interventi*. Milan: Bompiani, 1995.
Alterocca, Bona. *Pavese: dopo un quarto di secolo*. Turin: Società Editrice Internazionale, 1974.
Alvarez, Alfred. *The Savage God: A Study of Suicide*. New York: W.W. Norton and Co., 1990.
Angier, Carol. *The Double Bond: Primo Levi, A Biography*. New York: Farrar, Straus and Giroux, 2002.
Anissimov, Myriam. *Primo Levi: Tragedy of an Optimist*. Translated by Steve Cox. New York: Overlook Press, 1999.
Annoni, Carlo. 'Appunti di antifascismo e reistenza nella narrativa di Pavese.' *Vita e Pensiero: Rassegna Italiana di Cultura* 51 (1968): 205–13.
Antelme, Robert. *On Robert Antelme's The Human Race: Essays and Commentary*. Edited by Daniel Dobbels. Evanston, IL: Marlboro Press/Northwestern, 2003.
Arnone, Vincenzo. *Pavese: tra l'assurdo e l'assoluto*. Padua: Edizioni Messaggero, 1998.
Aspesi, Natalia. 'Arrall "Inedito" messaggio nella bottiglia.' *La Repubblica*, 11 February 1976: 10–11.
Balakian, Anna. *André Breton, Magus of Surrealism*. New York: Oxford University Press, 1971.
Baldacci, Alessandro. *Amelia Rosselli*. Rome-Bari: Gius. Laterza e Figli 2007.
Baratta, Stefano. *L'arte del morire: lettura simbolica del suicidio*. Bergamo: Moretti e Vitali, 1992.
Bárberi Squarotti, Giorgio. 'Il ragazzo e l'avventura: *Feria d'agosto*.' *Esperienze Letterarie: Rivista Trimestrale di Critica e Cultura* 25.3–4 (2000): 7–21.

Barthes, Roland. *Camera Lucida: Reflections on Photography*. Translated by Richard Howard. New York: Hill and Wang, 1981.

– *Critique et verité*. Paris: Editions du Seuil, 1966.

– 'From Work to Text.' In *The Norton Anthology of Theory and Criticism*. Edited by Vincent B. Leitch et al. New York: W.W. Norton and Company, 2001. 1470–5.

– *Image, Music, Text*. Translated by Stephen Heath. New York: Hill and Wang, 1977.

– *The Pleasure of the Text*. Translated by Richard Miller. New York: Hill and Wang, 1975.

Battin, M. Pabst, and David J. Mayo, editors. *Suicide: The Philosophical Issues*. New York: St Martin's Press, 1980.

Becker, Jillian. *Giving Up: The Last Days of Sylvia Plath*. New York: St Martin's Press, 2002.

Belpoliti, Marco, and Robert Gordon, editors. *The Voice of Memory: Interviews 1961–1987 Primo Levi*. Translated by Robert Gordon. New York: New Press, 2001.

Benedetti, Carla. *The Empty Cage: Inquiry into the Mysterious Death of the Author*. Translated by William Hartley. Ithaca: Cornell University Press, 2005.

Benedikt, Amelie Frost. 'On Reading Valedictory Texts: Suicide Notes, Last Wills and Testaments.' In ΠΑΙΔΕΙΑ, Contemporary Philosophy, http://www.bu.edu/wcp/Papers/Cont/ContBene.htm, accessed 18 August 2003.

Benjamin, Walter. *Reflections: Essays, Aphorisms, Autobiographical Writings*. Edited by Peter Demetz. Translated by Edmund Jephcott. New York and London: Harcourt Brace Jovanovich, 1978.

Biasin, Gian Paolo. 'L'inconscio di Pavese.' *Italica* 46.3 (1969): 310–21.

– *The Smile of the Gods: A Thematic Study of Cesare Pavese's Works*. Translated by Yvonne Freccero. Ithaca: Cornell University Press, 1968.

Billani, Francesca. 'Cesare Pavese in Gran Bretagna e Irlanda: 1949–2000.' *Esperienze Letterarie: Rivista Trimestrale di Critica e Cultura* 25.3–4 (2000): 163–80.

Binetti, Vincenzo. 'Contextualizing Marginality: Urban Landscape and Female Communities in Cesare Pavese's *Among Women Only*.' In *Italian Women and the City: Essays*. Edited by Janet Levarie Smarr and Daria Valentini. Madison/Teaneck, NJ: Fairleigh Dickinson University Press, 2003.

– 'Marginalità e appartenenza: La funzione dell'intellettuale tra sfera pubblica e privato nell'Italia del dopoguerra.' *Italica* 74.3 (1997): 360–74.

Blum, Cinzia Sartini, and Lara Trubowitz, editors and translators. 'Amelia Rosselli.' In *Contemporary Italian Women Poets: A Bilingual Anthology*. New York: Italica Press, 2001.

Bo, Carlo. 'La fede secondo Morselli.' *Corriere della Sera*, 16 October 1977: 10.

Bondy, François. 'Un romancier d'outre-tombe: L'œuvre et le destin post-humes de Guido Morselli.' *Commentaire* 5 (1979): 153–5.

Borghese, Giulia. 'Caro signor Morselli, mi duole comunicarle …' *Corriere della Sera*, 4 May 1998: 23.

Borgna, Eugenio. *L'attesa e la speranza*. Milan: Feltrinelli, 2005.

Borsa, Elena, and Sara D'Arienzo, editors. *Guido Morselli: I percorsi sommersi: Inediti, immagini, documenti*. Novara: Interlinea, 1999.

Bosetti, Gilbert. 'L'Intimité du journal pavesien: Ecrire pour vivre.' In *Le Journal intime et ses formes litteraires*. Edited by V. Del Litto. Geneva: Droz, 1978. 119–28.

Boym, Svetlana. *Death in Quotation Marks: Cultural Myths of the Modern Poet*. Cambridge, MA: Harvard University Press, 1991.

Brambilla Ageno, Franca. 'Un caso di utilizzazione funzionale delle fonti.' *Lettere Italiane* 28 (1976): 43–7.

Brand, Peter, and Lino Pertile. *The Cambridge History of Italian Literature*. Second edition. Cambridge: Cambridge University Press, 2001.

Brugnoli, Giorgio. 'Le arpie di Dante.' *Aevum* 71.2 (1997): 359–70.

Bruni, Pierfranco. *Cesare Pavese: interventi*. Cosenza: Pellegrini, 1986.

Burke, Seán. *Authorship: A Reader. From Plato to the Postmodern*. Edinburgh: Edinburgh University Press, 2004.

– *The Death and Return of the Author: Criticism and Subjectivity in Barthes, Foucault, and Derrida*. Edinburgh: Edinburgh University Press, 1998.

Butler, Judith. *Precarious Life: The Power of Mourning and Violence*. New York: Verso, 2004.

Caesar, Michael. 'The 1970s.' In *The Cambridge History of Italian Literature*. Second edition. Edited by Peter Brand and Lino Pertile. Cambridge: Cambridge University Press, 2001. 581–98.

Calvino, Italo. 'Pavese e i sacrifici umani.' *Revue des Etudes Italiennes* 12.1 (1966): 107–10.

Cambon, Glauco. 'Truth as Fiction: Pavese's Diary.' *Michigan Quarterly Review* 16 (1977): 1–10.

Campbell, Robert, and Diané Collinson. *Ending Lives*. Oxford: Basil Blackwell, 1988.

Cancogni, Annapaoli. Review of *Divertimento 1889*, by Guido Morselli. *New York Times*, 13 September 1987: BR 34–5.

Capello, Angelo Piero. 'La metafora negata: Il "Capitolo breve sul suicidio" di Guido Morselli.' *Otto/Novecento* 17.1 (1993): 129–41.

Caputo, Francesca. *Amelia Rosselli: una scrittura plurale*. Novara: Interlinea edizioni, 2004.

Carbognin, Francesco. 'Amelia Rosselli: prove d'autore.' *Strumenti critici* 105.2 (May 2004): 245–71.

Carrera, Manuel. 'Cesare Pavese.' *Revista de Occidente* 12 (1976): 13–22.

Carteri, Giovanni. *Al confino del mito (Cesare Pavese e la Calabria)*. Catanzaro: Rubbettino, 1991.

Caruth, Cathy. *Unclaimed Experience: Trauma, Narrative and History*. Baltimore: Johns Hopkins University Press, 1996.

Caserta, Giovanni. *Realtà e miti nella lirica di Pavese*. Matera: BMG, 1970.

Cases, Cesare. 'L'ordine delle cose e l'ordine dele parole.' In *Primo Levi: Un'antologia della critica*. Edited by Ernesto Ferrero. Turin: Piccola Biblioteca Einaudi, 1997. 5–33.

Catalano, Ettore. *Cesare Pavese: fra politica e ideologia*. Bari: De Donato, 1976.

Catalfamo, Antonio, editor. *La stanza degli specchi: Cesare Pavese nella letteratura, nel cinema e nel teatro: quarta rassegna di saggi internazionali di critica pavesiana*. Santo Stefano Belbo (Cuneo): CEPAM, 2004.

Ceserano, Giorgio. 'Riflessioni su Pavese.' *Paragone: Rivista Mensile di Arte Figurativa e Letteratura* 194.17 (1966): 102–7.

Chesler, Phyllis. *Women and Madness*. Garden City, NY: Doubleday Press, 1972.

Chiusano, Italo A. 'Il libro postumo che fa inopportunamente gridare al caso letterario: *Roma senza papa* di Morselli, una acuta satira socio-politica.' *Il Globo*, 22 November 1974: 5.

Cillo, Giovanni. *La distruzione dei miti: Saggio sulla poetica di Cesare Pavese*. Florence: Enrico Vallecchi, 1972.

Clerval, Alain. 'Cesare Pavese: De la naissance du mythe au suicide comme art de vivre.' *Nouvelle Revue Francaise* 239 (1972): 83–8.

Coletti, Vittorio. 'Guido Morselli.' *Otto/Novecento* 5 (1978): 89–115.

Cortellessa, Andrea. 'Il bosco, il sonno, la sipida musica.' *Galleria* 48.1–2. Edited by Daniele Attanasio e Emmanuela Tandello (1997): 96–112.

Costa, Simona. *Morselli*. Città di Castello: La Nuova Italia, 1981.

Costaz, Gilles. '*Rome sans pape* de Guido Morselli: Un romancier italien imagine l'Eglise à la veille de l'an 2000.' *Le Matin*, 24 March 1979: 24.

Couturier, Maurice. *La figure de l'auteur*. Paris: Seuil, 1995.

Crapanzano, Vincent. *Imaginative Horizons: An Essay in Literary-Philosophical Anthropology*. Chicago: University of Chicago Press, 2004.

Dal Bon, Piero. 'Sulla fortuna di Pavese in Spagna.' *Esperienze Letterarie: Rivista Trimestrale di Critica e Cultura* 25.3–4 (2000): 181–215.

D'Arienzo, Sara. 'Il cantiere della Dissipatio H.G.: ipotesi di lettura degli appunti preparatori.' *Autografo* 37 (1998): 9–21.

De Camilli, Davide. 'Pavese e altri diaristi.' *Italianistica* 5:1 (1976): 93–109.

– *Vita e Pensiero: Rassegna Italiana di Cultura* 51 (1968).

Dedet, Christian. 'Cesare Pavese.' *La Revue de Paris* 71 (1964): 121–5.

Della Colletta, Cristina. 'Amelia Rosselli (1930-).' *Italian Women Writers: A Bio-Bibliographical Sourcebook*. Edited by Rinaldina Russell. Westport, CN: Greenwood Press, 1994. 360–7.

de Man, Paul. 'Autobiography as De-Facement.' *MLN* 94. Baltimore: Johns Hopkins University Press, 1979. 919–30.

De March, Silvia. *Amelia Rosselli tra poesia e storia*. Naples: L'ancora del mediterraneo 2006.

Derrida, Jacques. *Aporias. Dying – awaiting (one another at) the limits of truth*. Stanford: Stanford University Press, 1993.

– *The Gift of Death*. Translated by David Wills. Chicago: University of Chicago Press, 1995.

– *Specters of Marx: The State of the Debt, the Work of Mourning, and the New International*. Translated by Peggy Kamuf. New York: Routledge, 1994.

– *The Work of Mourning*. Chicago: University of Chicago Press, 2001.

De Tommaso, Piero. 'Ritratto di Cesare Pavese.' *Rassegna della letteratura italiana* 69.3 (1965): 545–68.

Deutsch, Helen. *Loving Dr. Johnson*. Chicago and London: University of Chicago Press, 2005.

Di Biase, Carmine. 'Dal verso alla prosa: Autocritica e chiarificazione nel *Diario* di Pavese.' *Vita e Pensiero: Rassegna Italiana di Cultura* 51 (1968): 214–29.

– 'L'inconsolabile Orfeo in Cesare Pavese.' *Esperienze Letterarie: Rivista Trimestrale di Critica e Cultura* 25.3–4 (2000): 23–37.

– 'Morselli e il problema del male.' *Studium* 74 (1978): 251–65.

– 'Uno scrittore in cerca di Dio.' *L'Osservatore Romano*, 23 January 1978: 3.

Di Grado, Antonio. 'Mitteleuropa come utopia: Il "Contropassato" di Guido Morselli.' *Rassegna della Letteratura Italiana* 88.3 (1984): 457–63.

Dolce, Ester. 'Appunti dopo la lettura dell'epistolario pavesiano.' *Vita e Pensiero: Rassegna Italiana di Cultura* 51 (1968): 230–46.

Druker, Jonathan. 'On the Dangers of Reading Suicide into the Works of Primo Levi.' In *The Legacy of Primo Levi*. Edited by Stanislao Pugliese. New York: Palgrave Macmillan, 2005. 221–31.

Du Maurier, Daphne. *Rebecca*. New York: Harper Collins, 1938.

Durkheim, Emile. *Suicide: A Study in Sociology*. Edited by George Simpson. Translated by John A. Spaulding and George Simpson. New York: Free Press, 1997.

Enckell, Pierre. Review of *Le communiste*. Translated by Cl. Minot-Templier. *Les Nouvelles Létteraires*, 31 August 1978: 21.

Enciclopedia Zanichelli 2003. Bologna: Zanichelli Editore, 2002.

Erasmi, Gabriele. 'Negazione ed Adesione alla vita: *Tra donne sole* di Cesare

Pavese e *Le indulgenze* di Libero Bigiaretti.' *Studi Romani: Rivista trimestrale dell'Istituto Nazionale di Studi Romani* 45.1–2 (1997): 47–58.

Fales, Angela Bianchini. 'Cesare Pavese e le sue opere postume.' *Italica* 31.3 (1954): 160–70.

Fasano, Marina Lessona. *Guido Morselli: Un inspiegabile caso letterario.* Naples: Liguori Editore, 1998.

Felman, Shoshana. *The Juridical Unconscious: Trials and Traumas in the Twentieth Century.* Cambridge, MA: Harvard University Press, 2002.

– *Writing and Madness (Literature/Philosophy/Psychoanalysis).* Translated by Martha Noel Evans. Stanford: Stanford University Press, 2003.

Fernandez, Dominique. 'Lettres de Pavese.' *Les Temps Modernes* 23.268 (1968): 577–608.

– *L'échec de Pavese.* Paris: Grasset, 1967.

Ferrero, Ernesto, editor. *Primo Levi: un'antologia critica.* Turin: Giulio Einaudi Editore, 1997.

Ferretti, Gian Carlo. 'Pavese e la scelta del silenzio.' In *Studi in memoria di Luigi Russo.* Pisa: Nistri-Lischi, 1974. 477–85.

Ferrucci, Franco. 'La casa di Primo Levi.' In *Primo Levi as Witness: Proceedings from a Symposium Held at Princeton University April 30-May 2, 1989.* Edited by Pietro Frassica. Fiesole: Casalini Libri, 1990.

Fiorentino, Maria. *Guido Morselli tra critica e narrativa.* With a preface by Francesco D'Episcopo. Naples: Eurocomp Edizioni, 2002.

Fiori, Giuseppe. *Casa Rosselli: vita di Carlo e Nello, Amelia, Marion e Maria.* Turin: Einaudi Editore, 1999.

Flint, R.W. 'Translating Cesare Pavese.' *Delos: A Journal on and of Translation* 1 (1968): 152–64.

Fontes, Ignacio. 'Una interrogación sobre el suicidio de Pavese.' *Revista de Occidente* 142 (1993): 121–35.

Fortichiari, Valentina. *Guido Morselli: Immagini di una vita.* With an essay by Giuseppe Pontiggia. Milan: Rizzoli, 2001.

– 'Guido Morselli: *Un dramma borghese.' Uomini e Libri* 69 (1978): 33.

– *Invito alla lettura di Morselli.* Milan: Mursia, 1984.

Fortini, Franco. *I poeti del Novecento.* Bari: Laterza, 1977. 208–9.

Foucault, Michel. *Essential Works of Michel Foucault: Aesthetics, Method, and Epistemology.* Volume 2. Edited by James D. Faubion. New York: New Press, 1998.

Frassica, Pietro, editor. *Primo Levi as Witness: Proceedings from a Symposium Held at Princeton University April 30-May 2, 1989.* Fiesole: Casalini Libri, 1990.

Frattini, Alberto. 'Sulla poesia italiana degli anni Sessanta ad oggi.' *L'Osservatore Romano*, 12–13 July 1976: 5.

Friedlander, Saul, editor. *Probing the Limits of Representation: Nazism and the 'Final Solution.'* Cambridge, MA: Harvard University Press, 1992.

Frongia, Eugenio N. '"Letteratura parlata" e "ritmo del quotidiano": Appunti sulla prosa di Pavese da *Paesi tuoi* alla *Luna e i falò.'* *Canadian Journal of Italian Studies* 26–7.3–4 (1984): 29–49.

Gabellone, Lino. *L'oggetto surrealista: il testo, la città, l'oggetto in Breton.* Turin: Giulio Einaudi Editore, 1977.

Genette, Gérard. *Paratexts: Thresholds of Interpretation.* Cambridge and New York: Cambridge University Press, 1997.

Ghezzi, Aurelia. 'Life, Destiny, and Death in Cesare Pavese's *Dialoghi con Leucò.'* *South Atlantic Bulletin* 45.1 (1980): 31–9.

Gilbert, Sandra, and Susan Gubar. *The Madwoman in the Attic: The Woman Writer and the Nineteenth-Century Literary Imagination.* New Haven: Yale University Press, 1984.

Ginzburg, Natalia. 'Portrait of a Friend.' *London Magazine* 8.5 (1968): 21–7.

Gioanola, Elio. *Cesare Pavese: la poetica dell'essere.* Milan: Marzorati, 1971.

– *Cesare Pavese: La realtà, l'altrove, il silenzio.* Milan: Editoriale Jaca Book, 2003.

– *'Feria d'agosto*: alle origini della "prima volta."'* *Esperienze Letterarie: Rivista Trimestrale di Critica e Cultura* 25.3–4 (2000): 39–59.

– *Psicanalisi e interpretazione letteraria.* Milan: Editoriale Jaca Book, 2005.

Giovanetti, Luciana. 'Il "testamento" di Pavese.' *Italian Culture* 9 (1991): 273–80.

Giuliani, Alfredo. 'A Crisopoli sono spariti gli abitanti.' *La Repubblica*, 12 March 1977: 11.

– 'Comunista serio, deputato inutile.' *La Repubblica*, 3 March 1976: 10.

– *Le droghe di Marsiglia.* Milan: Adelphi, 1977.

– 'Guido Morselli, che buon romanziere!' In *Le droghe di Marsiglia.* Milano: Adelphi, 1977. 309–16.

Giuliani, Massimo. *A Centaur in Auschwitz: Reflections on Primo Levi's Thinking.* Lanham, MD: Lexington Books, 2003.

Gordon, Robert S.C. *Primo Levi's Ordinary Virtues: From Testimony to Ethics.* New York: Oxford University Press, 2001.

Gottlieb, Eli. *Now You See Him.* New York: William Morrow/Harper Collins Publishers, 2008.

Gross, John. Review of *Divertimento 1889*, by Guido Morselli. *New York Times*, 31 July 1987: C32.

Guglielminetti, Marziano, and Silvia Savioli. 'Un carteggio inedito tra Cesare Pavese e Mario Bonfantini.' *Esperienze Letterarie: Rivista Trimestrale di Critica e Cultura* 25.3–4 (2000): 61–85.

Guglielminetti, Marziano, and Giuseppe Zaccaria. *Cesare Pavese: introduzione e guida allo studio dell'opera pavesiana: storia e antologia della critica*. Florence: Le Monnier, 1976.

Guerrazzi, Vincenzo. 'Alle foci del Po con Pavese, Morselli ed Hemingway.' *Forum Italicum* 33.1 (1999): 273–80.

Guiducci, Armanda. *Il mito Pavese*. Florence: Enrico Vallecchi, 1967.

Gutierrez, Marìa Elena. 'La poetica del lapsus: inconscio e linguaggio nell'opera di Alberto Savinio.' *Forum Italicum* 312 (1997): 439–57.

Halbwachs, Maurice. *On Collective Memory*. Chicago: University of Chicago Press, 1992.

Harrison, Robert Pogue. *Dominion of the Dead*. Chicago and London: University of Chicago Press, 2003.

Harrison, Thomas. *1910: The Emancipation of Dissonance*. Berkeley and Los Angeles: University of California Press, 1996.

Heiney, Donald. 'Pavese: The Geography of the Moon.' *Contemporary Literature* 9.4 (1968): 522–37.

Hutcheon, Linda. 'Pavese's Intellectual Rhythm.' *Italian Quarterly* 60–1 (1972): 5–26.

Isotti Rosowsky, Giuditta. 'La luna e i falò, una rilettura.' *Narrativa* 22 (2002): 105–18.

– 'Pavese: il romanzo deludente.' *Esperienze Letterarie: Rivista Trimestrale di Critica e Cultura* 25.3–4 (2000): 87–101.

– *Pavese lettore di Freud*. Palermo: Sellerio, 1989.

– '(Re)lire Pavese.' *Études* 369.5 (1988): 487–96.

Jamison, Kay Redfield. *Touched with Fire: Manic Depressive Illness and the Artistic Temperament*. New York: Free Press, 1994.

Janet, Pierre. *L'Automatisme psychologique*. Ninth edition. Paris: Felix Alcan, 1921.

Jesi, Furio. 'Cesare Pavese, il mito e la scienza del mito.' *Sigma* no. 3–4 (December 1964): 95–120.

Kantorowicz, Ernst H. *The King's Two Bodies: A Study in Medieval Political Theology*. Princeton: Princeton University Press, 1997.

Kilmer, Nicholas. 'Indian Giving.' *Pequod* 16–17 (1984): 81–97.

Knapp, James A., and Jeffrey Pence. 'Between Thing and Theory.' *Poetics Today* 24:4 (Winter 2003): 641–71. Durham, NC: Porter Institute for Poetics and Semiotics, Duke University Press.

Kofman, Sarah. *Nietzsche and Metaphor*. Translated by Duncan Large. Stanford: Stanford University Press, 1993.

– *Rue Ordener, Rue Labat*. Translated by Ann Smock. Lincoln: University of Nebraska Press, 1996.

Kovacs, Laurand. Review of *Le Communiste* in *La Nouvelle Revue Française* no. 311(December 1978): 132–5.

Kremer, Roberta S., editor. *Memory and Mastery: Primo Levi as Writer and Witness*. Albany: State University of New York Press, 2001.

Lacan, Jacques. *Four Fundamental Concepts of Psychoanalysis*. New York: W.W. Norton, 1998.

Lajolo, Davide. *An Absurd Vice: A Biography of Cesare Pavese*. Translated by Mario and Mark Pietralunga. New York: New Directions, 1983.

– *Il vizio assurdo: Vita di Cesare Pavese*. Milan: Il Saggiatore, 1960.

– *Pavese*. Milan: Rizzoli, 1984.

Lanzillotta, Monica. *La parabola del disimpegno: Cesare Pavese e un mondo editoriale*. Rende: Centro Editoriale e Librario Università degli Studi della Calabria, 2001.

Laroche, Pierre. 'La réception de Pavese en France.' *Esperienze Letterarie: Rivista Trimestrale di Critica e Cultura* 25.3–4 (2000): 217–32.

Lazzaro, Claudia, and Roger J. Crum, editors. *Donatello among the Blackshirts: History and Modernity in the Visual Culture of Fascist Italy*. Ithaca: Cornell University Press, 2005.

Leake, Elizabeth. *The Reinvention of Ignazio Silone*. Toronto: University of Toronto Press, 2003.

– '"Nor do I want your interpretation: Suicide, Surrealism, and the Site of Illegibility in Amelia Rosselli's *Sleep*.' *Romanic Review* 97.3–4 (2006): 445–59.

Leitch, Vincent B., et al, editors. *The Norton Anthology of Theory and Criticism*. New York: W.W. Norton and Company, 2001.

Lejeune, Phillipe. *On Autobiography*. Minneapolis: University of Minnesota Press, 1989.

Leopardi, Giacomo. *The Poems of Leopardi*. Translated by Geoffrey Bickersteth. Cambridge: Cambridge University Press, 1923.

Leshem, Dan. 'The Question of Ethical Discorse: Emmanuel Levinas, Primo Levi, and Giorgio Agamben.' In *The Legacy of Primo Levi*. Edited by Stanislao Pugliese. New York: Palgrave Macmillan, 2005. 153–60.

Levi, Primo. *Ad ora incerta*. Milan: Garzanti, 2004.

– *If This Is a Man*. Translated by Stuart Woolf. Suffolk: Chaucer Press/Penguin Books, 1979.

– *Opere*. Vol. 1. Turin: Einaudi, 1997

– *Opere*. Vol. 2. Turin: Einaudi, 1997.

– *Opere*. Vol. 3. Turin: Einaudi, 1990.

– *Survival in Auschwitz and The Reawakening: Two Memoirs*. Translated by Stuart Woolf. New York: Summit Books, 1986.

– *Vizio di forma*. Turin: Einaudi, 1987.

Leys, Ruth. *From Guilt to Shame: Auschwitz and After*. Princeton: Princeton University Press, 2007.

– *Trauma: A Genealogy*. Chicago: University of Chicago Press, 2000.

Lopez, Guido. 'Guido Morselli: *Divertimento 1889.' Uomini e libri* 55 (1975): 26–7.

Macchione, P. 'La solitudine di Guido Morselli.' *La Prealpina*, 16 April 1988.

'A Man and His Novels.' *Times Literary Supplement*, 15 September 1961: 612.

Manganelli, Giorgio. *La notte*. Milan: Adelphi, 1996.

Manera, Manuela. 'L'"ydioma tripharium" di Amelia Rosselli: Ricognizioni linguistiche.' *Lingua e stile* 38 (2003): 233–67.

Mannoni, Octave. 'Je sais bien mais quand même.' In *Clefs pour l'Imaginaire ou l'Autre Scène*. Paris: Seuil, 1969.

Manzi, Attilio. 'El espacio y la palabra: Reflexiones acerca del exilio poético de Amelia Rosselli.' In *Exilios femeninos*. Edited by Pilar Cuder-Domínguez. Huelva, Spain: Universidad de Huelva, Instituto Andaluz de la Mujer, 2000. 339–45.

Margalit, Avishai. *The Ethics of Memory*. Cambridge, MA: Harvard University Press, 2004.

Mari, Michele. 'Estraneo agli angeli e alle bestie (lettura di *Dissipatio H.G.*).' *Autografo* 37 (1998): 49–58.

Mariani, Umberto. 'Del falso mito d'un Pavese contadino.' *Forum Italicum* 26.1 (1992): 150–70.

Marotti, Maria Ornella, editor. *Italian Women Writers from the Renaissance to the Present: Revising the Canon*. University Park: Pennsylvania State University Press, 1996.

Marshall, Robert G. 'Additional Items on Pavese's "American Criticism."' *Italica* 39.4 (1962): 268–72.

Matamoro, Blas. 'Cesare Pavese y la hermandad de la muerte.' *Cuadernos Hispanoamericanos* 605 (2000): 79–86.

Mattesini, Francesco. 'L'echec di Pavese.' *Vita e Pensiero: Rassegna Italiana di Cultura* 51 (1968): 201–4.

Maurois, André. *Mes songes che voici*. Paris: Grasset, 1933.

Mauroni, Elisabetta. 'Tre esempi di stile nominale: Morselli, Tobino, Volponi.' *Studi di grammatica italiana* 20 (2001): 255–86.

Mazzariol, Ferruccio. 'La narrativa del (caso) Morselli.' *L'osservatore romano*, 2 October 1976: 3.

McCarthy, Mary. *The Group*. New York: Harcourt, 1963.

McClellan, William. 'Levi, Agamben, and the New Ethics of Reading.' In *The Legacy of Primo Levi*. Edited by Stanislao Pugliese. New York: Palgrave Macmillan, 2005. 146–52.

McDowell, Edwin. 'Posthumous Acclaim.' *New York Times*, 3 April 1983: BR22.

Mengaldo, Pier Vincenzo. Introduction to poems by Amelia Rosselli. *Poeti italiani del Novecento*. Milan: Mondadori, 1981. 993–7.

– *Poeti italiani del novecento*. Milan: Mondadori, 1978.

Menninger, Karl. *Man against Himself*. 1966 reprint of original. New York: Harcourt, Brace and World, 1938.

Mercadante, Francesco. 'Guido Morselli o della fede senza teodicea.' *Studium* 74 (1978): 239–50.

Miccinesi, Mario. 'Guido Morselli: Incontro col comunista.' *Uomini e Libri* 81 (1980): 22.

Michelstadter, Carlo. *La persuasione e la rettorica*. Milan: Adelphi, 2005.

Middlebrook, Diane. *Anne Sexton: A Biography*. New York: Houghton Mifflin, 1991.

– *Her Husband: Hughes and Plath – A Marriage*. New York: Viking, 2003.

Minois, Georges. *History of Suicide: Voluntary Death in Western Culture*. Translated by Lydia Cochrane. Baltimore: Johns Hopkins University Press, 1999.

Moe, Nelson. 'At the Margins of Dominion: The Poetry of Amelia Rosselli.' *Italica* 69.2 (1992): 177–97.

Mollia, Franco. *Cesare Pavese: saggio su tutte le opere*. Florence: La nuova Italia, 1967.

Mondo, Lorenzo. 'Anni Settanta: tre outsiders.' In *L'arte dell'interpretare: Studi critici offerti a Giovanni Getto*. Cuneo: Arciere, c. 1984. 803–10.

– 'Le dernier roman de Pavese.' *Lettres Nouvelles* 13 (1965): 116–31.

Monod, Jacques. *Chance and Necessity: An Essay on the Natural Philosophy of Modern Biology*. Translated by Austryn Wainhouse. New York: Alfred A. Knopf, 1971.

Moravia, Alberto. 'Fu solo un decadente.' *L'Espresso*, 12 July 1970.

– 'Il mito di Pavese.' *L'Espresso*, 26 July 1970.

– *Pavese decadente. Corriere della Sera*, 22 December 1954.

– *L'uomo come fine e altri saggi*. Milan: Bompiani, 1964.

Moroni, Mario. *La presenza complessa: Identità e soggettività nelle poetiche del Novecento*. Ravenna: Longo, 1998.

Morselli, Guido. *Brave Borghesi. Romanzi* vol. 1. Milan: Adelphi Edizioni, 2002.

– *Il comunista*. Milan: Adelphi Edizioni, 1976.

– *Contro-passato prossimo*. Milan: Adelphi Edizioni, 1975.

– *Diario*. Edited by Valentina Fortichiari. Milan: Adelphi Edizioni, 1988.

– *Dissipatio H.G.* Milan: Adelphi Edizioni, 1977.

– *Divertimento 1889*. Milan: Adelphi Edizioni, 2000.

– *Un dramma borghese*. Milan: Tascabili Bompiani, 1988.

– *Fede e critica*. Milan: Adelphi Edizioni, 1977.

– *Incontro col comunista.* Milan: Adelphi Edizioni, 1980.

– *Proust o del sentimento*. Milan: Garzanti, 1943.

– *Realismo e fantasia: Dialoghi con Sereno*. Milan: Fratelli Bocca, 1947.

– *Roma senza papa.* Milan: Adelphi Edizioni, 1974.
– *Il suicidio e Capitolo breve sul suicidio.* Pistoia: I quaderni di Via del Vento, 2004.
– *Uomini e amori.* Milan: Adelphi Edizioni, 1998.
Morselli, Henry. *Suicide: An Essay on Comparative Moral Statistics.* New York: Arno Press, 1975.
Murrell, Duncan. 'Letters: Love Match.' *Harper's Magazine*, March 2009: 4.
Mutterle, Anco Marzio. 'Una forma virtuale di "Lavorare stanca."' *Esperienze Letterarie: Rivista Trimestrale di Critica e Cultura* 25.3–4 (2000): 103–19.
Nascimbeni, Giulio. 'Il comunista che contesta Marx.' *Corriere della Sera*, 2 March 1976: 3.
– 'Dalla casa di ringhiera, con amore.' *Corriere della Sera*, 14 September 1980: 9.
– 'Morselli, quel lago, quel mistero …' *Corriere della Sera*, 18 March 1979: 3.
– 'La notte in cui sparì il genere umano.' *Corriere della Sera*, 26 February 1977: 3.
– 'Quella febbre strana e sottile che arriva il pomeriggio.' *Corriere della Sera*, 21 May 1978: 11.
– 'Il romanza di fantateologia che sta diventando un caso letterario: C'è forse un Gattopardo del Nord.' *Corriere della Sera*, 21 October 1974: 3.
– 'Il terzo romanzo postumo conferma il caso Morselli: Re in incognito.' *Corriere della Sera*, 29 June 1975: 12.
Orlando, Saverio. 'Appunti su una lettera di Pavese.' *Giornale Storico della Letteratura Italiana* 146 (1969): 117–20.
Orr, David. 'Love, Your Ted.' *New York Times Book Review*, 16 November 2008: 15.
Ozick, Cynthia. 'The Suicide Note.' *New Republic* 198.12 (21 March 1988): 32–6.
Pampaloni, Geno. *Trent'anni con Cesare Pavese: Diario contro diario.* Milan: Rusconi, 1981.
Paolini, Alcide. 'Come sono vecchi I giovani narratori.' *Corriere della Sera*, 24 March 1975: 3.
– 'Romanzi di primavera.' *Corriere della Sera*, 16 March 1975: 15.
Paperno, Irina. *Suicide as a Cultural Institution in Dostoevsky's Russia.* Ithaca: Cornell University Press, 1997.
Parmeggiani, Francesca. 'Morselli e il tempo.' *Annali d'Italianistica* 19 (2001): 269–84.
Parussa, Sergio. 'A Hybridism of Sounds: Primo Levi between Judaism and Literature.' In *The Legacy of Primo Levi.* Edited by Stanislao Pugliese. New York: Palgrave Macmillan, 2005. 87–94.
Pasolini, Pier Paolo. 'Notizia su Amelia Rosselli.' *Il Menabò di letteratura* 6 (1963): 66–9.

Patruno, Nicholas. 'At an Uncertain Hour.' In *Memory and Mastery: Primo Levi as Writer and Witness*. Edited by Roberta S. Kremer. Albany: State University of New York Press, 2001.

Pautasso, Sergio. *Cesare Pavese, l'uomo libro: Il mestiere di scrivere come mestiere di vivere*. Milan: Arcipelago, 1991.

– *Cesare Pavese oltre il mito: Il mestiere di scrivere come mestiere di vivere*. Genoa: Marietti, 2000.

Pavese, Cesare. *Among Women Only*. Translated by D.D. Paige. London and Chester Springs: Peter Owen, 2004.

– *La bella estate*. Turin: Oscar Mondadori, 1999.

– *Lavorare stanca*. Turin: Einaudi, 2001.

– *Lettere 1924–1944*. Turin: Einaudi, 1966.

– *Lettere 1945–1950*. Turin: Einaudi, 1966.

– *Il mestiere di vivere – Diario 1935–1950*. Turin: Einaudi, 1952.

– *Notte di festa*. Turin: Einaudi, 2005.

– *Paesi tuoi*. Turin: Einaudi, 2001.

– *Le poesie*. Turin: Einaudi Tascabili, 1998.

Peterson, Thomas E. '*Il soggiorno in inferno* and Related Works by Amelia Rosselli.' *Rivista di Studi Italiani* 17.1 (1999): 275–85.

Philippe, Antoine. 'The Drowned as Saviors of Humanity: The Anthropological Value of *Se questo è un uomo*.' In *The Legacy of Primo Levi*. Edited by Stanislao Pugliese. New York: Palgrave Macmillan, 2005. 125–31.

Pietralunga, Mark. 'La fortuna di Pavese negli Stati Uniti (1990 al presente).' *Esperienze Letterarie: Rivista Trimestrale di Critica e Cultura* 25.3–4 (2000): 233–46.

Plath, Sylvia. *Ariel*. New York: HarperCollins Perennial Classics, 1999.

Pontiggia, Giuseppe. 'La Roma senza Papa di Morselli: l'altro ieri a Cortina il convegno sullo scrittore morto nel 1973.' *Corriere della Sera*, 26 August 1978: 3.

Ponzi, Mauro. *La critica e Pavese*. Bologna: Cappelli, 1977.

Procaccini, Alfonso. 'Pavese: Tangency and Circumspection.' *Lingua e Stile: Trimestrale di Filosofia del Linguaggio, Linguistica e Analisi Letteraria* 18.3 (1983): 457–77.

Pugliese, Stanislao. *Carlo Rosselli: Socialist Heretic and Antifascist Exile*. Cambridge, MA: Harvard University Press, 1999.

Pugliese, Stanislao, editor. *The Legacy of Primo Levi*. New York: Palgrave Macmillan, 2005.

Re, Lucia. '(De)Constructing the Canon: The Agon of the Anthologies on the Scene of Modern Italian Poetry.' *Modern Language Review* 87.3 (1992): 585–602.

– 'Mythic Revisionism: Women Poets and Philosophers in Italy Today.' In *Italian Women Writers from the Renaissance to the Present: Revising the Canon*. Edited by Maria Ornella Marotti. University Park: Pennsylvania State University Press, 1996. 187–233.

– 'Variazioni su Amelia Rosselli.' *Verri: Rivista di Letteratura* 3.4 (1993): 131–50.

Rensi, Giuseppe. *Le aporie della religione: Studio sul problema religioso*. Catania: Etna, 1932.

– *La filosofia dell'assurdo*. Milan: Adelphi, 1991.

Ricciardi, Alessia. *The Ends of Mourning*. Stanford: Stanford University Press, 2003.

Rimanelli, Giose. 'Myth and De-Mythification of Pavese's Art.' *Italian Quarterly* 49 (1969): 3–40.

– 'Pavese's Diario: Why Suicide? Why Not?' In *Italian Literature: Roots and Branches. Essays in Honor of Thomas Goddard Bergin*. Edited by Giose Rimanelli and Kenneth John Atchity. New Haven: Yale University Press, 1976. 383–405.

Rinaldi, Rinaldo. 'I romanzi a una dimensione di Guido Morselli.' *Critica letteraria* 24.91–2 (1996): 667–91.

Ritte, Jürgen. 'Die Gesellschaft: Eine schlechte Gewonhheit: Zu Guido Morsellis Romanen.' *Merkur: Deutsche Zeitschrift fur europaisches Denken* 39.2 (1985): 148–52.

Rosselli, Aldo. *La famiglia Rosselli: Una tragedia italiana*. Milan: Leonardo Paperback, 1992.

Rosselli, Amelia Pincherle. *Anima: Dramma in tre atti*. Edited by Natalia Costa Zalessow. Rome: Salerno Editore, 1997.

– *Memorie*. Edited by Marina Calloni. Bologna: Il Mulino, 2001.

Rosselli, Amelia. *Appunti sparsi e persi*. Rome: Empirìa, 1997.

– *Diario Ottuso*. Rome: IBN, 1990.

– *Documento*. Milan: Garzanti, 1976.

– *Epistolario familiare: Carlo, Nello Rosselli e la madre (1914–1937)*. Edited by Zeffiro Ciuffoletti. Milan: Sugar Co., 1979.

– *Le poesie*. Milan: Garzanti, 2004.

– *Serie ospedaliera*. Turin: Mondadori, 1969.

– *Sleep: poesie in inglese*. Translated by Emmanuela Tandello. Postface by Emmanuela Tandello. Milan: Garzanti, 1992.

– *Variazioni belliche*. Milan: Garzanti, 1964.

– *War Variations*. Translated by Lucia Re and Paul Vangelisti. Copenhagen and Los Angeles: Green Integer, 2005.

Ruschioni, Ada. 'Appunti su Pavese.' *Vita e Pensiero: Mensile di cultura dell'Università cattolica* 49 (1966): 601–10.

Salvatori, Mariolina. 'Elliptical Conversations: Writer's/Reader's Rapport in Cesare Pavese's Novels.' *Canadian Journal of Italian Studies* 26–7.3–4 (1984): 16–28.

Sanna, Paolo. *L'altro Pavese: Un 'misfatto' non solo letterario.* Sassari: Carlo Delfino, 2000.

Santner, Eric L. 'History beyond the Pleasure Principle: Some Thoughts on the Representation of Trauma.' In *Probing the Limits of Representation. Nazism and the Final Solution.* Edited by Saul Friedlander. Cambridge, MA and London: Harvard University Press, 1992. 143–54

Santoro, Marco. 'Per Cesare Pavese.' *Esperienze Letterarie: Rivista Trimestrale di Critica e Cultura* 25.3–4 (2000): 3–5.

Saunders, Max. 'Autobiografiction' *Times Literary Supplement*, 3 October 2008: 13–15.

Scarsella, Alessandro. 'Gualba: un dramma borghese.' In *La cultura catalana tra l'umanesimo e il barocco: atti del V Convegno dell'Associazione italiana di studi catalani (Venezia, 24–27 marzo 1992).* Edited by Carlos Romero and Rossend Arqués. Padua: Programma, c. 1994. 407–16.

Segre, Cesare. 'Lettura di *Se questo è un uomo*.' In *Primo Levi: un'antologia critica.* Edited by Ernesto Ferrero. Turin: Giulio Einaudi Editore, 1997. 55–75.

– 'Primo Levi nella Torre di Babele.' In *Primo Levi as Witness: Proceedings from a Symposium Held at Princeton University April 30–May 2, 1989.* Edited by Pietro Frassica. Fiesole: Casalini Libri, 1990.

Seinfelt, Mark. *Final Drafts: Suicides of World-Famous Authors.* Amherst, NY: Prometheus Books, 1999.

Severino, Emanuele. *Tautótēs.* Milan: Adelphi, 1995.

Shenk, Joshua Wolf. 'The Suicide Poem.' *New Yorker*, 14 and 21 June 2004: 62–5.

Shneidman, Edwin S. *The Suicidal Mind.* New York: Oxford University Press, 1996.

Showalter, Elaine. *The Female Malady: Women, Madness, and English Culture 1830–1980.* New York: Pantheon Books, 1985.

Sichera, Antonio. 'Pavese nei dintorni di Yoice: le "due stagioni" del *Carcere*.' *Esperienze Letterarie: Rivista Trimestrale di Critica e Cultura* 25.3–4 (2000): 121–51.

Silverman, Kaja. *Male Subjectivity at the Margins.* London: Routledge, 1992.

Simborowski, Nicoletta. 'From *La famiglia* to the *Taccuino* and *La casa in collina*: Pavese and the Need to Confess.' *Modern Language Review* 92.1 (1997): 70–85.

Smith, Zadie. 'Always Another Word.' *Harper's Magazine*, January 2009: 26–30.

Snodgrass, Ann. *Knowing Noise: The English Poems of Amelia Rosselli.* New York: Peter Lang, 2001.

– 'Rosselli's "Nouvelle Symphonie Littéraire": Erasure and Intertext, "Her Sense of Distances."' *South Atlantic Review* 63.4 (1998): 1–10.
– Soberón, Fabián A. 'Pavese y los ojos de la muerte.' *Espéculo: Revista de Estudios Literarios* 26 (2004): no pagination.
Solomon, Andrew. *The Noonday Demon: An Atlas of Depression.* New York: Touchstone, 2001.
Spackman, Barbara. *Fascist Virilities: Rhetoric, Ideology and Social Fantasy in Italy.* Minneapolis: University of Minnesota Press, 1996.
Tagliabue, John. 'Primo Levi, Holocaust Writer, Is Dead at 67.' *New York Times*, 12 April 1987.
Tandello, Emmanuela. *Amelia Rosselli: La fanciulla e l'infinito.* Rome: Donzelli Editore, 2007.
Terry, Jack. 'The Damaging Effects of the "Survivor Syndrome."' In *Psychoanalytic Reflections on the Holocaust: Selected Essays.* Edited by Steven A. Luel and Paul Marcus. New York: Holocaust Awareness Institute, Center for Judaic Studies, University of Denver; Ktav Publishing House, [Denver], 1984. 139–40.
Thompson, A.D. '"Slow Rotation Suggesting Permanence": History, Symbol, and Myth in Pavese's Last Novel.' *Italian Studies* 34 (1979): 105–21.
Thomson, Ian. *Primo Levi: A Life.* New York: Henry Holt and Company, 2002.
Todorov, Tzvetan. *The Fantastic: A Structural Approach to a Literary Genre.* Translated by Richard Howard. Cleveland: Press of Case Western Reserve University, 1973.
Toscani, Claudio. Review of *Contro-passato prossimo*, by Guido Morselli. *Uomini e libri* 54 (June-July 1975): 64–5.
Vaccaneo, Franco. *Cesare Pavese: biografia per immagini: la vita, i libri, le carte, i luoghi.* S. Stefano Belbo: Gribaudo, 1989.
Vattimo, Gianni. *The End of Modernity: Nihilism and Hermeneutics in Postmodern Culture.* Translated by Jon R. Snyder. Baltimore: Johns Hopkins University Press, 1991.
Vegliante, J.C. 'Guido Morselli.' *Magazine Littéraire* no. 165 (October 1980): 44–5.
Venturi, Gianni. 'Letteratura e vita: Per ricordare Cesare Pavese.' *Esperienze Letterarie: Rivista Trimestrale di Critica e Cultura* 25.3–4 (2000): 153–61.
Villani, Paola. *Il 'caso' Morselli: Il regisro letterario-filosofico.* Naples: Edizioni Scientifiche Italiane, 1998.
Vitelli, F. 'Un lago della memoria: Rocco Scotellaro e Amelia Rosselli.'*La Nuova ricerca* (1998): 6–7
Vittorini, Elio. *Diario in pubblico.* Milan: Bompiani, 1957.
Vittoz, Dominique. 'Guido Morselli e la figura dell'autore.' *Autografo* 37 (1998): 23–48.

– 'Mourir avant le 8 septembre 1943.' In *Umberto Eco; Le 8 septembre 1943 et les ècrivains italiens; Autobiographisme et intertextualité.* Grenoble: Centre d'études et recherches sur la culture italienne contemporaine, 1998. 129–42.

Wall, Thomas Carl. 'Au Hasard.' In *Politics, Metaphysics and Death: Essays on Giorgio Agamben's Homo Sacer.* Edited by Andrew Norris. Durham, NC, and London: Duke University Press, 2005.

Wexler, Mike. 'Land of Green Mysteries.' *Pequod* 45 (2002): 30–9.

Wlassics, Tibor. 'Una vita recitata: Problemi della biografia di Pavese.' *Nuova Antologia* 527 (1976): 404–19.

Ysmal, Pierre. Review of Pierre Courtade, *La place rouge* and Guido Morselli, *Il comunista. Magazine Littéraire* no. 141 (October 1978): 43–4.

Zanzotto, Andrea. 'Care, rischiose parole sibilline.' *Corriere della Sera*, 18 July 1976: 11.

Index

Agamben, Giorgio, 10, 135–6, 139, 150–2, 161, 216n97, 218n7, 220nn27–33, 224n68
Agosti, Stefano, 81–2, 83, 84, 85, 199nn38–9
Alesi, Eros, 27, 28
Alighieri, Dante, 50, 147, 155
Alvarez, Alfred, 11, 173n1, 178n31, 178nn33–4, 208n29, 208n32, 216n95
Améry, Jean, 144
Amiel, Frédéric, 186n49
Angier, Carole, 19, 217n4, 218n6, 218n9
Anissimov, Myriam, 217n4
Annoni, Carlo, 205n12, 206n17
Antelme, Robert, 97, 98
Antonioni, Michelangelo, 120, 214n80, 216n93
Arnone, Vincenzo, 203n1
Aragon, Louis, 199n44

Bachmann, Ingeborg, 67
Balakian, Anna, 200n48, 200nn53–4, 201n55
Baldacci, Alessandro, 192n12, 193n14, 194n17, 195n18

Barthes, Roland, 5, 7, 14–15, 27, 93, 113, 128, 132, 136, 141, 166, 167, 168, 169, 173n5, 173–4n6, 174n9, 175n12, 183n16, 215n81, 218n8
Baudelaire, Charles, 210n37
Beardsley, Monroe C., 14
Becker, Jillian, 175n11
Belpoliti, Marco, 217n2, 223n57, 223n59
Benedetti, Carla, 180n46
Benedikt, Amélie Frost, 174n10
Benjamin, Walter, 199n47
Berryman, John, 193n13
Bertolucci, Bernardo, 191n2
Bianchi, Alberto, 214n78
Biasin, Gian Paolo, 109, 206n15, 209n36, 210n38, 211n54, 213n67
Binetti, Vincenzo, 203n2, 212n59, 214n79
Blanchot, Maurice, 97, 98
Bo, Carlo, 183n20
Bosetti, Gilbert, 209n36
Breton, André, 83, 84, 199n44, 199n46, 200nn49–50, 200nn53–4
Broch, Hermann, 35
Buñuel, Luis, 199n47
Burke, Séan, 14–15, 180nn45–50

Burroughs, Augusten, 169
Burton, Richard, 74
Bush, George W., 176n17
Butler, Judith, 180n44

Caesar, Michael, 34, 184n29, 185n44
Calvino, Italo, 79, 112, 207n20
Cambon, Glauco, 210n37
Campbell, Robert, 102, 175n13,
   176n15, 192n9
Camus, Albert, 102
Caputo, Francesca, 194n17, 196n22,
   196n24, 197nn25–7, 199nn44–5,
   202n70
Carbognin, Francesco, 195n18
Carnevali, Emanuel, 27, 28
Carrera, Manuel, 207n21
Carter, Jimmy, 76
Caruth, Cathy, 6, 174n7
Caserta, Giovanni, 206n19
Cases, Cesare, 216n1, 220nn38–9,
   222nn45–6, 222n47
Cave, Marion, 68, 70–1, 74–5, 93,
   196n20
Celan, Paul, 142, 143, 144, 145, 148,
   225n73
Cheever, John, 170
Chesler, Phyllis, 179n39
Chiusano, Italo, 182n9
Cillo, Giovanni, 206n19
Cixous, Hélène, 179n39
Clerval, Alain, 206n19
Collinson, Diané, 102, 175n13,
   176n15, 192n9
Cortellessa, Andrea, 193n14
Costa, Simona, 181n2, 184nn31–3,
   185n38
Costaz, Gilles, 183n20
Couturier, Maurice, 22, 25, 180n46,
   182n11

Crapanzano, Vincent, 12, 179n36
Cros, Philippe, 97

De Camilli, Davide, 204n8,
   210nn37–8
Dedet, Christian, 206n18
Deleuze, Gilles, 167, 202n74
Della Coletta, Cristina, 197n33
de Man, Paul, 156, 169, 222n50
De March, Silvia, 192n3, 192n10,
   194n17
Derrida, Jacques, 7, 8–10, 13–14,
   15, 19, 38, 89, 93, 94–5, 99, 101,
   103, 114–17, 119, 134, 139, 166,
   167, 168, 172, 174n8, 177nn20–4,
   180n43, 180n51, 186n48, 201n62,
   202nn75–8, 202nn82–3, 210nn42–4,
   225nn1–6
De Tommaso, Piero, 208n18
Deutsch, Helen, 169, 225n8
Di Biase, Carmine, 183n20, 209n35
Dickinson, Emily, 67
Dolce, Ester, 209n35
Donne, John, 192n9
Druker, Jonathan, 216n2
Du Maurier, Daphne, 134, 216n96
Durkheim, Emile, 10, 42, 102,
   177n19, 178n28, 202n86

Eliach, Yaffa, 222n53
Eluard, Paul, 199n44
Enckell, Pierre, 185n39
Escher, M.C., 110

Fales, Angela Bianchini, 209n35
Falzoni, Giordano, 199n44
Fasano, Marina Lessona, 31, 32,
   181n2, 182n12, 184nn23–4
Felman, Shoshana, 13, 70, 77, 89,
   174n7, 179n38, 180n42, 196n21

Fernandez, Dominique, 108, 206n15
Ferretti, Gian Carlo, 208n30, 209n35
Ferrucci, Franco, 224n73
Fiorentino, Maria, 181n2, 182n8,
    184n28
Fiori, Giuseppe, 196n20
Flaiano, Ennio, 34, 35, 184n30
Flaubert, Gustave, 172
Flint, R.W., 203n6
Fontes, Ignacio, 208n31
Fortichiari, Valentina, 30, 32,
    181nn1–6, 184n22, 184nn25–7,
    186n59, 188n84, 188nn86–7,
    188n90
Fortini, Franco, 82, 84, 199n42, 201n56
Foucault, Michel, 7, 14, 15, 113, 152,
    166, 168, 169, 178n27, 202n84,
    210n40
Frattini, Alberto, 184n36
Freud, Sigmund, 6, 47, 84, 97
Frey, James, 169
Friedlander, Saul, 218n7, 221n42

Gabellone, Lino, 200nn49–51
Gautier, Xaviere, 170n39
Genette, Gérard, 22
Gide, André, 35
Gilbert, Sandra, 179n39
Ginzburg, Natalia, 206n14
Gioanola, Elio, 110–14, 155, 157,
    159, 207nn22–4, 208n26, 208n28,
    208n31, 211n56, 214n72, 214n77,
    218n15, 219n19, 221n43
Giuliani, Alfredo, 185n39, 186n58
Giuliani, Massimo, 217n2
Gordon, Robert S.C., 141, 217n2,
    218n7, 219n20, 223n57, 224n72
Gottlieb, Eli, 173n2
Grass, Günter, 169
Greene, Graham, 3

Gubar, Susan, 179n39
Guerazzi, Vincenzo, 208n27
Guglielminetti, Marziano, 204n9,
    206n13, 209n34
Guiducci, Armanda, 206n19
Gutierrez, Marìa Elena, 198n33

Harrison, Robert Pogue, 169, 173n3,
    225n7, 225n9, 225n11
Harrison, Thomas, 207n24
Heiney, Donald, 211n54
Hemingway, Ernest, 3, 111, 141
Highsmith, Patricia, 76
Hitchcock, Alfred, 5
Homer, 147
Hutcheon, Linda, 204n8
Huxley, Aldous, 35

Illyés, Gyula, 199n44

Jamison, Kay Redfield, 178n31,
    179n40
Janet, Pierre, 84, 200n49
Jesi, Furio, 206n19
Jung, Carl Gustav, 84

Kafka, Franz, 111
Kantorowicz, Ernst, 10, 177n25
Kennedy, John F., 66
Kennedy, John-John, 66
Knapp, James K., 179n41
Koestler, Arthur, 170
Kofman, Sarah, 17, 18, 67, 83, 93–101,
    114–17, 119, 132, 134, 139, 166, 167
Kovacs, Laurand, 185n37
Kozinski, Jerzy, 170
Kremer, Roberta, 221n42

Lacan, Jacques, 90, 92, 201n64,
    201n66

Lajolo, Davide, 108, 202n3, 206n14, 207n22, 208n28
Lansbury, Angela, 74
Lanzilotta, Monica, 205n12
Lawrence, T.E., 176n14
Leiris, Michel, 199n39
Lenin, Vladimir, 57
Leopardi, Giacomo, 83, 90–1, 109, 111, 201n68, 210n37
Leshem, Dan, 224n67
Levi, Primo, 4, 17, 18, 19, 138–64, 166, 168, 170, 172
Lévy-Bruhl, Lucien, 50
Leys, Ruth, 174n7, 219n19
Lincoln, Abraham, 176n16
London, Jack, 176n14
Lopez, Guido, 185n46
Lorenz, Konrad, 32
Lucentini, Franco, 172

Magris, Claudio, 219n21
Malinowski, Bronislaw, 50
Mallarmé, Stéphane, 14
Manera, Manuela, 194n17, 197n33
Manganelli, Giorgio, 10, 178n26
Mannoni, Octave, 202n71
Manzo, Attilio, 194n17
Marcus, Greil, 16
Margalit, Avishai, 17, 139, 149–52, 159, 161, 217n5, 219nn22–5, 220nn35–7, 224nn64–5
Martin, Robert 8, 177n18
Mattei, Enrico, 96n24
Mattesini, Francesco, 206n19
Maurois, André, 185n45
Mazzariol, Ferruccio, 183n19
McCarthy, Mary, 212n58
McClellan, William, 224n67
Mengaldo, Pier Vincenzo, 195n18, 198n34

Menninger, Karl, 176n17, 178n30
Michelstaedter, Carlo, 31
Middlebrook, Diane, 174–5n11
Miller, Richard Lawrence, 176n16
Minois, Georges, 175n13, 192n9
Moe, Nelson, 194n17, 197n31, 199n37
Monari, Gastone, 27, 28
Mondo, Lorenzo, 112, 202n2, 208n26
Monod, Jacques, 17, 26, 39, 40, 46, 56, 61, 64, 139, 186n49, 186nn51–4, 187n114, 188n74, 190n118
Montale, Eugenio, 38
Moravia, Alberto, 107, 191n2, 206n13, 206n19
Morselli, Guido, 4, 17, 18, 20–64, 69, 93, 101, 105, 111, 113, 139, 148, 150, 162, 166, 171, 172, 225n10
Murrell, Duncan, 204n8
Musil, Robert, 34, 35
Mussolini, Benito, 65

Nascimbeni, Giulio, 182n10, 183n21, 184n37, 185nn40–1, 185n47, 186n57
Nietzsche, Friedrich, 94, 97, 114

Offenbach, Jacques, 37
Orr, David, 192n11
Ozick, Cynthia, 217n2

Pampaloni, Geno, 204n9
Paolini, Alcide, 184n35
Paperno, Irina, 10, 12, 175n13, 177n25, 178nn29–30, 179n37
Parussa, Sergio, 221n40, 222n47
Pasolini, Pier Paolo, 27, 28, 66, 79, 81–2, 83, 84, 85, 100, 193n17, 197nn32–3, 198n35, 199n36, 199n41
Pasternak, Boris, 83

Patruno, Nicholas, 223n58
Pautasso, Sergio, 204n9, 205n 12, 207n22, 210n39
Pavese, Cesare, 4, 17, 18, 19, 21, 30, 31, 34, 104–37, 139, 150, 158, 163, 166
Pence, Jeffrey, 179n41
Petrignani, Sandra, 77
Philippe, Antoine, 224n67
Pinkus, Karen, 99
Pirandello, Luigi, 5, 111, 171, 188n88
Plath, Sylvia, 4, 17, 18, 30, 66, 67, 68, 76, 88–9, 93, 94–6, 99, 101, 141, 144, 201n61
Pontiggia, Giuseppe, 184n34, 185nn42–3
Ponzi, Mauro, 203n5, 204n9, 206n13
Presley, Elvis, 16, 152, 153
Proust, Marcel, 34, 35, 111
Pugliese, Stanislao, 157, 192n5, 222n53, 223n56, 224n67

Rabelais, François, 155
Ray, Nicholas, 178–9n35
Re, Lucia, 194n17, 196n18, 197n33, 198n34, 201n60
Rensi, Giuseppe, 17, 26, 32, 39, 40, 41, 49, 51–4, 56, 61–4, 139, 185n45, 186nn49–50, 188nn81–2, 188n86, 190n115, 190n118, 191n120
Reta, Vittorio, 27, 28
Ricciardi, Alessia, 180n44
Rimanelli, Giose, 203n4, 204n8, 209n35, 210n45
Rosowski, Giuditta Isotti, 106, 204n7
Rosselli, Aldo, 76, 77, 197n25
Rosselli, Amelia, 4, 17, 18, 19, 21, 30, 31, 34, 65–103, 105, 113, 139, 140, 141, 144, 166
Rosselli, Amelia Pincherle, 17, 70–1, 74, 93

Rosselli, Carlo, 65, 66, 68, 192n3
Rosselli, Nello, 65, 192n3
Ruschioni, Ada, 204n8

Salinari, Carlo, 206n13
Santner, Eric, 174n7
Sappho, 67
Satta, Salvatore, 27, 28
Saunders, Max, 186n62, 222n49
Savioli, Silvia, 209n34
Scotellaro, Rocco, 102, 194n17, 196n22
Segre, Cesare, 223n60, 224n69
Seinfelt, Mark, 176n14
Severino, Emanuele, 17, 118–19, 120, 132, 136, 139, 210nn48–9
Shenk, Joshua Wolf, 176n16
Silone, Ignazio, 4
Silverman, Kaja, 89, 201n64, 201nn65–6
Smith, Zadie, 204n8
Smock, Ann, 97, 202n73, 202n81
Snodgrass, Ann, 195n18
Socrates, 8, 9
Sodi, Risa, 140, 217n3
Solomon, Andrew, 11, 178nn31–2
Svevo, Italo, 111

Tagliabue, John, 217n2
Tandello, Emmanuela, 193n12, 194n17, 197nn29–30
Terry, Jack, 219n26
Thomson, Ian, 19, 157, 217n4, 223n54
Todorov, Tzvetan, 45, 187n70
Togliatti, Palmiro, 107
Tomasi di Lampedusa, Giuseppe, 23, 25, 31, 35
Toscani, Claudio, 189n94
Toole, John Kennedy, 4
Trakl, Georg, 142, 145, 148, 225n73

Trotsky, Leon, 57
Tzara, Tristan, 199n44

Vancini, Florestano, 185n41
Vandevaetere, Sara, 157, 222n51
Vattimo, Gianni, 17, 117–18, 132, 136,
    210n47
Vegliante, J.C., 183nn17–18
Vettori, Alessandro, 214n78
Vittorini, Elio, 79, 209n37

Wall, Thomas Carl, 225n74
Wallace, David Foster, 204n8

Wiesel, Elie, 140
Wilcock, Juan Rodolfo, 27, 28
Wimsatt, William K., 14
Windt, Peter, 177n19
Wood, David, 177n19
Woolf, Virginia, 67
Wordsworth, William, 19

Ysmal, Pierre, 184n35

Zaccaria, Giuseppe, 204n9, 206n13
Zanzotto, Andrea, 67, 195n18, 204n8